THE LOST ART OF DECLARING WAR

For Tom Fee

Here is a problem
that no one sees as a
problem.

Brien Hallett
Honolulu,
16 October 2002

THE LOST ART OF DECLARING WAR

Brien Hallett

UNIVERSITY OF ILLINOIS PRESS

URBANA AND CHICAGO

Library of Congress Cataloging-in-Publication Data
Hallett, Brien.
The lost art of declaring war / Brien Hallett.
p.   cm.
Includes bibliographical references and index.
ISBN 0-252-02418-4 (cloth : acid-free paper)
ISBN 0-252-06726-6 (paper : acid-free paper)
1. War, Declaration of—United States.
2. Executive power—United States.
3. War and emergency powers—United States.
I. Title.
KF5060.H355   1998
342.73'062—ddc21   98-8926
CIP

For Joseph J. Hallett, M.D.

Contents

Preface

My purpose is to rethink the power to declare war. The argument takes as its starting point a paradox. On the one hand, the Federal Convention of 1787 got it right. In a representative democracy the power to declare war must reside solely with the people's representatives. Otherwise the political regime is neither fully democratic nor fully representative. On the other hand, the people's representatives have never exercised this power in any clear-cut, unambiguous way in over two hundred years, which means that U.S. democracy has never been fully representative or fully democratic. During times of war it reverts to earlier feudal forms, placing the commander-in-chief "where kings have always stood."

This two-hundred-year-old gap between constitutional theory and the practical politics of wartime has been sustained, I will argue, by three factors: first, an inability to imagine an alternative to John Locke's "federative power," which stipulates that foreign affairs in general and the power to declare war in particular are "inherently executive functions"; second, an inability to imagine that unfamiliar trends and forgotten attitudes of the sixteenth and seventeenth centuries, not the familiar circumstances and well-known events of the nineteenth and twentieth centuries, provide the better explanation for Congress's failure to exercise its power to declare war; and third, an inability to imagine alternative perspectives and approaches to the traditional legalistic perspectives and approaches with which the topic has been discussed since 1793.

In response to these three factors, the book is divided into three parts. Part 1, "Breaking the Mold," contains two chapters in which I approach the topic, perhaps unexpectedly, from an autobiographical perspective. This abbreviated autobiography begins in chapter 1 with my naïve critique of the 1973 War Powers Resolution, which represents the final bankruptcy of the traditional legalistic approach to the congressional war powers, and then shifts to the more fundamental issue of war. Clearly no one can begin to discuss the power to declare war until after one determines the character of war. The dictates of democratic theory notwithstanding, perhaps wars are best fought without declarations, as has been argued since roughly the seventeenth century. If so, then the congressional power to declare war is as antiquated, vacuous, and meaningless as the congressional power to grant letters of marque and reprisal.

How should we conceive of war, then? Is war killing, conflict, or violence—or is it policy? Clausewitz naturally figures prominently in this discussion, but the bedrock of the analysis is a sharp distinction between combat and war, between the cinematographically most arresting part of war and the whole of war. I separate combat from war not so much because that distinction allows me to avoid a simplistic reduction of war to its violent fraction but rather because that is the way I experienced war, my service in Vietnam having been divided into a period of combat in the bush and a period without combat at division and air-wing headquarters. For this reason chapter 1 includes a section in which I describe my personal experience of war. The story is skewed, however. Instead of recounting the dramatic incidents that occurred during my time in the bush—the incidents that make *Going after Cacciato* (O'Brien 1978) or *Platoon* (Stone 1986) compelling—I recount the utterly banal incidents that occurred while I occupied different staff billets at headquarters. In other words, whereas Oliver Stone skewed *Platoon* in one direction by recounting the story of six patrols, which together would have occupied little more than a week of a fifty-six-week tour, I skew my story in the opposite direction by describing the tedious and trite events of my eighty weeks in staff positions while largely ignoring the patrols during which I was actually shot at. Stone uses the recipe for box-office success; I use the recipe for boredom. Nonetheless, by pushing my combat stories offstage in this way, I hope to engage the reader in both the perplexity and the paradox of my experience: how is it possible that my time in staff billets was both filled with war and bereft of combat?

A further advantage of this autobiographical approach is that it allows me to displace the traditional touchstone texts—James Madison's *Notes of the Federal Convention of 1787* and his 1793 exchange with Alexander Hamilton under the *noms de plume* "Helvidius" and "Pacificus"—with the Declaration of Independence in chapter 2. The importance of this displacement cannot be overemphasized. It was while comparing the Declaration of Independence to the five nineteenth- and twentieth-century congressional declarations of war that I realized why the latter possess neither form nor function. Indeed, it is only a slight exaggeration to say that my entire argument can be reduced to the Declaration of Independence: had the United States Congress done what the Second Continental Congress did, no controversy over its war powers would ever have arisen.

Many readers, however, will find my use of the Declaration of Independence eccentric. In particular, those who adhere to the interpretation begun with James Wilson in 1790, furthered by Justice Joseph Story, and culminating in Abraham Lincoln's Gettysburg Address and who thus view the declaration as the foundational document for the United States will be caught off guard (Wills 1992, 131). By returning the declaration to its original function, however, I have not sought to deny that it also embodies the proposition on which the new nation was conceived and to which it is dedicated. Rather, I have sought to draw from it only the form of a model declaration of war, there being no other example of an adequately reasoned declaration in U.S. history. My narrow purposes, therefore, dictated a narrower, more primitive interpretation.

My constricted use of the Declaration of Independence highlights another characteristic of the argument. Although long sections of the book are conceptual and historical in character, the argument is basically a textual analysis. This approach is dictated by the nature of the topic, for the power to declare war is emphatically not the power to initiate or start a war, as many believe it to be. Rather, it is the power to compose a text, to draft a document, to write a denunciation. An analysis of this power, therefore, resolves to an analysis of the quality of the text so produced. When one has isolated and identified the elements of a well-composed declaration of war—and this is done most easily through an analysis of the Second Continental Congress's declaration—one has, in a certain conceptual sense, exhausted the topic. This textual analysis of the Declaration of Independence is found toward the end of chapter 2.

Part 2, "Changing Attitudes," picks up and fleshes out the two key concepts identified in part 1. Chapter 3 is a brief historical sketch of the rise and fall of reasoned declarations of war. It documents the use of fully reasoned declarations of war from the earliest Sumerian times to the seventeenth century, when improvements in transportation technologies and changed diplomatic practices led to a decline in their use. This decline continued through the eighteenth, nineteenth, and twentieth centuries until, in a 1938 article, Clyde Eagleton was forced to conclude that declarations of war possess neither form nor function. The practical import of this conclusion is the modern consensus that there is never a need to declare war. To counter this consensus, one must return to the problem of war. If war is violence, then of course there is never a need to declare it. If war is policy, however, then there is an absolute need to articulate that policy and to do so both formally and publicly. Making this argument is the purpose of chapter 4, whose first section constitutes a lengthy argument for the distinction between war and combat; the second section tries to determine in what sense a formal reasoned declaration of war starts or initiates a war. Once this issue is resolved, it is then possible to develop a typology of war suitable for discussing and classifying wars based upon the quality of their declarations.

Finally, in part 3 ("Speculating on Solutions"), chapter 5 attempts to imagine ways in which the people's representatives might discharge their constitutional responsibility to declare war. Specifically the chapter focuses on how the three relevant groups—the professional military, the general public, and Congress—might organize themselves to make it possible for Congress to declare war. The touchstone of this speculation is the principle that war is not peace and hence that the current peacetime organization of Congress is demonstrably inappropriate for the declaring of war. In applying this principle, however, I have been guided in large part by the conduct of the Fifty-fifth Congress as it wrangled its way to a conditional declaration of war against Spain during April 1898. As a spectacle in partisan politics, this episode has few parallels and is a prime example of how not to declare war. With its eyes focused intently upon the upcoming midterm congressional elections, the Fifty-fifth Congress managed to ignore all the crucial strategic and diplomatic issues of the war.

—

Nothing is ever written by the author alone. Without the encouragement and criticism of others, the enterprise soon looses vitality and grinds to a halt. In my case my principal source of both encouragement and criticism was Peter Manicas. Not only did Peter provide the initial intellectual foundations from which I launched this project, but the unique way in which he tempered his excitement at each new insight with insistent critique of each new shortcoming did much to propel the project. In addition to Peter, Manfred Henningsen, Neal Milner, George Simson, and Carolyn Stephenson all labored through a less than fully coherent manuscript and made valuable contributions. Manfred kept a close eye on my "eccentricities," identifying if not correcting all of them. Neal worried about the ethical or moral foundations of my outlook and, not finding them, gently suggested that I uncover them and make them explicit to the reader. George, revealing a useful prejudice, found the autobiographical passages less fulsome than required and pushed me beyond that which reticence thought proper. Carolyn, in her Socratic way, edged me forward, question by question, to the realization that war cannot be defined, an insight that shaped chapter 4. I must also thank Louis Fisher and Edwin Firmage for their helpfully critical reviews, which identified many of the manuscript's shortcomings. That I failed to heed these well-aimed criticisms in all cases is, of course, my full responsibility, as are any other deficiencies in logic, fact, or style. Richard Martin at the University of Illinois Press was also indispensable for his support, his patience, and his persistence in shepherding the manuscript through review and production to publication.

And finally, there is the home team—my wife, LiLi, my daughter, Victoria, and my son, Kekoa—whose patience and support quite simply made this project possible.

PART 1

Breaking the Mold

1

"Something Else Is Needed"

Traditionally a study of the congressional war powers begins with a review of the standard works on executive authority, the presidential war powers, and the extensive constitutional law literature. This approach starts with the debates in the Federal Convention, proceeds to the 1793 exchange between Hamilton and Madison conducted under names "Pacificus" and "Helvidius," and then retells the story of the controversies and case law that arose in each of the United States' undeclared wars, concluding with the most recent one. But what is the relevance of this traditional approach? What can be learned from these studies, which are largely the story of presidential action and congressional inaction? For instance, what can be learned about the congressional war powers from the declarations of war that Congress did *not* write for the Quasi War against France, any of the numerous Indian wars, or the Korean and Vietnam Wars? The controversies that surround these wars teach us much about the presidential war powers, especially about the president's power to wage formally undeclared wars. But do these controversies tell us anything about the *congressional* war powers, except that they are easily circumvented? Hence, although it is true that the standard works cannot be ignored, it is equally true that "constitutional exegesis has done little to hold back the presidential juggernaut" and therefore that "something else is needed" (Draper 1991, 73).

This being the case, instead of beginning with the expected constitutional exegesis, I begin with a set of four personal experiences that have shaped my ideas and attitudes concerning the congressional war powers. These experiences stretch back over thirty years and are connected by nothing more solid than serendipity; taken together, however, they add up to an unexpected perspective.

The 1973 War Powers Resolution

I initially became interested in the congressional war powers as a result of the controversies that surrounded Commander-in-Chief Ronald Reagan's deployment of U.S. Marines to Lebanon in 1982–83. Briefly summarized, the events occurred as follows: On Monday, 20 September 1982, Reagan ordered the marines afloat with the Sixth Fleet back to Beirut to help restore civil order. Almost one year later, on Monday, 29 August 1983, the marines began taking hostile fire from the various factions quarreling in and around the city. The prospect of casualties revived long-dormant calls in the Ninety-eighth Congress for Reagan to comply with the provisions of the 1973 War Powers Resolution. Reagan refused, claiming that the resolution was unconstitutional, an unwarranted infringement on his own war powers. After six weeks of negotiations, the parties reached a compromise solution. Embodied in Senate Joint Resolution 159, the Multinational Force in Lebanon Resolution (Pub. L. No. 98-119, 97 Stat. 805), Reagan signed this compromise resolution on Wednesday, 12 October 1983. At the same time he also issued a statement specifically denying the validity of section 4 (a) (1) and section 5 (b), the operative sections of the 1973 act (Reagan 1985, 2:1444–45).

The Joint Resolution Concerning the War Powers of Congress and the President, to use the 1973 act's full title, is a piece of post-Vietnam legislation that was passed over President Richard Nixon's veto on 7 November 1973. It was an attempt to create a procedure whereby the commander-in-chief would be forced to report to Congress the introduction of any U.S. armed forces into a "hostile" situation within forty-eight hours of that introduction. This report, in turn, was intended to force Congress either to authorize the operation formally and officially within sixty days or, in the absence of a formal congressional authorization, to terminate the operation. After the veto fight, the resolution had rested peacefully on the books for nine years, until Reagan's deployment of the marines to Beirut created an opportunity for the procedures to be tested. As was to be expected, the procedures failed. Reagan denied their constitutionality, some members of Congress noisily upheld them, and the stage was set for the year-long controversy that reached its anticlimax during September and October 1983.

As is often the case, the news accounts shed little light upon the fundamental issues, concentrating instead upon the tit-for-tat posturing of the two sides.

Therefore, as the controversy raged and my confusion grew, I decided to go to the library and read the 1973 act. Since then I have learned of the specific drafting errors that render the War Powers Resolution inoperable. There are several of these, including the problem of defining "hostilities," but the most fatal arises as follows: The War Powers Resolution (Pub. L. No. 93-148, 87 Stat. 555) requires the commander-in-chief to file three different reports, only one of which—the so-called hostilities report mandated by section 4 (a) (1)—starts the clock (under §5 [b]) that "terminates" any further use of U.S. armed forces at the end of sixty day unless Congress has authorized continued use. However, the drafters neglected to require the commander-in-chief to stipulate in the letter which of the three reports is being transmitting to Congress. Consequently, when Reagan reported on 29 September 1983 that he had deployed 1,200 marines to Lebanon in September 1982, he left it up to Congress to decide whether his letter constituted a hostilities report or one of the other reports (see Glennon 1984). Deciding that what many thought to be a late report was indeed the required hostilities report, the Ninety-eighth Congress opened negotiations with the White House and eventually passed its 12 October 1983 resolution, even backdating it to August, when the marines first began to take incoming fire. Then, instead of keeping to the stipulated time limits, it allowed the clock to run unhindered for the next eighteen months, when a truck bombing finally precipitated the evacuation of the marines, which more or less put paid to the 1973 War Powers Resolution.

These drafting errors aside, what struck me most forcefully as I read the resolution was its conceptual incoherence. The most fundamental conceptual difficulty is the way the Ninety-third Congress sought to *force* the commander-in-chief to *force* Congress to discharge its duties under article 1, section 8, of the Constitution. Not knowing the constitutional literature at the time, I found this game of pass-pass bizarre in the extreme. I naïvely assumed that when the framers of the Constitution wrote, "The Congress shall have the power . . . to declare war," they meant just that. It therefore followed that there never was any need for Congress to attend upon anyone else to discharge its constitutional responsibilities. Most especially, there was never any need for Congress to wait until the commander-in-chief consulted with or reported to it before it could authorize the introduction of U.S. armed forces into a hostile situation.

Turning this coin over and phrasing the difficulty negatively, I was struck by the way the Ninety-third Congress conceived of the congressional war powers as being completely subordinate to and dependent upon the commander-in-chief. This dependency arose because, in both situations envisioned by the resolution, Congress is powerless to act unless and until the commander-in-chief acts first. Thus, in the first case the commander-in-chief "consult[s] with Congress *before* introducing United States Armed Forces into hostilities or into situations where imminent involvement in hostilities is clearly indicated by the circumstances" (§3; emphasis added). In this case Congress may either declare war in due form, or it may do nothing, awaiting the introduction of U.S. armed forces into hostilities, at which time the second case becomes operative. In the second case the commander-in-chief introduces U.S. armed forces into a hostile situation *first* and *then* consults with Congress, reporting within forty-eight hours (§4 [a] [1]). In this latter case, Congress has sixty days to authorize continuation of the operation; if it fails to do so, the operation must be terminated (§5 [b]).

In fine, the resolution does not envision Congress as acting independently of the commander-in-chief. In all cases congressional action is dependent upon the commander-in-chief's taking the initiative. Should the commander-in-chief not consult beforehand or refuse to report after the fact, as Reagan and many other commanders-in-chief have done, Congress is left high and dry, sputtering and protesting but unable to do much else. Since first reading the War Powers Resolution, I have learned that this dependence is sanctioned by a long tradition, stretching past Madison at least to Blackstone and Locke and their doctrines of royal prerogative. Not having read the standard literature at the time, however, it seemed to me self-evident that if Congress possesses any war powers at all, those powers must be exercised independently of the commander-in-chief, for powers that are dependent upon others for their exercise cease to be powers.

Naïvely, therefore, I imagined that Congress could discharge its war powers independently. I envisioned a scenario much more active than the two passive scenarios outlined in the 1973 resolution. For example, I could imagine a member of the Ninety-eighth Congress taking to the floor and announcing, "This morning, while driving to the Capitol, I heard on the radio that Commander-in-Chief Reagan had invaded Grenada. In light of this development, I move that all other business be suspended and a declaration of war against Grenada become the pending business of this chamber." Following the adoption of this motion, a debate would ensue. Several weeks later a declaration would be drafted, the draft would be debated fully over a period of days, if not weeks, and eventually it would be voted up or down. Should Congress find sufficient reasons to justify the invasion of Grenada, it would pass the declaration, thereby discharging its constitutional responsibilities and, not incidentally, sanctioning the commander-in-chief's decision. Should Congress find insufficient reasons to justify the invasion, however, it would not pass the declaration and move on to consider a bill of impeachment against the commander-in-chief for exceeding his authority.

The principal objections to my scenario of independent congressional action, I now know, are two: First, there exists no precedent for such independent action, such a direct attack upon the commander-in-chief's royal prerogative. However, a diminution of royal prerogatives does not strike me as an objection that should carry great weight in a democracy. Second, the consultations and reports envisioned by the Ninety-third Congress (and James Madison) are designed to act as checks and balances. However, consultations and reports are the weakest possible sort of check or balance. Moreover, such a scheme strikes me as both impractical and dangerous: impractical, because in two hundred years of U.S. history, these consultations have yet either to check or to balance the ambitions of a determined commander-in-chief; dangerous, because the scheme is too easily bypassed, like the safety on an M-16. By the simple expedient of never switching the selector off "semi" or "auto," the safety is bypassed and the M-16 functions just as well—some would even say better. By the simple expedient of never consulting with or reporting to Congress, these checks and balances are bypassed and the commander-in-chief is able to function just as well—some would say even better.

The second conceptual difficulty is the way in which the 1973 act envisions the congressional war powers as principally the "statutory authorization" of the commander-in-chief's power "to introduce United States Armed Forces into hostilities, or into situations where imminent involvement in hostilities is clearly indicated by the circumstances" (§2 [c]). Not only is the possibility of Congress's declaring war a subordinate concern in the act, but one has the strong impression that it was viewed by the Ninety-third Congress as but a different statutory form for authorizing the introduction of U.S. armed forces into hostilities. Yet given the results of the Ninety-eighth Congress's "compromise" with Reagan, not to mention the past two hundred years of U.S. history, the phrase *statutory authorization* appears to be but a euphemism for rubber-stamping a fait accompli. Whatever the congressional war powers might be, they must surely constitute something more substantial than statutory authorization.

Finally, closely related to the rubber-stamp problem, another conceptual difficulty that troubled me is the way in which the 1973 act focuses upon time and not substance. Not only is the act full of deadlines—"within forty-eight hours," "within sixty calendar days," "every six months," "extended for not more than thirty days"—but the whole purpose of the act is to fix the times at which the commander-in-chief will do this and Congress that. This emphasis upon *when* and not *what* possesses a long and distinguished lineage. I was later able to trace it back as far as James Madison. But again, my naïve reading of the Constitution led me to believe that the timing of the declaration of war—much less the timing of any statutory authorization—was unimportant.

What was important was content. That is, the first question that arose in my untutored mind when I read article 1, section 8, was not *when* Congress should declare war but rather *what* this declaration should say.

This question troubled me especially. Since nothing in the 1973 act answered it, I returned to the library, where, after several hours with the *Congressional Record* and its predecessors, I gathered a complete collection of absolute declarations of war, those of 1776, 1812, 1846, 1898, 1917, and 1941 (see Wormuth and Firmage 1989, ch. 4; see also the appendix for those declarations not cited in the text). Once these were in hand, the first thing I noticed was their lengths. The 1776 Declaration of Independence is long; the others are short. The reason for this difference soon became apparent when I read through them. The declaration of 1776 is long because it contains a lengthy analysis of the grievances that provoked the war. The declarations of 1812, 1846, 1917, and 1941 are short because they contain no analysis of grievances. Instead they simply declare, officially and formally, that a state of war exists between the United States and some other state—Great Britain, the Republic of Mexico, Imperial Germany, or the Empire of Japan. The conditional declaration of 20 April 1898 is a curious mixture. Although it is short, it also contains an analysis of the grievances that provoked the Spanish-American War. However, this analysis possesses neither the depth nor the detail of Jefferson's declaration, and it has a suspiciously hollow, rhetorical quality to it.

The conclusion I drew from this reading of the six declarations is that, just as there have been well-drafted laws and poorly drafted laws, likewise, there have been well-drafted declarations of war and poorly drafted declarations of war. A well-written declaration is a fairly long document that adequately analyzes the grievances that provoked the war, such as the Second Continental Congress's 1776 Declaration of Independence. A poorly written declaration is a relatively short document that either omits all analysis of grievances or provides an inadequate analysis, such as the five congressional declarations I had collected. By extension, the worst possible declaration of war is either no declaration at all or the "statutory authorization" of a fait accompli. I further concluded that, had the Ninety-third Congress concerned itself with content instead of timing when drafting the 1973 War Powers Resolution, it would have written a completely different resolution, one that required Congress to model its declarations of war upon the Second Continental Congress's Declaration of Independence. Specifically, the resolution would have followed Jefferson's dictum that "a decent Respect to the Opinions of Mankind requires that they should declare the causes that impel them to Separation." Moreover, should Congress ever model its declarations of war upon the Second Continental Congress's declaration, it would not only avoid the appearance of being little more than a rubber stamp for the commander-in-chief but also carve out a domain of action independent of that office. That is, the 1973 act stipulates among other things that the commander-in-chief set forth in the initial hostility report "the circumstances necessitating the introduction of United States Armed Forces [into hostilities]" (§4 [a] [A]). Needless to say, commanders-in-chief are never at a loss for circumstances necessitating their doing what they have done. However, if Congress ever took upon itself the responsibility to define and articulate these necessitating circumstances independently of the commander-in-chief, as the Second Continental Congress did in 1776, then not only would it have assumed a war power that would be more than a rubber stamp—not only would it begin acting as a real check upon the commander-in-chief's propensity to war—but it would, finally, break free of its subordination to and dependence upon the commander-in-chief as well.

Years later I would broaden and deepen my analysis of the Declaration of Independence. I would also learn that this type of declaration is called a "reasoned" declaration and that, by implication, the declarations of 1812, 1846, 1898, 1917, and 1941 are "unreasoned" declarations. But in 1983 I had exhausted my interest in these matters. The controversy had died down, and I had satisfied my curiosity concerning the War Powers Resolution. I now understood why its procedures would never work. I put my complete collection of absolute declarations of war in a folder and filed it away.

—

The next personal experience that shaped my attitudes and ideas on the congressional war powers occurred on Sunday, 20 January 1991, during the height of the Persian Gulf War. During December Rev. Phillip Reller asked me to help organize a program on the Gulf War for his Adult Education Ministry, which met at nine o'clock Sunday mornings between the early and late services. He was planning to spend two Sundays on this topic and was looking for two speakers. We easily identified the first speaker but were unable to think of a second. Finally I mentioned that I had done some work on the War Powers Resolution and could talk on that. He quickly agreed, no doubt because we had been unable to think of anything better, and the program was set.

At the appointed hour, I passed out copies of my complete set of absolute declarations of war and explained the difference between the Second Continental Congress's fully reasoned Declaration of Independence and the five unreasoned congressional declarations. I then suggested that, instead of having voted an "authorizing" resolution on 12 January 1991, the 102d Congress should have written a fully reasoned declaration of war modeled on the Second Continental Congress's 1776 declaration. Such a course of action, I continued, would have replaced the babble of conflicting justifications emanating from the administration with a single official explanation of the necessities that justified the war. In addition, since the congressional debate would have been public, unlike the private decisions being made within the White House, ordinary citizens would have been able to influence its course in the same way they influence all legislation that concerns them.

After a short question period, someone discretely mentioned that it was time for the service to begin, and most of the audience got up and left. A few people stayed back, however, which allowed the discussion to continue for another hour. One woman in particular was interested in what I had said. She was a fifth-grade schoolteacher who for some time had been struggling to explain the war to her class. Several of her students had fathers who were in Saudi Arabia, and the others could not avoid hearing about the war on television. All her students were worried, but she had discovered no good way to explain the war to them. President George Bush said this; Secretary of State James Baker said that. The United Nations Security Council did this; Congress did that. She was confused, and because of her confusion, she was doing nothing to allay the anxieties of her students. Her fifth graders, she told us, were not reassured when she told them their daddies were fighting a war for oil or jobs.

Her interest in my talk had been threefold, she explained: First, she liked what I had said about the Declaration of Independence. The distinction between reasoned and unreasoned declarations made sense to her. More important, however, it would make her task of explaining the Gulf War to her students much easier if she had a fully reasoned declaration like Jefferson's. She had taught the Declaration of Independence before, and her fifth-grade students had understood it. If she had a similar document, she should be able to use the same lesson plan with the same results. Second, she liked my idea that Congress would provide a single official voice that would speak with authority. The voice could have many tongues articulating the pros and the cons, but she needed a single source. She simply did not have the time to ferret out the information she needed. If she could read a competent summary of a congressional debate that was focused upon the *reasons* it was necessary for us to fight in the Persian Gulf—the grievances that had caused the war and the remedies that would end it—she could quickly and efficiently prepare herself to answer her students' questions and concerns. Third, as a citizen, she liked the idea that the congressional debate would be open. She was skeptical as to the amount of influence people could exert, but just being able to follow the debate, hear the reasons for and against the war, and decide for herself which were valid and which were not would be a great improvement from her point of view. She followed the news as closely as she could but was totally confused as to the reasons that made this war necessary. She had faith in President Bush, but she would have preferred to hear the reasons and decide for herself.

This experience did not change my attitudes toward the congressional war powers, but it did sharpen and clarify them. Before the talk I had conceived of the congressional war powers vaguely as doing what the Second Continental Congress did. After the talk I came away with a better, clearer, and poignant definition of those duties: the power to declare war is the power to debate and frame a fully reasoned declaration, that is, a document that articulates the grievances that necessitate a war and the remedies that will end it, such that a fifth-grade teacher can explain to his or her students why their fathers and mothers have left home. Nonetheless, increased clarity did not translate into increased motivation. Strangely, in retrospect, I was not motivated to develop my thoughts further. After a most gratifying two hours of discussion, I put my materials back in their folder and occupied myself with other concerns.

—

My apathy was jarred when I finally got around to reading Peter Manicas's *War and Democracy* (1989). It had been sitting on my "must-read" pile for over a year, but it was not until several months after the Sunday talk that I picked it up and started reading. As its title indicates, the book explores the relationship between war and democracy, sweeping from ancient Athens down to the present. It does not address the congressional war powers specifically; rather, it confronts the broader topic of war and democracy, thereby setting the narrow constitutional issue in a larger historical and philosophical context, providing the necessary background that is so often missing from the standard works. Most particularly, *War and Democracy* illuminates the continuing effects of the antidemocratic tradition that stretches from Plato and Aristotle through Madison into the present.

I found the book informative, provocative, and frustrating. Beginning on page 1, it was a "Yes, but . . ." book. Yes, the book's purpose was both timely and important: "This book is a historical study of war and democracy. Its main aim is to contribute to an understanding of our present situation" (1). Yes, "there was a time when no one who had to fight a war was excluded from the decision to go to war. Citizens ruled, and only citizens fought and died" (ibid.). Yes, "it may well be that the problem of 'democracy,' construed as an ideal, cannot be solved until there is a solution to the problem of war" (ibid.). Yes, the present dilemma is how to deal with "the Machiavellian imperative of modern politics: Namely, how an executive responsible for the national security [is] to deal with a recalcitrant, uninformed, and voting public" (157). Yes, in a democracy, "outcomes requiring conjoint action [such as war] require participation precisely because only the participants can decide whether a particular outcome is good for them" (375). Yes, yes, yes, . . . but what are the specific modalities by which this increased participation would take place? More democracy is always welcome, but unless this increase creates specific procedures and processes that connect the governed to their governors, it will do little to resolve the Machiavellian imperative of modern politics.

Since I thought I knew what these specific modalities should be, I was frustrated that Manicas limited himself to suggesting somewhat tentatively that Jeffersonian "ward republics" or some similar arrangement would be the solution. The only remedy for my frustrations, it soon became clear, was to build upon the foundation Manicas had laid and provide what I took to be the answer to the problem of war and democracy.

Thus challenged, I began reading the standard works on executive authority, the presidential war powers, and the constitutional law literature. As my reading progressed, I became more and more skeptical of the value of this standard literature for the questions I was pursuing. Take one of the smaller anomalies: why did such confusion result from the pursuit of a suitable adjective to describe a war for which a formal declaration in due form had not been issued? Prior to the seventeenth century, this had not been a problem. Toward the end of the seventeenth century, however, after the Thirty Years War, as formally declared wars became less and less frequent, it became necessary to develop an appropriate set of adjectives to capture this new circumstance. The Supreme Court's decision in the case of the *Eliza,* one of the earliest cases to address issues surrounding the congressional war powers, is a convenient place to observe these various alternatives. The case turned on whether France and the United States had been at war when the *Ganges* recaptured the *Eliza* from a French privateer on 31 March 1799. Justices Bushrod Washington and Samuel Chase both analyzed the case in the same way, differing only in the adjectives they used. For Justice Chase, the substantive issue was one of distinguishing between "a public general war, and a public qualified war." This led him to argue that "Congress is empowered to declare a general war, or congress may wage a limited war; limited in place, in objects, and in time. If a general war is declared, its extent and operations are only restricted and regulated by the *jus belli,* forming a part of the law of nations; but if a partial war is waged, its extent and operation depend on our municipal laws" (4 U.S. [4 Dall. 37] 44, 43). Justice Washington agreed with Justice Chase on the substantive issue but expressed himself with a greater variety of adjectives:

> It may, I believe, be safely laid down, that every contention by force between two nations, in external matters, is not only war, but public war. If it be declared

in form, it is called solemn, and is of the perfect kind; because one whole nation is at war with another whole nation. . . . In such a war all the members act under a general authority, and all the rights and consequences of war attach to their condition.

But hostilities may subsist between two nations more confined in its nature and extent; being limited as to places, persons, and things; and this is more properly termed *imperfect war;* because not solemn, and because those who are authorized to commit hostilities, act under special authority and, can go no further than to the extent of their commission. Still, however, it is *public war,* because it is an external contention by force, between some of the members of the two nations, authorized by the legitimate powers. (4 U.S. [4 Dall. 37] 40).

In addition to noting the adjectives used, it is perhaps appropriate to make the following three comments: First, Justice Washington's basic definition of war as a "contention by force" is the classic definition, handed down from Cicero (*De Officiis* I, xi, 34). Second, the distinctions drawn by the court are yet another example of how the congressional war powers have traditionally been analyzed in terms of formalities and not in terms of content. Congress is free to wage a war of whatever extent it may desire, but should this desire be expressed through the manipulation of formalities or through the manipulation of content? Should Congress declare war formally when it desires an extensive war but refrain from declaring war formally when it desires a more restricted war? Or should Congress declare war in every case, setting expansive war aims when it desires an extensive war and limited war aims when it wants a "partial" war? As I will argue in the next chapter, the proper method for Congress to control the extent of the war is by manipulating the content of the declaration. Third, the connotations implicit in Justice Washington's adjectives are too ironic for comfort. According to this terminology, World War II was not only a "good war" but a "solemnly perfect" one as well, whereas the Vietnam War will forever remain "imperfect" only because Congress failed to provide it with a "solemn" declaration. One understands why jurists finally settled on the terms (formally declared) *war* and (formally undeclared) *armed conflict* toward the middle of the twentieth century.

This amazing variety of adjectives hides a real distinction. Specifically, it obscures the distinction between the necessary and the sufficient conditions for declaring war. The necessary, but not sufficient, conditions are the need for a formal debate in a socially approved forum leading to a formal declaration; the sufficient, but not necessary, conditions are an order from the commander-in-chief to begin operations, such as the issuance of orders to the navy by Commander-in-Chief Ronald Reagan to deploy marines to Beirut, which is the meaning of Justice Washington's description of *imperfect war* as being limited to "those who are authorized to commit hostilities, [and] act under special authority." However, coming to terms with this real distinction requires the use of a less ironic language than that which Justices Chase and Washington had at their disposal.

—

Meanwhile, to return to my present concerns, this confused search for a suitable adjective is in itself a small matter. As I read further, however, I discovered not only that there were more fundamental difficulties but also that a fourth personal experience, my service in Vietnam, was going to exert a powerful influence upon my ideas and attitudes. In particular, I was amazed to learn that all the standard works assume without question that war is violence and that "unsolemn," "imperfect," "formally undeclared" wars are not only possible but often desirable. Because my experience in Vietnam had convinced me that war is not a synecdoche and cannot be reduced to the violence of combat, I was not prepared to accept the first assumption and was extremely skeptical of the second. Further reading confirmed my skepticism and made it clear, first, that these two assumptions have combined synergistically to vitiate Congress's power to declare war and, second, that the problem thus lies in our conception of war, not in our conception of democracy, precisely as Manicas had argued. I was also surprised to learn that both misconceptions grew out of changes that had occurred not during the nineteenth and twentieth centuries, as conventional wisdom holds, but rather during the seventeenth century.

Briefly, assuming that "formally undeclared" wars are both unavoidable and unexceptional means that, no matter how democratic a polity might be, the specific modalities for achieving enhanced participation are no longer relevant, no longer alive. They have ceased to function. Throughout history the debates, discussions, rites, and rituals that have surrounded formal declarations of war have been the specific means by which the tribe, the assembly, or the great council participated in the decision to war. Once an archon, a consul, a king, or a president is empowered to wage so-called imperfect, formally undeclared wars, however, these modalities become hollow and meaningless. They become hollow because the rulers seek formal declarations of war only when they are certain that they will obtain them. The modalities become meaningless because whenever the rulers are not certain, they wage an unsolemn, imperfect, formally undeclared war on their own authority, without consultations, restrained only by the need to ensure that the war is short, successful, and popular, as two hundred years of U.S. history demonstrate.

Hence the source of our confusion concerning the congressional war powers is not some defect in our constitutional arrangements but rather our unexamined belief that formally undeclared wars are unexceptional. And this belief in turn rests upon an unexamined belief that war is combat. For when we conceive of war as combat, then a hard-edged cynicism forces us to acknowledge that it is absurd to declare our intentions publicly, as Robert Ward has argued persuasively:

> These dazzling maxims [requiring a formal declaration of war before combat begins], have, however, long been abandoned: and since the rules of chivalry have ceased to be binding, they have met with no support either in law or practice. The common sense of mankind, demonstrates the impropriety of allowing an enemy to strengthen himself in the means of consummating mischief. It is either for injury committed, or to prevent that which is *proved* to be meditated, that we are driven to arms. Shall we then wait till he, who has deserved punishment, deserves it still more, with augmented power to resist our efforts? Or shall we give him, who wills our destruction, the force that is wanting to accomplish that will? The whole doctrine has long, and justly been exploded, by the soundest authorities and the wisest practice. (1805, 5; cf. 72)

A reevaluation of article 1, section 8, therefore, must first question whether war can indeed be reduced to the violence of combat and then, if that investigation proves positive, move on to investigate the sense in which "formally undeclared" wars must always be considered exceptional, unusual, and suspect. Since my experiences in Vietnam are the primary source for my belief that war cannot be reduced to the violence of combat, an explanation of how and why I came to this conclusion is perhaps appropriate.

Vietnam: Combat versus War

I arrived in Da Nang from Okinawa in December 1967. Like most freshly minted brown bar marines, I was sent from division to regiment to battalion to company and eventually put in command of the Second Platoon, Lima Company, Fifth Marines. During this initial phase of my tour, my platoon and I walked in the sun, slept in the rain, received a few potshots from friendly guerrillas now and again, and ran into serious trouble once or twice. When I returned from the hospital in June, I was reassigned to division headquarters as a Combat Operations Center watch officer, G-3 (Operations). With this assignment the second and more significant phase of my tour began.

My duties as a G-3 watch officer were straightforward. I sat in an air-conditioned reinforced bunker at a long desk next to the G-2 (Intelligence) watch officer, answered the telephone to my right whenever it rang, took down the report from whoever called, and saw that the incident reported was plotted on a large backlit map directly in front of our desk; near the end of each watch, I wrote a report for higher commands summarizing all the incidents, including the totals for both friendly killed, wounded, and missing and enemy killed, wounded, and captured. In addition, whenever I pulled the midnight to eight o'clock watch, I prepared and delivered the G-3's portion of the commanding general's morning briefing. In short, watch officers worked a normal eight-hour-a-day job that kept them in the know because they heard the reports first and could see the "big picture" with a glance at the map in front of them.

Another advantage to this billet was that I was free to do as I liked after my watch was over. In the afternoons a friend and I could hitch a ride down the road to the Freedom Hill PX to watch a film. In the evenings, when the headquarter's club became a little stale, we could visit one of the other officer clubs in the area. And every Sunday a group of us would head for the Navy Club for their roast beef dinner, a bottle of Mateus, and a film. There was also time to renew old acquaintances. One day I ran into my freshman dorm counselor, who was in Da Nang as a youth worker for USAID. We got together several times, mostly in the evenings, but one Sunday he invited me to join a group of USAID people who were planning to spend the day at China Beach. Sitting on a nearly deserted white sand beach, we talked, drank beer, watched the nurses from the German hospital ship *Helgoland* playing volleyball and sunbathing, and ate the enormous grilled prawns that the vendors were selling. Another time an air force nurse I was dating and I took a day off for some sightseeing. A next-door neighbor I had not seen for years flew helicopters for the 101st Airborne out of Phu Bai. This was a convenient staging area for a trip to Hue, so we caught a Chinook at Freedom Hill and flew to Phu Bai. After spending the night in the 101st cantonment, we drove into Hue the next morning, visited the palace and some other sights, returned to Phu Bai, and flew back to Da Nang early in the evening in an OH-6.

It was a very nice trip and quite a contrast with my previous excursion to Phu Bai and Hue. That time I had traveled with Lima Company. We arrived in Phu Bai late one night toward the end of the 1968 Têt offensive, several hours after a rocket attack. I remember how apologetic the mess sergeant was about the twenty-foot hole in the roof of his mess hall. This hole, he explained, was not from the most recent attack—the one that had occurred a couple of hours earlier—but from two days before. He also apologized for not having any hot food for us, but it was near midnight and no one had told him that 150 marines were coming, so he had no time to prepare. After gorging on canned peaches and bologna and processed cheese sandwiches, we were assigned to hooches and slept comfortably in cots, under a roof. The next morning we were trucked into Hue and, about noon, heloed across the Perfume River into the Forbidden City. I also remember, as our convoy left the Phu Bai airport in the morning for Hue, passing a freshly painted billboard erected by the Hue Tourist Authority that said "Welcome to Hue, Enjoy Your Stay" in Vietnamese, French, and English. My radio man and I thought this was somewhat ironic under the circumstances.

Although it was many years before I could articulate it, the lesson I learned from the contrasting parts of my tour was to distinguish combat sharply from war. Clearly, war is not combat any more than combat is war. The two sometimes occur at the same time in the same general vicinity, but the connection between them is tenuous at best. During the first phase of my tour, while serving as a platoon commander out in the bush, I was frequently involved in combat; there was often a very real prospect of getting seriously killed. During this time, however, the war was distant and remote, a muffled murmur that seldom intruded. Infrequently we had an opportunity to read about it in the *Stars and Stripes* or to hear about it when we tuned one of the PRC-25 radios to the Armed Forces FM station to listen to some music and the news. But these infrequent intrusions of that other reality were so incongruous, so surreal, so grossly irrelevant, that they made little or no impression. We had other more pressing concerns: where to set up for the night; how to cross to the far tree line; how to convince short-time med. evac. pilots that the LZ was not hot, that the houses and bamboo would shelter it from the sniper on the other side of the river if the pilot swooped in low from the west; how to keep the kids from stealing grenades or the odd M-16 magazine and the like.

In sharp contrast, during the second phase of my tour, while serving as a watch officer in the air-conditioned comfort and safety of the rear areas, combat was as distant, remote, and muffled as war had been when I was in the bush. The prospects of getting injured, much less killed, were remote. I copied down SPOT reports for eight hours every day, and I understood what 0 KIA, 2 WIA, meant as well as the G-2 watch officer sitting next to me, especially when the report came from an area in which I had operated, especially when the report was a carbon copy of a report I had transmitted six months earlier describing what was no doubt the exact same ambush—the fire coming from Câm Vân, the village to the left of the road, during the morning sweep for mines planted during the night. But none of these firefights had anything to do with either me or the G-2 watch officer. After the morning briefing, breakfast, and a couple of hours sleep, we had plans to see the new flick at Freedom Hill. The combat that was taking place as close as three or four kilometers from our air-conditioned bunker was irrelevant. It would not affect our plans, our lives.

In fine, combat happened to platoon commanders in the bush; war filled the duty hours of watch officers in the rear. The basic differences between the phenomena was their relative scale and the distance one had to travel to get there from civilian life, from "the real world," to use an old grunt expression. With respect to the latter dimension, the distance from "the real world" to combat is immeasurable. Indeed, the metaphor fails. Like shit, combat happens.* It is a peculiarly intense state of affairs in which the overwhelming complexity of life is reduced to elemental essentials—thirst, hunger, sleep, dry socks—punctuated at odd and unexpected moments by a slow-motion freeze-frame action that renders thirst, hunger, sleep, and even dry socks unimportant and irrelevant. In contrast, the distance from "the real world" to war is but a skip and a hop, or perhaps a slight stumble. After all, how much difference can there be between answering the telephone for eight hours a day as a watch officer in Da Nang and answering the telephone for eight hours a day as an order clerk at L. L. Bean's in Maine? Still, differences do exist. First, unlike "the real world," the war colored our existence with an unspoken fear, usually exaggerated, that the distant murmur of combat might move our way and disrupt our settled routine, our plans to see the new John Wayne flick. Second, because of this unspoken fear and the feeling of insecurity it created, our freedom of movement was sharply circumscribed. We could travel certain roads during the day but not at night. We could go to China Beach with friends and eat grilled prawns, but only as long as we stayed within the shadow of Monkey Mountain. Just three kilometers farther south there were no prawn vendors, and we went to the beach, if we went at all, riding atop Amtracs with preplotted artillery on call, to recall one operation I was on.

With respect to scale, war is a large, inclusive, all-encompassing phenomenon; it embraces entire populations in innumerable ways. Combat is a small, exclusive, discriminating phenomenon; it touches but a small fraction of a population in extremely restricted ways. The Vietnam War touched every

---

* The sentence derives from the all-purpose explanation used in Vietnam to explain everything: "Why are the helos late?" "I don't know, man. Shit happens." "Why is a button missing from your jacket?" "Gimmie a break, man. Shit happens." "Why is Boyd dead?" "Shit happens, man; 'uh know what I mean, man?" It is a matter of Zen meditation, but the koan "Shit happens" must be distinguished from the other, nihilistic, koan heard in Vietnam: "It don' mean nut'n, man. It don' mean nut'n."

American in one way or another, from the antiwar protester in Washington to the Army captain who won the MACV golf tournament in Saigon in 1968.* Combat in Vietnam touched few Americans, slightly above one-tenth of 1 percent. The difference between 99.9 percent and 0.1 percent begins to measure the difference in relative scale between war and combat. Indeed, to emphasize how small a fraction of war combat is, recall that of the 58,022 Americans who died in the Vietnam War, 10,700 died "nonhostile deaths" from malaria, truck accidents, helo crashes, and the like (Department of Defense 1985, 1). Even among the dead, combat touches many fewer than the dramatic television news clips suggest. Before World War II and the introduction of penicillin, the relation of hostile to nonhostile deaths was even more startling. For example, during the Civil War there were two nonhostile deaths for every hostile death.

The disorienting experiences of platoon commander and watch officer, however, are not the only way to experience the sharp distinction between war and combat. Noncombatant bystanders experience a similar disorientation. The distance they travel is not that which separates civilian life from combat, as with soldiers; rather, their journey is a momentary escape from both war and combat to an unnamed place of terror. While in Vietnam I never thought about the situation of the noncombatants, because like most Americans since 1865, I was never a bystander. That role fell to the Vietnamese. All I remember is that, judging from the expressions on their faces, they experienced great anxiety when combat was a little distant and great terror when combat was upon them, when they were caught in the crossfire. On reflection, however, their situation was most curious precisely because they were bystanders. Like all bystanders, coincidence drew them in without making them participants. Their experience was not of combat, although it arose out of combat. To be "of" combat, one must be a combatant. One must be active—or at least potentially so, when the artillery lifts, when dark comes, when the small-arms fire pauses. But noncombatant bystanders are passive, frozen by terror and their lack of training, discipline, leadership, and above all, an objective and a plan. Similarly, their experience was not of war, although it arose during a war. To

---

* MACV (Military Assistance Command Vietnam) was the command that had responsibility for all U.S. military activities in South Vietnam. I read about the golf tournament on the sports page of the *Stars and Stripes*. One copy for every five marines came in every resupply mission. After one resupply, when everything had been distributed, I sat down, leaned against the bamboo lining the side of the trail, and was surprised to learn that the people in Saigon had not only a golf course but the time to enjoy it. This was during the first phase of my tour, before I learned about the Freedom Hill theater and the Sunday roast beef buffets at the Navy Club.

be "of" war, one must also be active—supporting the war or protesting against it. But noncombatant bystanders are passive. They are simply standing by and praying.

Paradoxically, then, during their moments of greatest terror, noncombatant bystanders are simultaneously *in* the war and *in* the combat, yet they are *of* neither. They participate in neither. Their immediate status is one of suspense. Unable to join the combat and cut off from the war until the bombing stops or the battle moves on, they are removed and separated from both. Their entire existence is momentarily suspended in time and space. If they could protest what was happening to them, they would again be participating in the war. But they cannot protest. If they could join the combat, they would be no longer noncombatant bystanders but combatants. They would possess an objective and a plan, and the shape and focus of their terror would change dramatically to those of a soldier's. But they dare not join the combat. In a word, they represent a separate and distinct category that by its segregation from both war and combat tends to highlight the disconnection among all three. None of the categories—neither war, combat, nor noncombatancy—can be reduced to any of the others; the autonomy and suffering of each must be respected.

With respect to scale, even when noncombatants are added to the balance, combat is still much smaller and much more ephemeral than war, which is all-encompassing and persistent. In South Vietnam, for example, although the entire population was caught up in the war, some large fraction of it never endured combat, and of those who did, most were caught in the crossfire only once or twice. For instance, on the last day of operations in and around Hue during Tết 1968, the day I was wounded, our company was engaged in driving remnant guerrilla forces out of the all but deserted villages that lined Route 551 to the east of Hue. About two o'clock in the afternoon, my platoon came upon a charming T'ang-style villa set in a formal garden. As soon as the occupants heard us speaking English, one of the panels slid open and out stepped a tall slender man who greeted us in English, offered us one of his business cards, and asked if we had any cigarettes, explaining that he had smoked his last one that morning. Having secured a cigarette, he went on to say that he and his family had come up from Saigon, where he was an executive with IBM, to spend Tết with his father. Needless to say, their celebration had been less than joyful. Instead of celebrating a week-long family reunion, they had endured six weeks of fear after the North Vietnamese occupied the village.

Living in an occupied village, attending nighttime indoctrination sessions, and digging village defenses were common experiences during the Vietnam War, but they do not constitute combat. As is commonly the case, despite the fact that this holidaying IBM executive and his family had innocently stepped into the vortex of the North Vietnamese Spring Offensive, the gods of topography preserved them from combat. Because his father's villa was five or six kilometers east of Hue, they had escaped all the heavy fighting that took place within the city during the previous six weeks. Because his father's villa was set deep within the village, about two hundred meters from Route 551, next to the irrigation canal, both they and my platoon escaped the firefight that engaged the first platoon for the better part of the afternoon. Standing in his father's lovely garden, smoking his newly delivered cigarettes, and chatting with us, this vacationing IBM executive could hear the pop of the small arms, the thud of the artillery, and the scream of the A-4s as they came in to drop their bombs not three hundred meters away. But neither he nor we were in the line of fire. Deep within the village, we were protected from all that. Finally, because his father's villa was five or six hundred meters from the temple with the large polished bronze Buddha, just past the cemetery at the eastern end of the village, he and his family were also protected from the ambush that greeted my platoon as we pushed out of the village in an effort to come up behind the machine gun that was causing the first platoon so much trouble. In sum, combat is such a constricted and ephemeral phenomenon that, in a village of several thousand inescapably afflicted by all the terrors of war, two substantial firefights could occur in the course of a single afternoon and not more than a dozen noncombatants were actually caught in the crossfire.

But of course, I am speaking of only one afternoon. There would be, no doubt, other afternoons. On each afternoon only a handful of villagers would be caught in the narrow and ephemeral crossfire of combat; only two or three houses would be replaced by bomb craters. Significantly, though, the emptiness of the craters would remain long after the shock waves of the explosions had dissipated, so that after not too many afternoons, the village would change its appearance, and the scale of the accumulating devastation would grow and grow. Thus, although combat—as it ebbs and flows across the contested landscape—occupies a relatively limited and compact terrain at any given moment, the destruction that combat leaves in its wake during the course of the war steadily accrues and accumulates until it craters and scars vast areas.

Disentangling War from Combat

Once I had articulated my experience and began thinking of war and combat as distinct and discrete things, I began to notice how loosely we use the two words, treating them as synonyms and using them interchangeably. For example, I came across articles such as Commander David Hart-Dyke's moving account of his service during the Falklands War, of his psychic journey from peace to war to combat and back again. Although the essay is entitled accurately "HMS Coventry—The Day of Battle," Commander Hart-Dyke systematically speaks of war when he means battle, as is illustrated in the following passage, chosen because it is one of two in which he also uses the word *battle:* "The first few days of war were nervously exciting and cheers erupted throughout the ship when enemy aircraft were shot down. But we had not yet seen real war, we were naive and far from being battle-hardy" (1986, 17). If I may be annoyingly precise, Commander Hart-Dyke is describing not the first few days of "real war" but rather the first few days of real combat or real battle. The real war had begun several months earlier. Indeed, it was the start of the real war that had caused the HMS *Coventry* to sail from Portsmouth into the South Atlantic in the first place. If I may speak again with annoying precision, the shift from peacetime operations to wartime operations came when the Argentineans invaded the Falkland Islands, whereas the shift from a wartime sailing to a combat patrol came when the HMS *Coventry* crossed the line that brought her within the combat operating range of the Argentine air force. Having crossed that line but not yet having sustained an attack, the crew of the HMS *Coventry* was still naïve, still far from being "battle-hardy," a condition that would quickly change when the ship was sunk on Tuesday, 25 May 1982, with the loss of nineteen.

To be sure, I am imposing an inappropriate standard of precision upon Commander Hart-Dyke. Whether he was sailing to war, combat, or battle makes no difference. Everyone understands the emotions he is trying to convey. Still, even though precision is not important in this type of informal essay, one begins to see the shape of the problem. Commander Hart-Dyke tells the story of the journey he and his crew made from peacetime duty in Portsmouth to wartime operations in the South Atlantic to combat in the waters just west of the Falkland Islands and finally to peacetime duty back in England. This cycle is characteristic of all wars, which means that war is a nested phenomenon—war being nested inside peace and combat being nested inside war. But does it not create unnecessary confusion if two of the three nests are designated by the same word? For the sake of clarity, is it not necessary to speak of peace becoming war, war periodically flaring up into combat, which just as quickly subsides to war, and war eventually returning to peace, so as to describe accurately the nested quality of the full phenomenon?

Most particularly, is this precision not absolutely necessary when one begins a study of the congressional war powers? If the power to declare war is the power to transform peace into war, but not to initiate combat, then the war powers of Congress and the commander-in-chief are clearly marked out, Congress deciding that the peace shall be breached and the commander-in-chief deciding whether the initiation of combat is the most appropriate way to conduct the war. If, however, war and combat are artificially conflated such that it appears that the power to declare war is also the power to initiate combat and vice versa, then the war powers of Congress and the commander-in-chief are also conflated, which means that it becomes extremely unclear as to who should do what when. In this situation, the resulting confusion is most easily resolved by the commander-in-chief's assuming the powers of both branches and waging "formally undeclared" wars, as two hundred years of U.S. history demonstrate.

But it was not just in informal essays such as Commander Hart-Dyke's that I observed the conflation of war and combat. I also began to notice the same confusion in other contexts where precision was important, such as academic studies. In these contexts the conflation was achieved not so much by treating *war* and *combat* as synonyms but by reducing war to combat. This reduction was accomplished by defining war as conflict or violence or some variant on this theme, such as armed conflict, organized violence, the destruction of the enemy, or most simply, killing. For example, the Brookings Institution once published a study entitled *Force without War: U.S. Armed Forces as a Political Instrument* (Blechman et al. 1978). Noting that since World War II U.S. armed forces had not always been deployed to fight wars such as in Korea and Vietnam, the study's authors wished to determine the effectiveness of forces deployed in situations not qualifying as a war. The study examined six cases in which U.S. armed forces had been used as "a political instrument," the implication being that they had not been used as a political instrument during the Korean and Vietnam Wars. But the operative difference between the Korean and the Vietnam Wars and, for example, the 1958 deployment of the Sixth Fleet marines to Lebanon or the two Berlin crises is not that the former two were wars whereas the latter two were political instrumentalities.* Rather, it is that the former two resulted in combat, whereas the latter two did not.

---

* I knew a master gunnery sergeant who had been with the Sixth Fleet in 1958 and had stormed the beaches in Beirut. He said that it was the most dangerous landing he had ever made. The landing took place on a warm Sunday afternoon, and the marines had been briefed to expect the worst. Consequently, when the ramps of the landing craft banged down, they charged out with their weapons cocked and loaded and nervous fingers on the safeties. Instead of finding barbed wire, mines, and machine guns, however, they discovered something more dangerous. The beach was full of families out for a Sunday swim. Since many of these families contained young ladies in attractive bikinis, the landing nearly turned into a rout. There are few things more dangerous than a distracted marine with a loaded weapon stumbling around a beach gawking at the sights.

The reduction of war to combat is misleading, to say the least. A more accurate title would have been something on the order of "War without Combat: A Study of Six Cases." A more recent study that is also guilty of reducing war to combat is Alexander George's (1991) *Forceful Persuasion: Coercive Diplomacy as an Alternative to War*. Examining seven cases from Pearl Harbor to the Persian Gulf, George asks why "coercive diplomacy" (principally economic sanctions) avoided combat in some instances but not in others. A less reductionist title would have been something like "Forceful Persuasion: Economic and Diplomatic Sanctions as an Alternative to Combat" or to better illustrate the complexity of the nested quality of war, "Forceful Persuasion: Economic and Diplomatic Sanctions as a Prelude to Combat, but Not Always."

In fine, war cannot be reduced to its most dramatic fraction, to combat. This is the case because it is a nested phenomenon. Moreover, if war is combat, then there is never any good reason for Congress (or anyone else) to declare war, and several excellent reasons not to, as "realists" have argued for millennia. Indeed, the only rational course is to follow the advice of Atreus, an unusually violent man, who urged, "Attack your enemy without delay, before he can strengthen himself or get forces together" (Seneca, *Thyestes* II, 201; cited in Gentili 1933, 135; cf. Maurice 1883, 8, 12 n‡, 32–33).

After I started to separate combat from war, I also began reading Carl von Clausewitz's great book *On War* with greater confidence. The book is demanding for a number of reasons. As Bernard Brodie points out in his reader's guide at the back of the 1976 translation, although the ideas discussed are not difficult, the text itself is. Many long sections are of historical interest only, other sections deal with outmoded technologies or tactics, and faulty organization and a disturbing tendency for "metaphysical" reflection distract readers as well (Clausewitz 1976, 641). Compounding these shortcomings is the fact that the manuscript was unfinished at the time of Clausewitz's unexpected death in 1831. Normally no one would bother to read a text plagued by this many flaws and imperfections. Yet compensating for all its defects and deficiencies is Clausewitz's common sense, sparking like diamonds in a mine. Consequently, the best way to use *On War* is as a mine from which aphorisms and dicta may be extracted to introduce, criticize, or conclude some common-sense point one wishes to make. One of the best examples of this aphoristic use of *On War* is Colonel Harry G. Summers's 1982 book *On Strategy: A Critical Analysis of the Vietnam War*. In this book Colonel Summers's method is to cite an appropriate passage from *On War* and then use it as a foil to criticize some aspect of the Vietnam War. For example, taking aim at the Pentagon bureaucracy, Summers begins:

The problem was that Secretary McNamara's Planning, Programming, and Budgeting System (PPBS) approach was only half the equation [needed to conduct the war in Vietnam]. To return again to Clausewitz:

> ... We see clearly that the activities characteristic of war may be split into two main categories: those *that are merely preparation for war, and war proper.* The same distinction must be made in theory as well. [1976, 131]

> ... [PPBS] did an excellent job in "getting control of the lines of supply." It was and is a useful system for "preparing for war" [but not for "war proper"]. (44–45)

But even though this "returning again to Clausewitz" in search of common sense may be the best way to use *On War,* one cannot accept everything Clausewitz says uncritically. This is especially true in regard to his most famous dictum—namely, that "war is merely the continuation of policy by other means" (1976, 87). Its undeniable truth notwithstanding, the dictum is profoundly ambiguous. What other means? If the other means are taken to be violent means, as is always the case, then the dictum struggles to describe not war but combat (or battle, as Clausewitz would no doubt prefer to say). I say "struggles to describe" because to describe combat as violence, or even as violent, is to misread the phenomenon, to fail to appreciate the plans and objectives that undergird the chaos of combat and that in turn depend upon extensive training, discipline, and leadership for their execution. However, if the other means are taken to include means *other than* combat, then one begins to see how the dictum might serve to define war. Specifically, if the phrase is interpreted as the means made available by a formal declaration of war, then new horizons begin to open, for a formal declaration of war creates the condition of war, putting certain legal, economic, and diplomatic sanctions into place in addition to threatening the possibility of combat. Interestingly, when one combines Grotius with Clausewitz in this way, a useful division of labor develops. As prescribed by the Constitution, Congress creates the legal, economic, diplomatic, and military condition of war through a formal declaration. From this menu of various means, the commander-in-chief then chooses those most appropriate for securing the policy objectives defined in the declaration. In some cases condemnation in the United Nations coupled with intensified negotiations may suffice. In other cases economic sanctions of one sort or another may be needed to supplement the diplomacy, whereas for the recalcitrant, it may be necessary to go a step further and initiate combat. In short, war is a matter of policy. But if so, then there exists an absolute need to articulate that policy, a war without a clearly articulated policy being like a play without a script or a book without a text. Furthermore, since it is the function of a fully reasoned declaration of war to articulate that policy, as the Second Continental Congress's Declaration of Independence demonstrates, then there also exists an absolute need to make a fully reasoned declaration of war, which not incidentally would fulfill requirements of article 1, section 8, of the Constitution.

2

Ignoring Democracy and the Constitution

The power to create the condition and state of war is one of the enumerated powers assigned to Congress in article I, section 8, of the Constitution. This section begins "The Congress shall have the power" and continues, in its eleventh clause, "to declare war, grant letters of marque and reprisal, and make rules concerning captures on land and water." Discussions of the power to grant letters of marque and reprisal lead in one of two directions. On the one hand, during the sixteenth, eighteenth, and early nineteenth centuries, the law of war stipulated that "solemnly perfect" "big" wars were to be initiated with a formal declaration of war, whereas "unsolemn imperfect" "little" wars—what are today called "armed conflicts"—were to be initiated by issuing letters of marque and reprisal. Consequently, as a matter of constitutional theory, the power to grant letters of marque and reprisal retains a residual significance for demonstrating that the Federal Convention intended the congressional war powers to encompass all types of war, imperfect as well as perfect wars, little as well as big wars, and covert wars as well as openly acknowledged wars (Gudridge 1995; Lobel 1995; Wormuth and Firmage 1989, 36–39, 261, 300). On the other hand, as a matter of international practice, letters of marque and reprisal are now antiquated, the practice having been outlawed by the 1856 Declaration of Paris. The United States never signed this declaration, but it has observed it, and the North did not commission privateers during the Civil War, although the South did. Since the Civil War, with the advent of iron bottoms and steam engines, the design and equipage of merchant and naval ships has become so radically different that it is no longer technically or financially feasible to convert merchant ships into ships of war.

The power to declare war, however, has not been outlawed by international convention. To the contrary, it has been mandated in article 1 of convention 3 of the 18 October 1907 Hague Peace Conference, Relative to the Opening of Hostilities, which was ratified by the Senate on 10 March 1908 and approved by President William Taft on 23 February 1909 (36 Stat. 2259). Since both the Constitution and convention 3 mandate Congress to declare war, its failure to do so more that twice or thrice a century is perplexing. Yet this failure is not just a domestic shortcoming. No representative democracy has done better. I will focus narrowly upon the U.S. Constitution and U.S. history, but it is important to note at the beginning that parliamentary regimes have been no more successful in involving the full legislature in the decision to war. For example, on Tuesday, 12 December 1826, the British Foreign Secretary George Canning stood at the dispatch box to describe the exemplary speed with which the government's decision to send troops and ships to Portugal was taken: "'It was only on last Friday night that this precise information,' of the actual invasion of Portugal [by Spain], 'arrived. On Saturday His Majesty's confidential servants came to a decision. On Sunday that decision received the sanction of His Majesty. On Monday it was communicated to both Houses of Parliament; and this day [Tuesday], Sir, at the hour in which I have the honour of addressing you, the troops are on the march for embarkation'" (cited in Maurice 1883, 48).

Over one hundred years later parliamentary practice was no more democratic, the inner cabinet still exercising the royal prerogative to declare war at its sole discretion. For example, on Monday, 8 December 1941, at the same time that Commander-in-Chief Roosevelt was delivering his famous "A Date Which Will Live in Infamy" speech requesting a congressional declaration of war against Japan, Prime Minister Winston Churchill was addressing Parliament, prefacing his remarks with admirably democratic sentiments: "As soon as I heard last night that Japan had attacked the United States I felt it necessary that Parliament should be immediately summoned. It is indispensable to our system of government that Parliament should play a full part in all the important acts of state, and at all crucial moments in the conduct of the war, and I am glad to see so many members have been able to be in their places in spite of the shortness of notice." A little further on in his address, however, we learn that the indispensable part that Parliament was to play in this important act of state consisted entirely of gathering to listen to the prime minister tell it what he had already done: "The Cabinet, which met at 12:30 today, therefore authorized an immediate declaration of war upon Japan. Instructions to this effect were sent to His Majesty's Ambassador in Tokyo, and a communication was dispatched to the Japanese Chargé d'Affaires at 1 o'clock today to this effect" (Churchill 1941, 14). By "Cabinet," Churchill presumably meant the war cabinet and not the full cabinet. To be sure, in a parliamentary system, where the threat of a no-confidence vote always hangs over a government, a war cabinet is more directly accountable to the entire parliament than a U.S. president is to Congress. But there is more nuance than substance in this systemic difference. In both systems executive control is effectively complete. In both systems the executive never requests or promulgates a declaration of war unless it is absolutely certain that Congress or Parliament will endorse it. (For a more recent perspective, see Seymour-Ure 1984.) As a result representative democracies in general and U.S. democracy in particular have never lived up to their democratic pretensions, and unlike a direct democracy or a monarchy, representative democracy has always been a sometimes thing, functioning tolerably well during peacetime but reverting to previous feudal forms during wartime.

Locating the Problem: Before 1789 or After?

This reversion to feudal forms in times of crisis is perhaps not so surprising after all, for representative democracy did not evolve out of direct democracy in some natural and organic way. Rather, it evolved out of the polar opposites of democracy, feudalism and absolutism as filtered through Britain's unique "mixed constitution." Under absolutism, according to its great theorist, Jean Bodin, the power to denounce war was the sovereign's second "mark of sovereignty," just after the right to ordain law and just before the right to appoint the higher magistrates (1962, 163 [162]). To be sure, there was some confusion as to the exact position of the power to denounce war. Earlier Bodin had listed it as the sovereign's third mark, behind appointing the higher magistrates and propagating law (1951, 174–75). Whatever its exact rank order, Bodin and his contemporaries were certain that the power of denouncing war belonged to the sovereign, not the legislature. In England identical views prevailed, although the term *mark of sovereignty* never took hold. In its place the English spoke of "royal prerogatives," which John Locke (1963) defined in chapter 14 of his *Second Treatise* as follows: "This power to act according to discretion for the public good, without the prescription of the law, and sometimes even against it, is that which is called prerogative." This definition neatly describes the manner in which U.S. commanders-in-chief have declared war since 1789. In the *Second Treatise* Locke does not specifically list the declaring of war as one of the king's prerogatives (the calling of Parliament is the only prerogative mentioned), but William Blackstone (1969, I, vii, 3) did, listing it as the king's third prerogative.

More to the point, however, in chapter 12 of the *Second Treatise,* Locke classifies foreign affairs in general and the power of war and peace in particular as one of the "federative" powers, which, although distinct from the executive powers, "yet . . . are almost always united" in the same hands. The reasons for uniting the executive and federative powers are, first, the fact that "what is to be done in reference to foreigners, depending much on their actions, and the variation of designs, and interests, must be left in great part to the prudence of those who have this power committed to them" and, second, the fact that the federative power "is much less capable to be directed by antecedent, standing, positive laws, than the executive." These two characteristics led Locke to warn against allowing the federative and executive power to "be placed in [different] persons that might act separately, whereby the force of the public would be under different commands; which would be apt some time or other to cause disorder and ruin." Although Locke's first characteristic of the federative power is benign and correct, his second strikes at the heart of the congressional war powers. Locke, it appears, was unable to imagine a legislature doing anything other than passing "antecedent, standing, positive laws." Fully reasoned declarations of war possessing substantive military and moral functions were beyond his experience and imagination. Like commentators since, Locke viewed formal declarations of war as precisely that—a mere formality. This fundamental flaw in Locke's analysis of the division of powers notwithstanding, his treatise reaffirmed and reinforced the belief that the power to declare war is a royal prerogative, beyond the competence of the legislative power.

This royal legacy, of which the members of the Federal Convention were fully aware and to which they were philosophically opposed, led, after 1789, to one of the earliest ways of framing the war powers debate as a dispute over the essence or nature of inherently executive powers versus the essence or nature of inherently legislative powers. First formulated in this way by Alexander Hamilton and James Madison during their 1793 Pacificus/Helvidius exchange, Hamilton argued in his "First Letter of Pacificus" that

> . . . if the Legislature have a right to make war on the one hand—it is on the other the duty of the Executive to preserve Peace till war is declared. . . .
>
> It deserves to be remarked, that as the participation of the senate in the making of Treaties and the power of the Legislature to declare war are exceptions out of the general "Executive Power" vested in the President, they are to be construed strictly—and ought to be extended no further than is essential to their execution. (1969, 40, 42)

Madison responded in his "First Letter of Helvidius": "Those who are to *conduct* a *war* cannot in the nature of things, be proper or safe judges, whether *a war ought* to be *commenced, continued,* or *concluded.* They are barred from the latter functions by a great principle in free government, analogous to that which separates the sword from the purse, or the power of executing from the power of enacting laws" (1906, 148). Although the consensus is that Hamilton's views have by and large prevailed (e.g., "Congress, the President, . . ." 1968, 1777), this belief is based less upon Hamilton's views than on Locke's and, more important, upon the practical reality that Congress so seldom declares war.

Another popular and traditional way in which the dispute has been rendered since 1789 is to try to divine the "original intentions" entertained by the Constitution's framers. Although the intentions of the members of the Federal Convention were many and mixed, there is general agreement that their primary intention was to avoid placing too much power in the hands of one person. This point was perhaps best captured by Abraham Lincoln in a letter dated 15 February 1848 to his law partner, William H. Herndon:

> The provision of the Constitution giving the war-making power to Congress was dictated, as I understand it, by the following reasons: Kings had always been involving and impoverishing their people in wars, pretending generally, if not always, that the good of the people was the object. This our convention understood to be the most oppressive of all kingly oppressions, and they resolved to so frame the Constitution that no one man should hold the power of bringing this oppression upon us. But your view* destroys the whole matter, and places our President where kings have always stood. (Lincoln 1907, 1:111–2)

The great irony of Representative Lincoln's critique of Commander-in-Chief James Polk's war against Mexico is that, thirteen years later, after he had become commander-in-chief in his turn, Lincoln would himself inflict this "most oppressive of all kingly oppressions" upon the United States. The Civil War is not only America's largest undeclared war but also its most costly war in terms of casualties suffered. Lincoln's letter is also of great interest because James Wilson, a delegate to the Federal Convention from Pennsylvania, had previously used strikingly similar language in the Pennsylvania ratifying convention: "This [new] system will not hurry us into war; it is calculated to guard against it. It will not be in the power of a single man, or a single body of men, to involve us in such distress; for the important power of declaring war is vested in the legislature at large: . . . from this circumstance we may draw a certain conclusion that nothing but our national interest can draw us into a war" (cit-

---

* Herndon's view, expressed earlier in the letter, was that the "President [Polk] may, without violation of the Constitution, cross the line and invade the territory of another country [Mexico], and that whether such necessity exists in any given case the President is the sole judge."

ed in Lofgren 1972, 685). More important than the fact of similar language, both passages speak to the question of intent, as Arthur Schlesinger Jr. has pointed out: "Lincoln's doctrine of '*no one man*'—an unconscious restatement of James Wilson's view that it should not be in the power of "a single man" to bring the country into war—unquestionably expressed the original intent [of the Federal Convention]" (1973, 43).

Without denying for a moment that this was indeed the original intent of the Federal Convention, on closer examination this intention, original or otherwise, is also seen to be tangential to the questions I am pursuing. Both Lincoln's "one man" and Wilson's "single man" doctrines speak more directly to the questions of how to organize the executive power and how to maximize accountability than to anything else. As Schlesinger also makes clear (1973, 5, 382–83), it was in this context, not in a discussion of the power to declare war, that this doctrine was first raised and most frequently discussed. Most of the delegates to the Federal Convention desired a plural executive, agreeing with Edmund Randolph of Virginia that a singular executive would be "the fœtus of monarchy." As a result, when James Wilson first proposed and Charles Pinckney seconded a singular executive on Friday, 1 June 1787, the proposal produced a shocked silence. Nonetheless, Wilson's views eventually won out, and the executive power was vested in one person, creating thereby a "vigorous" executive without sacrificing accountability.

A variation on or extension of the one-man doctrine that also figured among the framers' original intentions is the presumption that the executive branch possesses a special propensity for war. This being the case, article 1, section 8, is prescribed as the antidote. This line of argumentation was taken up by Madison in his "Fourth Letter of Helvidius":

> In no part of the Constitution is more wisdom to be found, than in the clause [article 1, section 8] which confides the question of war or peace to the legislature, and not to the executive department. Beside the objection to such a mixture to heterogeneous powers, the trust and the temptation would be too great for any one man; . . . War is in fact the true nurse of executive aggrandizement. In war, a physical force is to be created; and it is the executive will, which is to direct it. In war, the public treasures are to be unlocked; and it is the executive hand which is to dispense them. In war, the honours and emoluments of office are to be multiplied; and it is the executive patronage under which they are to be enjoyed. It is in war, finally, that laurels are to be gathered; and it is the executive brow they are to encircle. The strongest passions and most dangerous weaknesses of the human breast; ambition, avarice, vanity, the honorable or venial love of fame, are all in conspiracy against the desire and duty of peace.

> Hence it has grown into an axiom that the executive is the department of power most distinguished by its propensity to war; hence it is the practice of all states, in proportion as they are free, to disarm this propensity of its influence. (Madison 1906, 174)

Since 1793 this passage has been much quoted by those opposing this or that "presidential war." One of the earliest recitations of it was by Representative Robert Winthrop of Massachusetts on 8 January 1847, during a debate on the House floor to raise ten additional regiments for the Mexican War (*Congressional Globe* 1847, 144). Like those members of Congress who voted for the Gulf of Tonkin Resolution only to find out later that Commander-in-Chief Lyndon Johnson had stampeded them by providing less than accurate information, Representative Winthrop had also voted for the resolution declaring war against Mexico on 13 May 1846 based upon President Polk's less than accurate information concerning General Zachary Taylor's march on Matamoros. The previously deceived Winthrop now opposed the war. To bolster his attack, he denounced the way in which Polk had obtained his declaration of war, citing Madison to dramatize the dangers of such methods. More recently, Theodore Draper has used the passage to warn of the dangers of executive aggrandizement (Draper 1990, 42). Nonetheless, the argument, although plausible and comforting, is both tangential and suspect. It is suspect because its axiom cannot be accepted. If nothing else, the proclivities of the Athenian Assembly during the Peloponnesian War would cast considerable doubt upon Madison's axiom. It is tangential because it is democratic theory that drives article 1, section 8. Even if the executive department were the most pacific of all the departments of government, a representative democracy could still not confide the power to declare war to it. To do so would destroy the representative character of U.S. democracy during wartime, if not during peacetime.

An interesting variation on this theme of an executive propensity for war is found in part 1 of Thomas Paine's *Rights of Man:* "On the question of war, three things are to be considered; 1st, the right of declaring it; 2d, the expense of supporting it; 3d, the mode of conducting it after it is declared. The French constitution places the *right* where the *expense* must fall, and this union can be only in the nation. The mode of conducting it, after it is declared, it consigns to the executive department. Were this the case in all countries, we should hear but little more of wars" (1989, 88).

Perhaps Paine is correct; however, it is not necessary to catalog further the shortcomings of the various ways in which the war powers debate has been framed since 1789. Whichever of the many perspectives one examines, their most striking characteristic is their endlessly repetitive sterility. As Abraham Sofaer, who considered only the first forty years of the debate, has observed:

> Virtually every conceivable constitutional argument was advanced repeatedly, at times one feels almost ritualistically [during the first forty years of the republic, from 1789 to 1829]. Even the statements of the most important and influential leaders provide little definitive guidance. Most are offset by equally significant statements of opposing spokesmen. Other statements must be discounted as the product as much of party politics as of principle, or because the spokesman acted inconsistently with his pronouncement. The actions of early leaders [and later leaders as well] reflect their positions on issues more reliably than their constitutional rhetoric. . . . Actions may speak "louder" than words, but not necessarily as clearly or as authoritatively. And the acts of this nation's early [and later] leaders were at times as inconsistent and politically motivated as their words. (1976, xiv; cf. Lehman 1976, 38–39)

There are many reasons for this endless sterility. The largest reason, however, is the simple fact that the custom of formally declaring war had gone out of fashion at least a hundred years before the Federal Convention met in Philadelphia. By 1789 no nation was regularly and consistently declaring war formally. By 1789 the realities of international practice and custom had already rendered the power to declare war with due ceremony vacuous. Alexander Hamilton recognized this vacuity in *The Federalist No. 25* when he observed that "the ceremony of a formal denunciation of war has of late fallen into disuse." Just how far "the ceremony" had fallen was documented a hundred years later by Brevet Lieutenant Colonel J. F. Maurice in an influential and much quoted 1883 study of European and North American wars for the British Board of Trade. In his study Colonel Maurice found that between 1700 and 1870, there had been no fewer than 107 formally undeclared wars and no more than 10 formally declared wars (Maurice 1883, 4).* These findings shocked a good number of people, beginning with Colonel Maurice:

---

* The importance of Colonel (later General Sir Frederick) Maurice's study is difficult to overestimate. It is the definitive empirical study in English. It is cited whenever one wishes to demonstrate empirically that formal declarations of war no longer served any useful function after the seventeenth century. For example, one finds it cited in Takahashi (1908, 2–5), who reproduces the bulk of the report's "executive summary"; de Louter (1920, 236); Hall (1924, 448 n. 1), who adds, "Most of the wars of the seventeenth century began without declaration, though in some cases declarations were issued during their continuance" (447 n. 1); Wright (1932, 365); Eagleton (1938, 20); Department of State (1971, 12 n. 58); and Schlesinger (1972, 83). A summary listing of Colonel Maurice's study containing 81 of his 107 cases is reproduced in *The American Journal of International Law* 2, no. 1 (Jan. 1908): 57–62, which refers the reader to "House Report 754, p. 9, 52d Congress, 1st session."

The result of the investigation, as the work has gone on, has been to completely change its character. It was commenced under the impression that here and
there a casual case might be discovered in which the ambition of a Napoleon
or of a Frederick had led to some breach of established usage. The result is to
show conclusively that there has not been, unless in mere theory, and in the
tone adopted by historians as to what ought to have been, any established usage whatever on the subject. (1883, 4)

Since 1870 the disproportion of formally undeclared wars to formally declared
wars has not changed. Indeed, between 1945 and 1970 only one war was formally declared, and then by only a few of the belligerents involved. On 5 June
1967 Algeria, Iraq, Kuwait, Sudan, and Syria appear to have made formal declarations of war against Israel (Committee on Foreign Affairs 1970, 24 n. 2).

What are the consequences of this incontestable fact? The primary consequence is the need to relocate the problem, displacing it from its traditional locus in the changing circumstances of the nineteenth- and twentieth-cen-
turies and situating it in the ill-explored mists of the seventeenth century.
Indeed, once the problem has been relocated to the seventeenth century, the
failure of Congress to declare war more frequently than it has is readily explained: philosophical and constitutional inhibitions notwithstanding, the
United States is a country that respects and upholds the rules and customs that
govern international relations. Since the nation's inception in 1607, those
rules and customs have dictated that wars be declared formally on only the
rarest of occasions, which is precisely what the United States has done
throughout its history. Talk of executive prerogative, an imperial presidency,
and such take on a new perspective as soon as one recognizes that, had Congress declared war more frequently than two or three times a century, the
United States would have been seen as an oddity, possibly a disruptive oddity, in the eyes of the world community.

Therefore, the problem—or more precisely, the primary problem—is not
located in what the Constitution says or does not say. It is not located in what
the Founding Fathers intended or did not intend. Neither is it located in the
precedents and opinions, the disputes and squabbles, of the nineteenth and
twentieth centuries. Rather, the foremost problem—or better, the foremost
mystery—is located in the seventeenth century. Since before the dawn of history, in all cultures, it had been a sacred custom, infrequently violated, to begin *every* war with a formal declaration. Then "suddenly" the European powers stopped issuing formal declarations of war during the course of the
seventeenth century. Herein lies the challenge, for as soon as one can explain
why *all* nations stopped declaring their wars formally during the seventeenth

century, it then becomes an easy matter to explain why any one of them did so. More important, once one can explain this phenomenon, it becomes possible to explore how Congress might break away from this four-hundred-year-old internationally imposed norm. In other words, by relocating the problem to the seventeenth century, one takes the first steps toward exploring how representative democracy might transform itself in the twenty-first century into a system of representation that functions not only in times of peace but in times of war as well.

A Mere Formality?

As I already indicated in the previous chapter, I believe that the root cause of this change in attitudes toward formal declarations of war was a change in attitudes toward war. As soon as people began reducing war to the violence of combat, formal declarations of war no longer made any sense. The trajectory of this change in attitudes toward formal declarations of war will be taken up in the next chapter, whereas chapter 4 will argue more extensively the case for believing that war cannot be reduced to the violence of combat. For the present, however, I will largely ignore the question of why and simply accept as an empirical fact that formal declarations of war had gone out of fashion one hundred years or more before the Federal Convention met in Philadelphia, developing the argument from there.

Let me begin with a paradox: whereas it is incontestable that all nations stopped making *formal* declarations of war regularly and consistently during the seventeenth century, this does not mean that they stopped making declarations of war. Instead they began resorting to "functional equivalents." I discuss the infinite variety of functional equivalents toward the end of the next chapter, but for now it is their simple existence that intrigues me. In particular, I am intrigued by the circularity of the resulting situation: the moment one admits the existence of functional equivalents, such as a presidential message to Congress or a televised presidential address, one must also acknowledge that *all* wars are declared wars, some formally and others informally. Consequently the term *undeclared war* is cruelly misleading. It does not mean that the war in question is actually undeclared; rather, it means that no *formal* declaration has been made with due solemnity and ceremony, the declaration having been contained in some functional equivalent, such as a proclamation.

But if all wars are declared wars, then why would anyone accept a functional equivalent when the real thing is so easily had? Since at least the seventeenth century, the conventional response has been that formal declarations of war can and should be dispensed with whenever expediency or circumstances so dictate because they add nothing of substance to the hostilities, because they *are* nothing but meaningless ceremonies, cynical solemnities, and empty formalities. In addition, since 1789 the conventional response has been that substituting functional equivalents for the meaningless formalities of a formal declaration of war is the only or at least the best way to resolve what Manicas called "the Machiavellian imperative of modern politics"—namely, that an elected executive charged with the responsibility for national security can best deal with a recalcitrant, uninformed, and voting public by ignoring it.

For the sake of completeness, however, I should note in passing that those upholding the conventional wisdom supplement the empirical evidence that formal declarations of war are unnecessary by offering a number of policy reasons. John Adams was the first president to wage an undeclared war as a matter of conscious policy, in his case against revolutionary France (see Sofaer 1976, ch. 3). But whether one talks about 1793 or 1973, the policy reasons given are essentially the same. A summary of them can be elicited by recalling the controversies that surrounded the repeal of the Gulf of Tonkin Resolution. For example, the State Department argued:

> Formal declarations of war are often deliberately avoided because they tend to indicate both at home and abroad a commitment to total victory and may impede settlement possibilities. The issuance of a formal declaration can also have certain legal results: Some treaties may be canceled or suspended; trading, contracts, and debts with the enemy are suspended; vast emergency powers become operative domestically; and the legal relations between neutral states and belligerents can be altered. (Department of State 1971, 12 n. 58)

John Moore has summarized several other considerations, beginning with the assertion that the constitutional requirement for Congress to declare war is not really a requirement:

> As Under Secretary Katzenbach puts it "[a joint resolution is] a functional equivalent of a declaration of war."
>
> There are also numerous policy arguments why the formal declaration of war is undesirable. . . . Arguments made include increased danger of misunderstanding of limited objectives, diplomatic embarrassment in recognition of nonrecognized guerrilla opponents, inhibitions of settlement possibilities, the danger of widening the war [e.g., by activating secret treaties between North Vietnam and the Soviet Union or China], and unnecessarily increasing the President's domestic authority [e.g., by authorizing wartime censorship to curb dissent]. Although each of these arguments has some merit, probably the most compelling reason for not using the formal declaration of war is that there is no reason to do so. As Former Secretary of Defense McNamara has pointed out

"[T]here has not been a formal declaration of war—anywhere in the world—since World War II." (Moore 1969, 33)*

As John Moore indicates, the policy reasons for not formally declaring war have always formed a secondary line of defense. Based mainly upon expediency and convenience, they lack the hard edge of the incontestable empirical evidence that there is never reason to declare war formally.

With the new democratic theory conflicting so openly and directly with such an empirical reality, with such a well-established international custom and practice, one or the other obviously had to give. Unfortunately, neither option was palatable. Who, after all, would dare to advocate openly that representative democracy must be sacrificed to international custom during times of war? Alternatively, who would dare to state frankly that the United States must violate the norms of international relations merely to abide by the legal dictates of the Constitution and the philosophical requirements of representative democracy? As a consequence, the principal method for resolving this conflict since 1789 has been to ignore it. When the abstract philosophical demands of the Constitution conflict with the practical realities of the well-established principles and conventions of international relations, pragmatic people prefer settled practices to unsettling philosophies—and change the topic. A recent example of this question-begging approach is Eugene Rostow's 1972 attack upon the then-pending War Powers Bill. The problem, according to Rostow, is found not among the philosophical demands of representative democracy but rather in the overriding need to maintain long-established methods for the conduct of foreign affairs:

> Responding to the bitterness and tragedy of Vietnam, a group of Senators led by Jacob K. Javits of New York proposes fundamentally to change the constitutional relationship between President and Congress in the field of foreign affairs. . . . These men have offered a Bill which in their view would correct nearly two hundred years of error, strip the Presidency of many of its most essential powers, and restore what they fondly imagine was the constitutional model of 1789. (1972, 833–34)

But if the "constitutional relationship between the President and the Congress in the field of foreign affairs" is sound and not in need of realignment, then it follows that the real problem lies elsewhere:

---

* Secretary McNamara was speaking in May 1966, which means that the 5 June 1967 formal declarations of war by Algeria, Iraq, Kuwait, Sudan, and Syria against Israel noted previously were yet to occur.

> The relevant Congressional Committees, and the Congress as a whole, should
> be leading the nation in a courteous and sustained debate, through which we
> could hope to achieve a new consensus about foreign policy, as vital, and creative,
> as that which sustained the line of policy which started with the Truman Doc-
> trine, the Marshall Plan, NATO and its progeny, and the Four Point Program.
>
> Instead, the Senate Foreign Relations Committee has chosen to escape from
> the demanding but manageable task of reality by retreating into the insoluble
> and dangerous realm of constitutional myth. . . . The Javits Bill would turn the
> clock back to the Articles of Confederation, and destroy the Presidency which
> was one of the chief aims of the men of Annapolis and Philadelphia to create.
> (Rostow 1972, 900)

In sum, the Vietnam War created not a constitutional crisis but rather a crisis
of consensus. As soon as consensus is restored, the "imagined" constitutional crisis will recede into the background, where it belongs.

However, Senator Jacob Javits and his group were not the first people who
could not ignore "the insoluble and dangerous realm of constitutional myth."
Since 1789 the alternative to ignoring the conflict between democratic theory and international practice has been to suggest that article 1, section 8, was
never meant to require that Congress actually declare war. Rather, the requirement is for full and frequent consultation. With suitable consultations between the commander-in-chief and the congressional leadership, one should
be able to bridge the gap between democratic theory and international practice. After all, consultations not only avoid the dangers of "executive aggrandizement" but also accommodate the various policy considerations that are
often said to militate against a formal declaration of war, do they not?

This conception of the congressional war powers as consultations has always been particularly appealing because it appears to work well. Beginning
with John Adams, most commanders-in-chief have assiduously consulted
with Congress. Even on those few occasions when they were less than forthcoming, such as James Polk's manipulation of the Twenty-ninth Congress in
1846, the damage to democracy has not been excessive. Indeed, so strong is
the appeal of this conception of the congressional war powers that Senator
Javits and his group enshrined it in law, the 1973 War Powers Resolution being no more than an attempt to force the commander-in-chief to consult with
the Congress at thirty-, sixty-, and ninety-day intervals. In the final analysis,
however, conceiving of the power to *declare* war as an injunction for consultations about the war is unsatisfactory. Since it is the commander-in-chief who
deigns to consult with the congressional leadership, not the other way
around, can such consultations be construed as a congressional power, much
less an autonomous war power?

This dilemma was first hinted at in the spring of 1793, when the congressional war powers first became a matter of public concern. At that time, the French minister, Edmond Genêt, was publicly demanding that the fledgling U.S. government honor articles 17 and 22 of the Franco-American Treaty of Amity and Commerce of 1778 and support the French Revolution militarily. President George Washington, fearing British retaliation, responded by issuing a presidential proclamation on 22 April 1793 indicating that the United States would follow a policy of strict neutrality. To defend Washington's widely unpopular actions, Hamilton wrote a number of newspaper articles known as the "Letters of Pacificus." At Jefferson's urging, Madison took up the challenge, responding to Hamilton under the name of Helvidius. Traditionally it has been held that Hamilton "won" the exchange and hence that his views on the need for a strong executive who need not consult with Congress carried the day. Hamilton was never elected president, however; Madison was. Moreover, in 1812 Madison was the president who made the very first request for a declaration of war. Letters and opinions are one thing; actual precedents are another. Consequently, what Madison thought and did is of more than passing interest.

What did Madison think? In his second "Letter of Helvidius," we learn that, with respect to the congressional power to declare war, "the executive has no other discretion than to convene and give information to the legislature." (Madison 1906, 160). Not surprisingly, this is precisely what Madison did in 1812, thereby giving the weight of precedent to his words. After consulting with key members secretly, he then consulted with the Twelfth Congress publicly, initiating the process by sending a long message to Congress on 1 June 1812 informing it of his reasons for requesting the declaration of war. Seventeen days later the Twelfth Congress gave him the following unreasoned declaration of war on 18 June 1812:

> *Be it enacted by the Senate and House of Representatives of the United States in Congress assembled,* That war be and the same is hereby declared to exist between the United Kingdom of Great Britain and Ireland and the dependencies thereof, and the United States of America and their Territories; and that the President of the United States is hereby authorized to use the whole land and naval force of the United States to carry the same into effect, and to issue to private armed vessels of the United States commissions or letters of marque and general reprisal, in such form as he shall think proper, and under the seal of the United States, against the vessels, goods, and effects, of the Government of the said United Kingdom of Great Britain and Ireland, and the subjects thereof. (Pub. L. No. 12-102, 2 Stat. 755)

Since all wars require a public statement of their causes and goals, Madison's message constitutes the fully reasoned declaration of war—that is, the declaration that makes the unreasoned declaration of the Twelfth Congress nothing but a mere formality. Still, it is not this that concerns me here. Rather, it is the importance of Madison's precedent, which cannot be overemphasized. John Adams had previously established the necessity of close consultation with Congress for formally undeclared war. Yet crucially, consultations in this case do not compromise the autonomy of the congressional war powers. In theory at least, Congress could have formally declared war against France. Now, however, Madison extended the practice to formally declared wars, to wars in which the commander-in-chief desires Congress to exercise its war powers. In all cases Congress would now be dependent on and subordinate to the commander-in-chief. By custom and precedent Congress could not act except at the request and with the permission of the commander-in-chief.

The full extent of congressional dependency is well understood by anyone who has served on a board of directors. One does not need much experience to know that an executive officer who controls the timing of a debate and the information used in it controls the debate. Timing is especially important. Such executives need only delay the debate until the crisis has reached its peak and then stampede the board into doing whatever they desire to be done. In effect, then, conceiving of the *congressional* war powers as an injunction for consultation places control of the *congressional* war powers in the hands of the commander-in-chief. This subversive dependency of Congress upon the commander-in-chief is best illustrated by the joint resolution of 2 June 1858 against Paraguay, a conditional declaration of war that did not eventuate in combat. In response to a request made by commander-in-chief James Buchanan in his annual address of 8 December 1857, on 21 April 1858 the Thirty-fifth Congress began debate on the following conditional declaration of war:

> A Resolution for the Adjustment of Difficulties with the Republic of Paraguay.
> *Resolved by the Senate and House of Representatives of the United States of America in Congress assembled,* That for the purpose of adjusting the differences between the United States and the republic of Paraguay, in connexion with the attack on the United States steamer Water Witch, and with other matters referred to in the annual message of the President [Buchanan], he be, and is hereby, authorized to adopt such measures and use such force as, in his judgment, may be necessary and advisable, in the event of a refusal of just satisfaction by the government of Paraguay. (Pub. Res. No. 35-15, 11 Stat. 370)

"And with other matters referred to in the annual message of the President"— this phrase shows Congress clearly acting as the commander-in-chief's handmaiden. Buchanan, not Congress, has determined when and why a declaration of war is required and is now simply asking for congressional approval of his decision. There is no thought that Congress might play an autonomous role in the drama, that the *congressional* war powers could or even should be exercised by Congress at its sole discretion. Instead, following Madison's words and precedents, the commander-in-chief controls both the timing of the request and the information used in the congressional deliberations, such as they are.

The problem, as can be seen from the 1812 and 1858 declarations just cited, lies within the texts themselves. Clearly, if declarations of war contain no more substance than these two examples—and none of Congress's five absolute declarations have contained more—then they *are* nothing but mere unreasoned formalities. Lacking all substance, they can and should be ignored, as the seventeenth century had long since come to realize. However, it was not always thus. As I describe in the next chapter, from before the dawn of history until the seventeenth century, declarations of war were fully reasoned. In particular, this older tradition distinguished between an absolute and a conditional declaration, which in turn may be either reasoned or unreasoned. An absolute declaration of war, such as the 1812 declaration, proclaims absolutely, as a matter of uncontested fact, that a state of war exists between two parties. In contrast, a conditional declaration, such as the 1858 declaration, argues that certain grievances have caused a breech of the peace that can be mended only if certain conditions are met. It then concludes that war is unavoidable "in the event of a refusal of just satisfaction by the government of" the offending nation. When a time limit is attached to the fulfillment of the conditions, the conditional declaration becomes an ultimatum. The distinction between absolute and conditional declarations is an ancient one, stretching beyond Cicero, who tells his son in *De Officiis* that "all the rights and duties of war have been rigorously established by the Roman Fetial Laws, from which it is abundantly clear that no war is just unless preceded by an absolute or conditional declaration" (1967, I, xi, 36). Both the distinction and this passage from Cicero were well known before the twentieth century. For example, Grotius (1925, 2:633) and other seventeenth-century jurists quoted this passage frequently with approval.

Cicero neglects to mention that declarations of war also need to be reasoned. He does this for the simple reason that unreasoned declarations were completely beyond his experience. He could not imagine anyone writing one. After all, why would anyone simply proclaim that a state of war now exists between countries X and Y? Since wars announce themselves loudly and clearly, such declarations are always unnecessary and frequently undesirable, as we have already seen the State Department argue. They are, for all practical purposes, without consequence or effect. More recently, then, the terms *motivated* or *reasoned* have been introduced. For example, in article 1 of convention 3 of the 18 October 1907 Hague Peace Conference, Relative to the Opening of Hostilities, one reads:

> Les Puissances contractantes reconnaissent que les hostilités entre elles ne doivent pas commencer sans un avertissement préalable et non équivoque, qui aura, soit la forme d'une déclaration de guerre *motivée*, soit celle d'une ultimatum avec déclaration de guerre conditionelle. [The contracting powers recognize that hostilities between themselves must not commence without previous and explicit warning, in the form either of a *reasoned* declaration of war or of an ultimatum with a conditional declaration of war.] (Emphasis added.)

The only example of a reasoned declaration in U.S. history is the Declaration of Independence, which I analyze in detail subsequently. For the moment, however, what interests me is the fact that this earlier tradition of reasoned declarations of war—that is, declarations that do more than merely declare war formally—opens up the possibility that not all declarations of war are vacuous, that Congress might possess a realm of autonomous activity separate and independent from the commander-in-chief's power to conduct war. To recover this lost tradition, it is perhaps best to return to the beginning—to Friday, 17 August 1787—and see whether a fresh look at those seminal events in Philadelphia might not lead in new directions.

Searching for Substance

Unlike their subsequent history, the birth of the congressional war powers was not controversial. The clause—originally framed as the power "to make war"—was discussed in the Federal Convention on Friday, 17 August 1787, at the end of a busy day filled with other matters. The discussion was neither very long nor very contentious. Charles Pinckney of South Carolina began by urging that this power be vested in the Senate alone so as to consolidate in that body the powers to make both war and peace. This suggestion was countered by Mr. Pinckney's colleague from South Carolina, Pierce Butler, who argued "for vesting the power in the President, who will have all the requisite qualities, and will not make war but when the Nation will support it" (Farrand 1911, 318).

Neither of these suggestions provoked any interest, and the discussion soon focused upon a motion by James Madison of Virginia and Elbridge Gerry of Massachusetts that *declare* be substituted for *make*. Supported by Rufus King of Massachusetts, Oliver Ellsworth of Connecticut, and George Mason of Virginia, the delegates finally approved the motion on a second vote (ayes: 8; noes: 1; absent: 1) for the following reasons: first, they believed that "the Executive shd. be able to repel and not to commence war," and second, they wanted to forestall any misunderstanding "that '*make*' war might be under-stood [as] to 'conduct' it which is an Executive function" (Farrand 1911, 318, 319). The Madison-Gerry amendment having been passed, Charles Pinckney next moved to delete the whole clause. However, the delegates rejected the idea without even taking a vote. Pierce Butler also moved to add "and peace" after "war," a suggestion that was voted down unanimously. With this the delegates adjourned for the day, and the matter was settled as far as they were concerned.

Given the simplicity of its birth, one can only wonder at the controversy and complexity that has surrounded the congressional war powers since. On the face of it, the Federal Convention clearly envisioned a separation of the sovereign's war powers; the commander-in-chief was to repel sudden attacks and to conduct all wars, whereas Congress was to deliberate and write the declarations of war, it being—to all appearance—self-evident that one cannot declare war until after the declaration has been written and the declaration cannot be written until after suitable deliberations. I say "to all appearance" because for two hundred years the need for Congress to write its own declara-tions, or even to deliberate, has not been self-evident at all. For example, the two twentieth-century declarations, those of 1917 and 1941, were both writ-ten by functionaries in the State Department, and the 1941 declaration passed without any deliberations whatsoever.

Needless to say, relieving Congress of the burden of writing its own decla-rations of war does make sense when one misconceives of the congressional war powers as an injunction for the commander-in-chief to consult. Since it is commanders-in-chief who initiate the process and control the information given to Congress, it makes sense for them also to provide the texts of the declarations. Not surprisingly under this inadequate conception, the com-manders-in-chief have always submitted unreasoned absolute declarations for congressional approval because, by doing nothing more than declaring war, such documents give them the widest latitude in conducting wars.

But what if one conceived of the *congressional* war powers as an autono-mous *congressional* power to deliberate and write its own declarations of war, independently of the commander-in-chief? Furthermore, what if Congress deliberated on and wrote only fully reasoned declarations of war? That is, what if Congress did not simply declare the brute fact of war with an unreasoned absolute declaration, as it has done for the last two hundred years, but instead devoted itself to analyzing the grievances that called for the resort to arms and, more important still, the conditions that would restore peace, as the Second Continental Congress did in 1776? In other words, what if the Congress ig-nored the last four hundred years of international custom and practice and instead revived the practices and customs that governed the declaring of war before the seventeenth century?

In such a case, it would be possible to move beyond our modern conception of the power to declare war as a mere formality and to identify the military and moral functions of a declaration of war. The primary military functions of a fully reasoned declaration are to justify cogently the resort to war and to establish the meaning of peace and victory—the war aims. That is, in a more military language, the military purpose of a fully reasoned declaration of war is to articulate the grand strategy for the war. The primary moral function is to distinguish a good from a bad declaration. A good declaration is a cogently argued grand strategy, one that provides not only persuasive grievances justifying the resort to war but also sensible remedies or peace terms to end the war. A bad declaration is either an unreasoned declaration—that is, a declaration providing neither grievances to justify nor war aims to end the war—or a poorly argued set of grievances and aims.

In addition, when the *congressional* war powers are understood in this way, one soon discovers that war, not democratic theory, that Clausewitz, not Montesquieu, provides the rationale for dividing the sovereign's war powers. As the seventeenth century came to recognize, because an unreasoned absolute declaration of war does no more than declare war formally, there is no compelling reason ever to issue one. In contrast, a reasoned declaration of war, or its functional equivalent, is absolutely essential to the proper conduct of all wars. This is so because, as Clausewitz advises, a well-articulated grand strategy is absolutely essential: "No one starts a war—or rather, no one in his senses ought to do so—without first being clear in his mind what he intends to achieve by that war and how he intends to conduct it. The former is its political purpose; the latter its operational objective" (1976, 579). But how is the grand strategy to become clear in anyone's mind unless the responsible parties articulate cogently the grievances that have provoked the war, on the one hand, and the conditions that will restore peace, on the other hand—that is, unless they make a reasoned declaration of war? Indeed, the absolute need to become clear in one's mind is the primary lesson learned from the Vietnam War, as found, for example, in the 1984 revision of *AFM 1-1, Basic Functions and Doctrine of the United States Air Force:* "The fabric of our society and the character of our national values suggest that the decision to employ US military forces depends on a clear declaration of objectives and the support of the American people" (Department of the Air Force 1984, p. 1-1).

Of even greater interest, though, is the fact that grand strategy guides and directs strategy. That is, the political purposes articulated in a reasoned declaration guide and direct the operational objectives, with the result that "war is merely the continuation of policy by other means," to repeat Clausewitz's famous dictum (1976, 87). But if the political purposes control the operational objectives, then whoever articulates these war aims controls the conduct of the war "down to the smallest operational detail" (579), which seems to be precisely the sort of control a legislature would want to exercise over a commander-in-chief, controlling the means used by dictating the ends sought.

To avoid confusion, however, we must distinguish between the micromanagement of a war and the manner in which the political purposes of a war control the conduct of the war down to the smallest operational detail. Clausewitz would be the last person in the world to recommend that the political authorities attempt to micromanage a war. Micromanagement for him would just be an unwarranted interference in the professional conduct of the war. However, Clausewitz also understood the subtle way in which the ends always direct the means. For example, to use the confusion over the goals of the Vietnam War as an illustration, if the purpose of U.S. involvement was to defeat a North Vietnamese invasion, then U.S. forces should have been deployed in large units along or just over South Vietnam's frontiers, with all the operational consequences that that entails. If, however, the purpose of U.S. involvement was to stop an insurgent guerrilla movement, then U.S. forces should have been deployed in small patrolling units, stalking the villages by night and day so as to beat the guerrillas at their own game, with all the operational consequences that that entails. And if U.S. involvement had other purposes, then U.S. forces would have had to be deployed in other ways, which again would have entailed completely different operational consequences. The point is that this is the type of grand strategic decision about which Clausewitz is talking, not unwarranted micromanagement such as a congressional edict that all units deployed to Vietnam will be of some specific size. By simply articulating the purpose, Congress thereby fixes the optimal size of the deployed units. It need do no more. The professional military will unfurl the operational consequences of the congressionally articulated purpose.

Finally, Clausewitz also believed that the conduct of war "depends on the particular character of the commander and the army; but the political aims are the business of the government alone" (89). The implication here is that the business of war divides naturally into strategy, that is, the power to *conduct* war, and grand strategy, that is, the power to *declare* the political purposes of the war. That is, he believed that articulating the purposes of a war (i.e., grand strategy) is a different and distinct function from the conduct of a war (i.e., strategy), calling upon different qualities and requiring different agencies. Even when the head of government and the commander-in-chief are one and the same person, this functional division is still crucial. Indeed, it was precisely because Frederick the Great understood this difference that he died with honor after a long reign, whereas Bonaparte, who allowed the strategically possible to determine the politically desirable, died in ignominious exile. Frederick formulated his political objectives first and then sought a successful strategy; Bonaparte formulated a successful strategy and then imposed an ephemeral victor's peace upon the vanquished. Perhaps surprisingly, this same Clausewitzian division of war as between the commander and the government is found in *The Federalist No. 69,* written by Hamilton:

> The President is to be Commander in Chief of the army and navy of the United States. In this respect his authority . . . would amount to nothing more than the supreme command and direction of the military and naval forces, as first General and Admiral of the confederacy; while that of the British King extends to the *declaring* of war and to the *raising* and *regulating* of fleets and armies; all which by the Constitution under consideration would appertain to the Legislature.

In short, it is the demands of war itself, not the philosophical demands of democratic theory, that requires a division of the sovereign's power to *make* war. It is Clausewitz, not Montesquieu, who provides the most cogent reasons for reserving the power to *declare* war to Congress. Indeed, were Congress ever to conceive of its war powers as the power to articulate grand strategy by writing only reasoned declarations of war, then it could move beyond both the requirements of democratic theory and the four-hundred-year-old customs of international relations. It could begin controlling the actual conduct of war down to the smallest operational detail, for, whoever dictates grand strategy by that very act guides and directs strategy.

A problem now arises. The delegates to the Federal Convention, although well versed in Montesquieu, were innocent of Clausewitz, who was but seven years old in 1787. Neither did they recognize the distinction between an unreasoned and a reasoned declaration of war. They were, in fine, incapable of imagining the possibility of Congress controlling the commander-in-chief by controlling the articulation of the political purposes of the war. Consequently, when we conceive of the congressional war powers as the power to deliberate and write reasoned, and only reasoned, declarations, we cannot claim the sanction of the Founding Fathers. They spent only a short time on the matter and never thought through the implications of their decision.

Nonetheless, although the constitutional arguments may be nonexistent, the military and moral arguments are overwhelming. Just how overwhelming they are can perhaps best be demonstrated by moving from the abstract to the concrete, by turning our attention to actual texts, for example, the alpha and the omega of formal U.S. declarations of war: the Declaration of Independence and the declarations of 1941. Including the Declaration of Independence may strike many as an odd choice, since we never think of it as a declaration of war. Indeed, ever since Lincoln transformed its preamble into the "proposition" upon which the American experiment is founded in his Gettysburg Address, it has been, in Lincoln's words, "the electric cord . . . that links the hearts of patriotic and liberty-loving men together" (cited in Wills 1992, 86). Still, in both form and function, it remains a fully reasoned declaration of war, America's *lettre de défi* to George III. Therefore, my purpose in comparing it to the 1941 declarations is not to ignore or minimize its other historical and philosophical dimensions. Rather, my purpose is to return it to its original pragmatic function, which then allows me to build my comparison upon the fact that, because there is always a need to articulate a war's grand strategy, a reasoned declaration was made in both 1776 and 1941. In this respect, the only differences between the two are, first, *who* articulated the war's grand strategy and, second, the *quality* of the reasoning used. The question of who fixes grand strategy goes to the heart of the military functions of a declaration of war; the question of quality, to the moral functions. A comparison of the 1941 and 1776 declarations will illustrate these claims.

The 1941 Declaration

Pearl Harbor was attacked on Sunday, 7 December 1941. The next day Commander-in-Chief Roosevelt convened Congress to give it information. As the *New York Times* breathlessly reported:

> Congress, with only one dissenting vote, approved the resolution [declaring war] in the record time of 33 minutes after President Roosevelt denounced Japanese aggression in ringing tones. . . . There was no debate like that between April 2, 1917, when President Wilson requested war against Germany, and April 6, when the declaration of war was approved by Congress.
>
> President Roosevelt spoke only 6 minutes and 30 seconds today, compared with Woodrow Wilson's 29 minutes and 34 seconds.
>
> The vote today against Japan was 82 to 0 in the Senate and 385 to 1 in the House. The lone vote against the resolution in the House was that of Miss Jannette Rankin, Republican, of Montana. Her "No" was greeted with boos and hisses. In 1917 she voted against the resolution for war against Germany. (Kluckhohn, 1941, 1)

There are two ways to regard this report. On the one hand, the report is remarkable for how well it conforms to the conception of the congressional war powers as consultation. Roosevelt and many other Americans had known for over a year that the United States would have to enter the war against Germany sooner or later. However, isolationist sentiment was ferociously against another large-scale war in Europe. In the face of this opposition, Roosevelt did what he could around the margins in the way of the Lend-Lease Act, a new conscription law, an undeclared naval war against German U-boats in the Atlantic, and so on, biding his time until the inevitable crisis broke and he would be able to stampede the Seventy-seventh Congress. The crisis occurred on 7 December 1941 in the Pacific, and not the Atlantic as was expected. Then, like Commanders-in-Chief Madison, Polk, and Wilson before him, he "consulted" Congress, convening it and giving it information.

On the other hand, to a Clausewitz, this report would be of little or no interest, its description of procedure, who consulted with whom and when, being unimportant. Since *"war is nothing but the continuation of policy with other means,"* a Clausewitz would be much more interested in hearing a clear articulation of the nation's grand strategy. What were the grievances that justified the resort to war? What were the terms that would restore peace? In fine, he would want to hear a reasoned declaration of war. Who, therefore, was taking responsibility for articulating grand strategy, Commander-in-Chief Roosevelt or the Seventy-seventh Congress? Roosevelt spoke first, addressing a joint session at 12:30 P.M.:

> Mr. Vice President, Mr. Speaker, members of the Senate and the House of Representatives:
>
> Yesterday, December 7, 1941—a date which will live in infamy—the United States of America was suddenly and deliberately attacked by naval and air forces of the Empire of Japan.
>
> The United States was at peace with that Nation and, at the solicitation of Japan, was still in conversation with its Government and its Emperor looking toward the maintenance of peace in the Pacific. Indeed, one hour after Japanese air squadrons had commenced bombing in the American island of Oahu, the Japanese Ambassador to the United States and his colleague delivered to our Secretary of State a formal reply to a recent American message. And while this reply stated that it seemed useless to continue the existing diplomatic negotiations, it contained no threat or hint of war or of armed attack.
>
> It will be recorded that the distance of Hawaii from Japan makes it obvious that the attack was deliberately planned many days or even weeks ago. During the intervening time the Japanese Government has deliberately sought to deceive the United States by false statements and expressions of hope for continued peace.
>
> The attack yesterday on the Hawaiian Islands has caused sever damage to American naval and military forces. I regret to tell you that very many American lives have been lost. In addition, American ships have been reported torpedoed on the high seas between San Francisco and Honolulu.

Yesterday the Japanese Government also launched an attack against Malaya.

Last night Japanese forces attacked Hong Kong.

Last night Japanese forces attacked Guam.

Last night Japanese forces attacked the Philippine Islands.

Last night the Japanese forces attacked Wake Island.

And this morning the Japanese attacked Midway Island.

Japan has, therefore, undertaken a surprise offensive extending throughout the Pacific area. The facts of yesterday and today speak for themselves. The people of the United States have already formed their opinions and well understand the implications to the very life and safety of our Nation.

As Commander in Chief of the Army and Navy I have directed that all measures be taken for our defense.

But always will our whole nation remember the character of the onslaught against us.

No matter how long it may take us to overcome this premeditated invasion, the American people in their righteous might will win through to absolute victory.

I believe that I interpret the will of the Congress and of the people when I assert that we will not only defend ourselves to the uttermost but will make it very certain that this form of treachery shall never again endanger us.

Hostilities exist. There is no blinking at the fact that our people, our territory, and our interests are in grave danger.

With confidence in our armed forces—with the unbounding determination of our people—we will gain the inevitable triumph—so help us God.

I ask that the Congress declare that since the unprovoked and dastardly attack by Japan on Sunday, December 7, 1941, a state of war has existed between the United States and the Japanese Empire. (Roosevelt 1938–50, 10:514–15)

After this address, the Senate returned to its chambers, where it passed in fifteen minutes an unreasoned absolute declaration of war drafted by the State Department. The House took a little longer, not passing it until 1:10 P.M. Typing and other paperwork meant that Vice President Henry Wallace could not sign the resolution until 3:23 P.M., and it took another forty-seven minutes to organize the small ceremony at which Commander-in-Chief Roosevelt affixed his signature in the presence of congressional leaders at 4:10:

Declaring that a state of war exists between the Imperial Government of Japan and the Government and the people of the United States and making provisions to prosecute the same:

Whereas the Imperial Government of Japan has committed unprovoked acts of war against the Government and the people of the United States of America; therefore, be it

Resolved by the Senate and the House of Representatives of the United States of America in Congress assembled, That the state of war between the United States and the Imperial Government of Japan which has thus been thrust upon the United States is hereby formally declared; and the President is hereby authorized and directed to employ the entire naval and military forces of the United States and the resources of the Government to carry on the war against the Imperial Government of Japan; and, to bring the conflict to a successful termination, all of the resources of the country are hereby pledged by the Congress of the United States. (Pub. L. No. 77-328, 55 Stat. 795)

Clearly it was Commander-in-Chief Roosevelt who fixed the nation's grand strategy by making the functional equivalent of a reasoned declaration of war. Anyone, such as a subordinate military commander, seeking an authoritative, official statement of the war's causes and goals had to turn to his statement. Little or nothing can be learned from the congressional declaration, which was indeed nothing but a mere formality. At each and every point, the commander-in-chief provided more precision, more specificity, and more detail. Where the Seventy-seventh Congress speaks of "unprovoked acts of war," Roosevelt not only provides a detailed list but also mentions the failed diplomatic negotiations that form the essential background for the attacks. Where the Seventy-seventh Congress speaks thinly of bringing "the conflict to a successful termination," Roosevelt speaks forthrightly of winning "through to absolute victory." Consequently, it was the commander-in-chief, and not the Seventy-seventh Congress, who would guide the conduct of the war down to the smallest operational detail. When subordinate commanders drafted their battle plans, they would take no notice of the vague and empty congressional sentiments. Instead, they would base their plans upon the commander-in-chief's grand strategy of winning "through to absolute victory."

In defense of the Seventy-seventh Congress, one must acknowledge that, on this occasion at least, it did meet its absolute minimal constitutional requirement to declare war. Yet its unreasoned absolute declaration is both redundant and superfluous. It lacks all substance. It confuses more than it clarifies. Instead of reinforcing the natural division between the government and the commander, that is, between those who articulate the grand strategic purposes of the war and those who derive the strategic objectives from those purposes, this division has been erased, both functions being consolidated in the hands of the commander-in-chief. Indeed, had Roosevelt deleted "ask the Congress that" from his last sentence, he could have reduced the confusion and declared war on his own authority, as kings have always done and presidents usually do. In the final analysis, therefore, Roosevelt made the only declaration that counted. The Seventy-seventh Congress, unlike most other

Congresses, was not completely silent, but its words were unheard. The headlines roared with Roosevelt's dramatic "A Date Which Will Live in Infamy," not with Congress's tepid "Declaring that a state of war exists."

The 1776 Declaration

In 1776, needless to say, the situation was different. The Second Continental Congress spoke and Commander-in-Chief Washington listened. The world has long forgotten anything Washington may have said; it still rings with Jefferson's words. More important than its incomparable rhetoric, however, by adopting a fully reasoned declaration of war, the Second Continental Congress created a properly subordinate relationship between itself and Commander-in-Chief Washington, between the government and the commander, between grand strategy and strategy. In the subtle way in which the ends sought always direct the means employed, the Second Continental Congress asserted its authority over the conduct of the war down to the smallest operational detail.

Politically the Declaration of Independence justified officially and authoritatively a war that heretofore had been largely a spontaneous reaction against certain undefined aspects of British policy in North America. Out of the babble of large and small grievances, out of the plethora of possible purposes, an authoritative voice—"the Representatives of the UNITED STATES OF AMERICA, in General Congress, Assembled"—had spoken. Closure had been achieved. All those who both denounced the grievances enumerated and believed in the declared political purpose were now unified in a way that was impossible before. Now General Washington, his soldiers, and every citizen knew why they were fighting and when peace would return. Before 4 July 1776 they were just fighting, just destroying the enemy for no particular purpose; now they were fighting for well-articulated reasons to achieve a well-articulated purpose—independence.

Militarily the Declaration of Independence allowed Commander-in-Chief Washington to develop a strategy "down to the smallest operational detail." Before 4 July 1776 his mission had been vague and undefined. He was to end the occupation of Boston and then, more or less, to counter whatever moves the British army made. Merely reacting to the enemy's initiatives, however, is not the way to win a war, as General William Westmoreland will testify. In order to win, one must take the initiative; one must put the enemy in a position of extreme disadvantage. But the initiative can be taken only after the commander-in-chief knows what the political object of the war is. Only with a clear goal in mind can forces be deployed so as to secure that goal. Needless to say, it was not until 4 July 1776 that General Washington learned authoritatively of his goal. After that point he was able to devise an eminently suitable strategy to achieve it—trading space for time without allowing the British either to split the colonies or to occupy any significant expanse of territory.

The military level is particularly interesting from the constitutional point of view. Lacking guidance from the Second Continental Congress, Washington might well have selected independence as his personal war aim and gone on to develop his war-winning strategy on his own initiative. In this case, however, he would have become an American Caesar instead of an American Cincinnatus. Who articulates the war's political object is crucial for the health of a democracy.

Equally crucial is the quality of reasoning used by the Second Continental Congress. In form it follows the plan of the just-war criteria; in content it combines solid philosophy with detailed specificity. With respect to form there exists an interesting coincidence. Although Jefferson was no doubt familiar with the just-war criteria from his studies in international law, it is unlikely that he had them consciously in mind when he drafted the Declaration of Independence. Yet the declaration addresses six of the seven *jus ad bellum* criteria. The principal reason for this is that his assignment—to justify the war then in progress—is precisely the task for which the just-war criteria were developed, which meant that he had to address the same concerns that are codified in the *ad bellum* criteria. How else was Jefferson to justify this resort to war except by demonstrating (1) that the colonists possessed a just cause; (2) that their cause was significantly more just than that of the British; (3) that the colonists possessed a legitimate authority to wage war; (4) that the colonists' intentions were right, the war not having been commenced for self-serving motives; (5) that there existed a high probability of success without a resort to excessive means, it being axiomatic that excessive means destroy the justice of any cause, whereas a war without hope of success is futile and pointless; (6) that a due proportionality existed between the inevitable destruction caused in the war and the good that the colonist hoped to achieve; and (7) that the war was truly a last resort, an honest effort to exhaust all other means having been made? In fine, the *jus ad bellum* criteria are inescapable; they must be raised and responded to, as Jefferson did.*

With respect to content, Jefferson was concerned first and foremost with demonstrating the justice of the colonists' cause. He devoted over half his

---

* Since its publication in 1977, Michael Walzer's *Just and Unjust Wars: A Moral Argument with Historical Illustrations* has been the most popular work on the topic. For most purposes, however, James T. Johnson's (1981) *Just War Tradition and the Restraint of War: A Moral and Historical Inquiry* is the more useful text.

composition to doing so, presenting both philosophical and practical reasons. In terms of philosophy, the rebellion was justified because the Crown had frustrated the basic purpose of all government, denied the colonists their "inalienable rights," and thereby lost all legitimacy. In terms of practical politics, Jefferson listed twenty-seven specific grievances, ranging from "He [George III] has refused his Assent to Laws" to "He has excited domestic insurrections amongst us." Consequently, the document argues, the U.S. cause was just, not only in general philosophical terms, but in terms of specific grievances as well.

His second concern was to demonstrate that the colonies possessed the authority to wage war. For well-established governments, the competence of their authority is not usually called into question. It is already one of the principal marks of their sovereignty. In the case of rebellious colonies, however, it is a great problem, since colonies are not recognized sovereigns. To establish their competence, Jefferson used three approaches: First, he makes a formal assertion of competence by making the Declaration of Independence in the name of the Congress "of the thirteen united States of America." Second, in the very first sentence, he asserts competence under the natural law: "When in the course of human events, it becomes necessary for one people to dissolve the political bands which have connected them with another, and to assume among the Powers of the earth, the separate and equal station to which the Laws of Nature and of Nature's God entitle them . . ." Finally, in the concluding paragraph, he bases their competence upon the rock of representative democracy: "We, therefore, the Representatives of the united States of America, in General Congress, Assembled, appealing to the Supreme Judge of the world for the rectitude of our intentions, do, in the Name, and by authority of the good People of these Colonies, solemnly publish and declare, That these United Colonies are, and of Right ought to be Free and Independent States."

Jefferson's third concern was to compare the relative justice of each side. He makes this comparison implicitly throughout, but in his transition from the philosophical to the practical reasons for independence, he explicitly emphasizes the gross imbalance in comparative justice. Whereas the Americans are seeking "Life, Liberty, and the pursuit of Happiness," "The history of the present King of Great Britain is a history of repeated injuries and usurpations, all having in direct object the establishment of an absolute Tyranny over these States. To prove this, let Facts be submitted to a candid world."

His fourth concern was to establish the right intentions of the colonists, the rectitude of which Jefferson not only asserts formally in his concluding paragraph (cited previously) but also demonstrates by means of the colonists' prudence and long-suffering: "Prudence, indeed, will dictate that Governments long established should not be changed for light and transient causes; and accordingly all experience hath shewn, that mankind are more disposed to suffer, while evils are sufferable, than to right themselves by abolishing the forms to which they are accustomed. But . . ." The qualification is inevitable, for prudence and long-suffering must eventually give way before a radical imbalance in the relative justice that separates each side's cause. Hence, Jefferson continues: "When a long train of abuses and usurpations, pursuing invariably the same Object evinces a design to reduce them under absolute Despotism, it is their right, it is their duty, to throw off such Government, and to provide new Guards of their future security.—Such has been the patient sufferance of these Colonies; and such is now the necessity which constrains them to alter their former Systems of Government."

Jefferson's fifth concern was to show that the war was truly a last resort, a point that he had no difficulty documenting. The colonists had been more than just prudent:

> In every stage of these Oppressions We have Petitioned for Redress in the most humble terms: Our repeated Petitions have been answered only by repeated injury. A Prince, whose character is thus marked by every act which may define a Tyrant, is unfit to be the ruler of a free people.
>
> Nor have We been wanting in attentions to our British brethren. We have warned them from time to time. . . . We have reminded them. . . . We have appealed to their native justice and magnanimity, and we have conjured them.

But to no avail: "They too have been deaf to the Voice of Justice and of Consanguinity." Consequently, as a last painful resort, "We must, therefore, acquiesce in the Necessity, which denounces our Separation, and hold them, as we hold the rest of Mankind, Enemies in War, in Peace, Friends."

Jefferson's sixth concern was to demonstrate that the great evil of war would be outweighed by a greater good to be accomplished after the war was won. His handling of this point is quite weak. His only explicit reference allows "that mankind are more disposed to suffer, while evils are sufferable, than to right themselves by abolishing the forms to which they are accustomed." However, the entire declaration is also suffused with a feeling that royal tyranny has become entirely unacceptable and hence that a return to good government is well worth the evils of war. Perhaps this is enough.

The only *jus ad bellum* criterion that Jefferson omits from his text is the calculation that success was probable. As they must for any government embarking upon a war, the chances for success must have weighed heavily upon the Second Continental Congress, yet the declaration makes no mention of it. The reasons for this omission appear to be three. Partly, as a simple rhetorical matter, a declaration of war is not the place to analyze the probability of success. In the declaration one must always assume success. Partly, too, a declaration of war is itself an assertion that its authors believe that success is most probable. Otherwise they would not wage war. Finally, one must assume that the Second Continental Congress had already calculated their chances for success the previous year when they appointed George Washington as commander-in-chief on 15 June 1775 and authorized the raising of an army and a navy. In 1776 the question of the probability of success was moot.

To summarize then, the Second Continental Congress cogently addressed six critical concerns. It argued that (1) if its cause was just, (2) if it was competent to wage war, (3) if the weight of justice was on its side, (4) if its intentions were right, (5) if the war was waged truly as a last resort, and (6) if the justice to be gained from the independence sought in the war would be proportionally greater than the injustices inflicted by the war, then both the war and its declared purpose were justified. Therefore, in addition to conforming to the general rule of articulating the grievances that call for a resort to arms and terms that will restore peace, the Second Continental Congress's declaration exhibits six specific criteria that distinguish good from bad declarations of war. Those declarations that address each of these six concerns in a persuasive manner, as the Declaration of Independence did, are useful declarations. Those that do not are not. Applying this standard to the five congressional declarations, one discovers to no great surprise that, as unreasoned absolute declarations, they are neither good, adequate, nor useful. They address no concern; they fix no grand strategic objectives. They simply declare the brute fact of war. They *are* nothing but mere formalities.

Equally unsurprising, these six criteria also provide an excellent measure of the quality of the messages by which Commanders-in-Chief Madison, Polk, Wilson, and Roosevelt consulted with Congress, since those messages are in effect the reasoned declarations that articulated the grand strategic purposes of the relevant war. For example, Roosevelt's declaration was strong on articulating the causes for warring against Japan (but not against Nazi Germany or Italy), the purity of our intentions, and how this war was well and truly a last resort. However, he failed to mention the competence of our authority to wage the war, to compare the relative justice of each side, and to weigh the ends for which each side was fighting. In addition, his call for absolute victory is more than a little problematic.

Denouncing War and Declaring Peace

In assessing just how problematic Roosevelt's call for absolute victory was, one must shift from the military function of a declaration of war to its moral functions. If in strictly military terms the power to declare war is the power to articulate grand strategy—controlling the military means used by dictating the political ends sought—then does a declaration's moral significance not lie in the power to declare peace and denounce the necessity that forces war upon us? Unlike Roosevelt and the Seventy-seventh Congress, the Second Continental Congress did not *simply* declare war. Thus, whereas Roosevelt asked simply "that the Congress declare that since the unprovoked and dastardly attack by Japan on Sunday, Dec. 7, 1941, a state of war [had] existed between the United States and the Japanese Empire," and the Seventy-seventh Congress responded simply by "declaring that a state of war exists between the Imperial Government of Japan and the Government and the People of the United States and making provisions to prosecute the same," the Second Continental Congress took a slightly more complex approach. First it articulated the many causes that justified the war. Then it acquiesced in the necessity that *denounced* a separation of the United States of America from Great Britain: "We must, therefore, acquiesce in the necessity, which denounces our Separation, and hold them, as we hold the rest of mankind, Enemies in War, in Peace, Friends." Finally, it *declared* its preferred peace terms—independence: "We, therefore, . . . solemnly publish and declare, That these United Colonies are, and of Right ought to be Free and Independent States. . . ." The difference between *denouncing* one's acquiescence in the necessity for a war before *declaring* one's peace terms and simply *declaring* war is not merely procedural. It is also transformative, turning Roosevelt's angry call for "absolute victory" and Congress's thoughtless and unreasoned declaration into a reasoned plea for peace. How, therefore, should we conceive of the moral purpose of the congressional power to declare war? Should we not conceive of it as the power to denounce war and declare peace? Should we not conceive of it as the power to denounce the necessity that justifies a breach of the peace, but more important still, as the power to publish and declare the conditions that will restore peace?

PART 2

Changing Attitudes

3

Declarations of War:

A Brief Historical Sketch

In the previous chapter I argued that one should look not to Montesquieu or Madison to understand the meaning of the congressional war powers but rather to Clausewitz and Jefferson. In particular, one should pay attention to the military functions of a fully reasoned declaration of war, to Clausewitz's observation that no reasonable person would begin a war "without first being clear in his mind what he intends to achieve by that war and how he intends to conduct it." For everyone to get "clear in his mind," some authority must articulate those intentions in a fully reasoned formal declaration of war or its functional equivalent.

In this chapter I will puzzle over the fact that until the seventeenth century, fully reasoned denunciations of war were the rule and not the exception. Sovereigns and potentates were neither shy nor ashamed to state their grievances and declare their aims in due form, although cynicism, hypocrisy, and crass opportunism often made their denunciations less than candid. Attitudes subsequently changed, however, and formal reasoned declarations of war as the mode for articulating grand strategy gradually went out of style, to be replaced by their functional equivalents. In America after the adoption of the Constitution, this meant a public message from the commander-in-chief that on infrequent occasions ended with a request to Congress for an unreasoned absolute declaration.

The problem, then, is to understand this shift in attitudes. Why, in the course of the last four hundred years, have formal reasoned declarations of war gone out of fashion? There appear to be both historical and conceptual reasons. The conceptual reasons involve an inability to accept, much less articulate, the ambiguity inherent in the word *war*. The historical reasons revolve around two processes: first, a radical simplification of the complex formalities that had previously been a prelude to war; second, contemporaneous with the rise of absolutism, the disappearance of the councils, assemblies, and parliaments in which declarations of war had previously been debated. The disappearance of councils and assemblies meant that by the end of the seventeenth century, there no longer existed a place in which fully reasoned declarations of war could be debated. The simplification of the formalities meant that declarations of wars seemed to have lost all their political and diplomatic functions, without anyone appreciating that they still possessed military and moral functions.

Further aggravating this lack of venue and apparent lack of function was the inability of jurists and others to come to terms with the conceptual complexity of the word *war*. After the end of the seventeenth century, with the growth of the new scientific spirit, it was no longer considered respectable to permit the word *war* to represent simultaneously and ambiguously both a "condition" and a "contest," two terms that derive from Grotius, as I will show in a moment. Instead the empirical spirit of the age deemed it necessary to end the ambiguity decisively by conceiving of war as a contest only, the condition of war being regarded either as a legal fiction or as derivative of the contest. Having resolved the ambiguity in this way, from the beginning of the eighteenth century two juridical tendencies then developed, both of which led to dead ends. The first tendency consisted of a diminishing band of traditionalists who, citing Grotius and Cicero, insisted that declarations of war were still a necessity, despite their apparent lack of function. The second tendency consisted of modern, instrumentally rational, empirically minded positivists who, citing the undeniable facts of eighteenth-, nineteenth-, and twentieth-century diplomatic usage, insisted that declarations of war were never necessary and hence were outmoded relics of the past.

In fine, I wish to tell a story of inattention and reduction to absurdity: inattention both to the need to justify the war in governing forums and to the possibility that fully reasoned declarations of war might serve indispensable military, moral, and even democratic functions; reduction to absurdity by conceiving of war solely as a contest, which produces nothing but murderous nonsense. Only when the complex ambiguity of the word *war* is restored is it possible to make sense of war. By telling this confused and disappointing story, I hope to arrive at an appreciation of the attitudes and concepts that animate reasoned declarations of war, that lead people to believe they are always necessary. Clearly something has been lost over the last four hundred years, something that rendered the congressional war powers hollow and ineffective a hundred years or more before the Federal Convention met in Philadelphia, something that must be recovered if we are ever again to breath life into the power to denounce war and declare peace.

Simplifying a Complex Negotiating Strategy

Until roughly the seventeenth century, initiating war involved elaborate, complex, and lengthy formalities that were cloaked in religious formulas and legalistic jargon. Nonetheless, hiding beneath these sacred rites and judicial forms were exceedingly pragmatic political and diplomatic processes in which the formal declaration of war was an integral and crucial element. Politically the rites for declaring war usually required extensive public debate in governing forums that culminated in the writing of a fully reasoned declaration of war. The practical reality sustaining these public debates was the fact that war chiefs held relatively little political power and therefore had to defer to the council of elders, the assembly, the senate, or the great council before they could take up their spears. Diplomatically these ceremonies involved dispatching a special emissary to the potential adversary empowered to negotiate over the grievances and remedies articulated in the formal declaration that the emissary carried. The practical reality undergirding this negotiating mission was the essential autonomy of each tribe, city, or kingdom, on the one hand, and the difficulties in transportation and communication, on the other hand, which made contacts between potential adversaries sporadic. Indeed, war was for all practical purposes the only question important enough to force diplomats to break this isolation and risk the dangers of traveling to distant lands.

As the seventeenth century approached, however, both the political and diplomatic realities changed remarkably. Improvements in transportation and communications led to the development of permanent diplomatic representation in foreign courts and hence to continuous interchanges between monarchs. This meant that it was no longer necessary to send a special emissary with full panoply to explain the grievances and negotiate over the remedies articulated in a formal denunciation of war. The permanently resident ambassador could now whisper these concerns into the adversary's ear daily during intimate tête-à-têtes. But if the adversary already knew of the grievances from the resident ambassador and had already rejected the proposed remedies, then what was the point of dispatching a special envoy with a formal declaration? Improved communications and a more intensive diplomacy rendered the old ways redundant and irrelevant in the eyes of most, as Emerich de Vattel observed in his 1758 *Droit des gens:* "In former times the European powers sent heralds, or ambassadors, to declare war; at present they content themselves with announcing it in their capital, in their principal towns, or upon the frontier. Manifestos are sent out, and now that communication has become so quick and easy owing to the establishment of a postal service, the news is soon spread on all sides" (1916, 255).

Likewise, as the power of the monarch gradually increased and that of governing councils decreased over the centuries, the need for extensive public debate in official forums also diminished. The development of an absolutist theory of monarchy eliminated public debate completely, decisions for war and peace now being made in secret in the king's privy council. And so, again, insofar as there no longer existed a need to reach closure in a public debate by formally voting on a formal declaration of war, what was the purpose of a fully reasoned declaration? Would not some functional equivalent serve just as well to announce the monarch's private decision to his subjects and the world?

In fine, the disappearance of parliaments and changes in diplomatic and political practices meant that the practical realities underpinning these complex formalities appeared to lose all meaning and function. Lacking all meaning and function—to all appearances, at least—formal declarations of war soon came to be viewed as irrelevant to the important business of war. Of the two factors, however, the elimination of the need to send special envoys to the adversary was by far the more decisive factor. There had always been tyrants of one sort or another who had declared war on their own authority without reference to a ruling council. Until improved communications made permanent diplomatic representation possible, however, these tyrants seldom failed to dispatch heralds with reasoned declarations of war, the hypocrisy of the reasoning notwithstanding. Interestingly, one of the reasons tyrants were so punctual in declaring war formally is that observing the diplomatic formalities that precede war is what distinguishes tyrants from pirates, war from brigandage, for war requires policy, whereas brigandage does not. Consequently, pirates—those "powerful men" motivated by "their own cupidity and to support the needy" (Thucydides 1982, I, 5)—lacking policy, never wage war. Instead they raid, pillage, and plunder, descending upon a town without warning and making off with whatever they can carry. Tyrants, possessing a policy, wage war—but first they negotiate. After all, as Hitler's advisers no doubt argued during the 1938 Munich negotiations, if Czechoslovakia would fall without a shot, why not save the army for Poland?

Finally, I must comment upon the narrow scope and bias of the documents I will be examining. With one exception, they come from judicial and religious authors. Military authors are conspicuously absent. The complete absence of military authors highlights one of the greatest weaknesses in traditional discussions of declarations of war—if only the priests and the lawyers see a need to declare war formally, then obviously there can be no good reason ever to do so. In the fifth century B.C. or in the fourteenth century A.D., priestly or juridical reasons might have persuaded, but not in the seventeenth century or later. Today it would take a hearty priest to cite Deuteronomy 20:10 or a nostalgic lawyer to cite the *jus fetiale* in defense of the congressional power to declare war.

Consequently, the purpose of discussing the texts that form this chapter's focus is not to adduce religious or legal reasons for the congressional war powers. After having argued in the previous chapter that only solid military and moral functions can justify splitting the sovereign's personality and granting the power to declare war to Congress, such a course is not possible. Rather, my purpose is first to document the ubiquity, persistence, and complexity of the political and diplomatic processes that sustained a belief in the necessity of writing fully reasoned formal declarations of war until the seventeenth century and then to trace the subsequent rapid disintegration of all conviction in the need to denounce war formally. Incidentally, because of the religious and legal sources of the texts cited, we shall not see any evidence of the technological changes that undermined the diplomatic need for formal declarations of war, although we shall see traces of the political changes.

To Proclaim Peace

From the earliest times, in all cultures, declarations of war were an integral part of an elaborate system of negotiations characterized by three formal elements: First, the decision to war was taken only after extensive public debate in governing councils. Second, the declaration itself promised peace to the enemy if the grievances detailed were remedied. Third, battle was joined only after this formal, reasoned declaration was carried to the enemy by heralds and they had returned with a counterdeclaration denying the justice of those grievances. All three of these elements can be found in the five-thousand-year-old Sumerian epic *Agga and Gilgamesh,* which begins with the arrival of heralds from Agga of Kish informing Gilgamesh in Erech of the casus belli. Before he can respond, however, Gilgamesh must go before not one but two councils— a council of elders and a council of "men," probably meaning "armed men." His initial attempt to convince the council of elders to declare war is unsuccessful. Desiring peace, they resolve not to fight: "Submit to the house of Kish, let us not smite it with weapons" (in Pritchard 1955, 44–47, l. 14). The council of men is more receptive, however. After a second debate in that council, Gilgamesh secures a decision for war: "Do not submit to the house of Kish, let us smite it with weapons" (l. 29). His heralds having returned with this defiant counterdeclaration, "Agga, son of Enmebaraggesi besieged Erech" shortly thereafter (l. 49). Unfortunately, though, the fighting went against Erech, and the city was saved only through the kindness and mercy of Agga.

A second and fuller source for the functioning of this complex process is the Old Testament. With the greater detail available there, one can also see the reasons that the ancient cultures gave for employing this complex negotiating process—the gods demanded it. For example, among the Hebrew, Yahweh commanded: "When thou comest nigh unto a city to fight against it, then proclaim peace unto it. And it shall be, if it make thee answer of peace, and open unto thee, then it shall be, that all the people that is found therein shall be tributaries unto thee, and they shall serve thee. And if it will make no peace with thee, but will make war against thee, then thou shalt besiege it" (Deut. 20:10–12, AV). Not only did this injunction to "proclaim peace" result in a fairly complete *jus belli* (20:13–20), detailing the treatment of the vanquished, plunder, and so forth, but it also resulted in elaborate negotiations and fully reasoned declarations of war, as is seen in Judges 11 when the Ammonites threaten war against Israel. In response to this threat, the elders of Gilead recall Jephthah, the son of a harlot, to "be our captain, that we may fight with the children of Ammon" (Judg. 11:6). Having assumed command:

> Jephthah sent messengers unto the king of the children of Ammon, saying, What hast thou to do with me, that thou art come against me to fight in my land? And the king of the children of Ammon answered unto the messengers of Jephthah, Because Israel took away my land, when they came up out of Egypt, from Arnon even unto Jabbok, and unto Jordan: now therefore restore those lands again peaceably.
>
> And Jephthah sent messengers again unto the king of the children of Ammon: And said unto him, Thus saith Jephthah, Israel took not away the land of Moab, nor the land of the children of Ammon: But when Israel came up from Egypt, and walked through the wilderness unto the Red sea, and came to Kadesh; Then Israel sent messengers unto the king of Edom, saying, Let me, I pray thee, pass through thy land: but the king of Edom would not hearken thereto. And in like manner they sent unto the king of Moab: but he would not consent: and Israel abode in Kadesh.
>
> Then they went along through the wilderness, and compassed the land of Edom, and the land of Moab, and came by the east side of the land of Moab, and pitched on the other side of Arnon, but came not within the border of Moab: for Arnon was the border of Moab. And Israel sent messengers unto Sihon king of the Amorites, the king of Heshbon; and Israel said unto him, Let us pass, we pray thee, through thy land into my place. But Sihon trusted not

Israel to pass through his coast: but Sihon gathered all his people together, and pitched in Jahaz, and fought against Israel.

And the Lord God of Israel delivered Sihon and all his people into the hand of Israel, and they smote them: so Israel possessed all the land of the Amorites, the inhabitants of that country. And they possessed all the coasts of the Amorites, from Arnon even unto Jabbok, and from the wilderness even unto Jordan. So now the Lord God of Israel hath dispossessed the Amorites from before his people Israel, and shouldest thou possess it?

Wilt not thou possess that which Chemosh thy god giveth thee to possess? So whomsoever the Lord our God shall drive out from before us, them will we possess. And now art thou any thing better than Balak the son of Zippor, king of Moab? did he ever strive against Israel, or did he ever fight against them, While Israel dwelt in Heshbon and her towns, and in Aroer and her towns, and in all the cities that be along the coasts of Arnon, three hundred years? Why therefore did ye not recover them within that time?

Wherefore I have not sinned against thee, but thou doest me wrong to war against me: the Lord the Judge be judge this day between the children of Israel and the children of Ammon. (Judg. 11:12-27)

Among the Romans, the gods were just as insistent that war be for the purpose of peace. For example, in *De Officiis* Cicero begins with what became the standard definition of war until well into the nineteenth century: "There are two ways of contending [*decertandi*] an issue—one is by force [*vim*], and the other is by reason [*disceptationem*, "debate," "discussion," or "controversy"]. The former is the prerogative of beasts, the latter of men, so that we should only have recourse to the former when the latter is no avail" (Cicero 1967, I, xi, 34). He then concludes: "Therefore the only justification for war is that peace and justice should afterwards prevail. . . . All the rights and duties of war have been rigorously established by the Roman Fetial Laws, from which it is abundantly clear that no war is just unless preceded by an absolute or conditional declaration" (I, xi, 35, 36). Needless to say, the thought that the purpose of war is that peace and justice should afterward prevail was not original with Cicero. Both Plato (*Laws,* I, 628d) and Aristotle (*Politics* 1333ᵃ35), among many others, had said the same thing. Augustine also held that the purpose of war is peace (*City of God* XV, 4; XIX, 12). In contrast, the *jus fetiale* was a uniquely Roman institution. True, there is some doubt as to whether the *collegium fetialis* actually performed the rituals described by Livy (Wiedemann 1986; see Watson 1993, 56–58, for a convincing rebuttal). What is not in doubt, however, is the influence that these accounts had upon jurists during both the Middle Ages and the early modern period. For example, Grotius (1925) quotes Livy at III, iii, 5. As with the Deuteronomic law, the *jus fetiale* decreed elaborate negotiations and fully reasoned declarations of war. Livy, the principal source, explains that when some controversy arose, one or more *legati* would be sent to the offending people. Arriving at the frontier, the envoy

> covers his head with a bonnet—the covering is of wool—and says: "Hear, Jupiter; hear ye boundaries of"—naming whatever nation they belong to;—"let righteousness hear! I am the public herald of the Roman People; I have come duly and religiously commissioned; let my words be credited." Then he recites his demand, [e.g., "Whereas Perseus, son of Philip, King of Macedonia, contrary to the treaty made with his father Philip and renewed with himself after the death of his father, had invaded allies of the Roman people, had devastated their land and seized their cities, and whereas he had entered on plans for preparing war against the Roman people, and had assembled arms, soldiers and fleet for the said purpose, resolved that unless he offered satisfaction in these matters, war against him be undertaken" (XLII, xxx, 10–11)] after which he takes Jupiter to witness: "If I demand unduly and against religion that these men and these things be surrendered to me, then let me never enjoy my native land." (I, xxxii, 6)

The *legati* repeated this demand several times in the principal towns until they arrived in the capital city, where they again repeated it. Remaining in the enemy's capital for thirty-three days, the envoys negotiated for satisfaction. If the negotiations failed, they then declared war conditionally: "'Hear, Jupiter, and thou, Janus Quirinus, and hear all heavenly gods, and ye, gods of earth, and ye of the lower world; I call you to witness that this people'—naming whatever people it is—'is unjust, and does not make reparation. But of these matters we will take counsel of the elders in our country, how we may obtain our right'" (I, xxxii, 10). Upon their return to Rome, they denounced the enemy, and the question of war or peace was immediately put to the vote. When the decision went for war:

> It was customary for the fetial to carry to the bounds of the other nation a cornetwood spear, iron-pointed or hardened in the fire, and in the presence of not less than three grown men to say: "Whereas the tribes of the Ancient Latins and men of the Ancient Latins have been guilty of acts and offenses against the Roman People of the Quirites; and whereas the Roman People of the Quirites has commanded that war be made on the Ancient Latins, and the Senate of the Roman People has approved, agreed, and voted a war with the Ancient Latins; I therefore and the Roman People declare and make war on the tribes of the Ancient Latins and the men of the Ancient Latins." Having said this, he would hurl his spear into their territory. This is the manner in which at the time redress was sought from the Latins and war was declared, and the custom has been received by later generations. (I, xxxii, 13–14)

During the Middle Ages this elaborate negotiating tradition continued unbroken, no chivalrous knight ever thinking of participating in an undeclared war. The form changed slightly, however. Instead of reading a *clarigatio* such as Livy described, now the herald read *lettres de défi* (*diffidatio*). But continuity was the hallmark. For example, Honoré Bonet begins his ca. 1387 work *The Tree of Battles* by echoing Cicero: "War is nothing other than discord or conflict that has arisen on account of certain things displeasing to the human will, to the end that such conflicts should be turned into agreement and reason, and there is a law which provides this" (Bonet 1949, I, 1). He then assumes without discussion or question that "a general [i.e., public] war is declared after great council, and decreed by the lord" (IV, 114). Although Bonet does not trouble to describe the functions of a "great council," Christine de Pisan does so in great detail in her ca. 1434 work *The Book of Fayttes of Armes and of Chyualrye:*

> He [a prince] shall assemble grete counseyl of wysemen in his parliament / or in the counseil of his souerayn yf he be subgette / . . . [and] shal purpose or doo be purposed all the trouth & without ony fauour for god may not be deceyued all suche right & suche wronge that he may haue / & in concludying shal saye þᵗ of all he wyll reporte hym & holde to the determinacion of ryght / shortly for to saie by this manere / this thynge put in right wel seen & discuted so & by suche waye that it appere by true iugement that he hath iuste cause / Thenne he shal doo sommone his aduersarye for to haue of hym restytucion & amendes of thyniures & wronges by hym receyued / Thenne yf it happene / that þᵉ said aduersarye delyuer deffences & wyll gaynsaye it / that he be entirely herd without fauour to hym self in ony wise ne propre wyll ne haynous courage / These thynges & that whiche apperteyneth duely made / in caas that the said aduersarie be founde refusying to come to right & lawe / the prynce may Iustely & surely entrepryse warre / the whiche ought not be called vengeaunce / but pure execution of rightful Iustyce /. (1937, bk. I, ch. 4)

Christine's account is of particular interest because she goes on to say that the blessing of the prince's privy council is insufficient for undertaking war. Instead a wise prince should follow the example of the Romans and "assemble to counseil the four estates of his countree whiche ought to be called or he emprise so chargeable a thyng [as war]" (I, 5). According to Christine, the principal reason for this is to ensure the loyalty of his people by involving them in the decision, for "O how is that a proffitable thynge in seygnourye / Royame / or Cyte to haue true subgettis / & of grete loue" (ibid.). As a modern illustration of this principle, she cites the "wel gaaf ensample the good wyse kyng charles the fythe of that name," who in 1369

assembled at parys [Paris] at his parliament the forsaid foure estates / . . . / and
to theym purposed his reasons ayenst thenglyssh men [against the English
men] demaundyng theyr aduys / yf he had cause to bygynne warre / for without iuste cause / the regarde & deliberacion emonge theym / and the consente
& wylle of his good subgetts in no wyse he wold doo it at whiche counseyl by
long deliberacion was concluded that he had good & iuste cause to begynne
agayn the warre & thus the good wise kynge entreprysed it. (ibid.)

Needless to say, Christine's example is remarkable because it demonstrates
how easily and early the ancient precedents were misunderstood, a misunderstanding that transmogrified the power to declare war from an inherently legislative function into a royal prerogative.

Christine says that a wise prince should follow the example of the Romans.
Unfortunately, though, Charles V did not follow the Roman example. Her
ancient and modern examples are only superficially comparable, the role of
the Roman Senate in the fetial rituals described by Livy being profoundly different from the role of the Four Estates in 1369. In 1369 Charles V asked the
Four Estates first to assemble in Paris; next to listen to their sovereign's justification for renewing the war against the English and then to deliberate the
matter; and finally, to give their assent, after which he would declare war. Although it was unnecessary, Charles V also bound himself to abide by their
decision. Needless to say, this was a most gracious and politic gesture on his
part and was no doubt an important factor in obtaining the assent of the Four
Estates. In contrast, during the early republic the Senate (like the Athenian
Assembly) was not convened by a king to give its assent. Instead, it called itself into session, it deliberated, it wrote the *clarigatio,* and finally, it voted on
whether the fetials should take the *clarigatio* to the enemy's capitol to be negotiated. Should the adversary refuse satisfaction, the Senate again convened
itself, debated the question of war or peace once again, and again voted. When
the vote was for war, the Senate then authorized the consuls or some other
general to lead the legions out to war.

In fine, there is all the difference in the world between a self-activating
assembly deciding the question of war or peace by itself *before* it appoints the
commander-in-chief and an advisory panel giving its assent to a war that their
commander-in-chief has already decided to wage. Historically, of course, one
understands how and why Christine failed to see the incompatibility of her
ancient and modern examples. By the time of the early empire, the Roman
Senate had indeed degenerated into an advisory panel that did little more
than rubber-stamp the emperor's decisions. Moreover, during the thousand
years since the fall of Rome, nothing had happened to challenge the assumption that feudal assemblies possessed only an advisory function with respect

to the question of war or peace, as Locke confirmed when he assigned the question of war or peace to the federative power. Consequently, by the fourteenth century no one could imagine that the power to declare war had ever been exercised solely and exclusively by a legislative assembly. Long before the fourteenth century, it was assumed by one and all that the power to declare war was a royal prerogative. This unanimity of experience and opinion led Locke, Montesquieu, Hamilton, and many others to argue that the power to declare war is an inherently executive function. The only restraint that anyone could now imagine on this newly minted executive prerogative was the commonsense observation that a wise ruler should secure domestic support for a war before engaging any enemies abroad. Since one of the best ways to ensure domestic support for a war is to obtain the assent of the Four Estates, political realism dictated that, after having decided to wage a war but before declaring the intention formally, the wise ruler should assemble them in council.

Thus, through the alchemy of feudal practice, the power to declare war was transmogrified from an inherently legislative function into an inherently executive function, an undisputed royal prerogative. This being the case, the only question open to dispute was the issue of formality: are formal declarations of war always required, or can informal declarations be substituted? As long as diplomatic practice still required heralds to carry declarations back and forth between adversaries, formal declarations were still required. The need for heralds soon diminished and finally ceased, however, which meant that the need for formal declarations of war also appeared to diminish and then to cease altogether.

Thus, as the feudal kingdoms of western Europe slowly began to evolve into modern nation-states during the twelfth, thirteenth, and fourteenth centuries, their medieval *curiae regis* had haltingly transformed themselves into parliaments, estates general, and cortes. This evolution was reversed during the fifteenth, sixteenth, and seventeenth centuries as sovereigns began to claim a divine right to exercise an absolute power over their subjects. As a result, after the unification of the Spanish crown in the fifteenth century, the Cortes met infrequently and then only to pay homage to the king, while in France the Estates General did not assemble for 175 years, between 1614 and 1789. England was the great exception. Unlike its continental analogues, the English Parliament had gained firm control over the raising of nonfeudal revenues by the reign of Edward III in 1377. This "power of the purse" meant that an English king could not ignore his parliament as the Spanish and French kings could. But although the English kings' constant need for increased revenues meant that Parliament was frequently called into session, it did not mean that Parliament thereby possessed the power to declare war—quite the contrary, for the power to declare war was well established as a royal prerogative. In addition, the army and navy were also the monarch's, thereby further removing Parliament from matters military. As a result, although English kings often had to request increased taxes from Parliament to continue a war, they had no need whatsoever to consult Parliament before starting one.

The crucial example of course is the Bishops War of 1639–40. For a number of personal, political, and ideological reasons, including his belief in the divine right of kings, Charles I initiated a period of personal rule after the contentious parliamentary session of 1629. He did this by the simple expedient of refusing to summon Parliament for the next eleven years. Toward the end of this period, in an effort to achieve religious uniformity within his two realms, Charles I decided to impose the Church of England's ecclesiastical hierarchy (which is why the war was called the "Bishops" War) and its Book of Common Prayer upon the Presbyterian Scots. When the Scots objected vigorously, Charles I declared war upon them in 1639. To finance this invasion, the king resorted to a number of dubious devices, including a feudal levy, which much displeased the "militarily (though not politically) impotent" nobility (Fissel 1994, 153). This first campaign was indecisive, ending with the Pacification of Berwick, which stipulated that a free assembly of Scots would meet to decide whether Presbyterian Scotland would adopt the Church of England's hierarchy and Book of Common Prayer. When this assembly rejected both ideas, Charles I summoned Parliament for the first time in over a decade to obtain supplementary revenues to finance a second invasion of Scotland. Not having met for ten years, Parliament was more interested in obtaining redress for a long list of grievances than in voting new taxes for the king's unpopular war. Desiring only money and not wanting to hear grievances, Charles I soon dismissed this Parliament, which came to be known as the "Short" Parliament. Denied parliamentary revenues, the king nonetheless undertook a second campaign in 1640, relying again upon his own resources. This second campaign was even less successful than the first.

Since 1640 two schools of thought have developed to explain the English defeats in the Bishops War. Some, such as Mark Fissel (1994), place the blame squarely upon Charles's incompetent shoulders; others, such as Kevin Sharpe (1992), are less inclined to blame Charles I, emphasizing instead the enormous difficulties—both domestic and foreign—that he faced and the shortcomings of his advisers and commanders. However the defeats are explained, Charles was forced to pay the Scots an indemnity by the Treaty of Ripon. Having exhausted his own resources in these two ill-fated excursions into Scotland, Charles I was forced to recall Parliament to vote the additional taxes needed to pay the indemnity. Once recalled, this "Long" Parliament immediately demanded redress for numerous grievances before voting the additional revenues demanded by Charles. Charles's refusal led to the English Civil Wars. Parliament, having now declared war against the king, was suddenly faced with the realization that it possessed no army with which to oppose the king, who still commanded the Royal Army. In the short run Parliament solved this problem by co-opting the trained bands, thereby raising its own army. In the long run, however, this proved to be Parliament's undoing. In 1653 Oliver Cromwell dissolved the Rump Parliament, accepted the Instrument of Government from the Parliamentary Army, and ruled as lord protector until his death in 1658. In 1660 Parliament was restored under Charles II, but the power to declare war remained a royal prerogative, and the army and navy continued to pledge allegiance to the person of the king, not to Parliament. Thus, by the end of the seventeenth century, even in England, where absolutism did not triumph, both the army and the power to declare war remained firmly in the hands of the king.

The eclipse of parliaments and estates general in practice was accompanied by a parallel rise in political theories that justified the imposition of absolutism. In *The Prince* (1532) Machiavelli's sovereign declares and fights wars but never consults with a great council, if perchance there is one to consult. Likewise, Jean Bodin (1530–96) saw no need for an assembly. He listed the first three marks of sovereignty as (1) the right to ordain law, (2) the right to denounce war, and (3) the right to appoint the higher magistrates, but these marks established the personality of the sovereign, who necessarily was an absolute monarch and who could not derogate these marks of sovereignty to a council or parliament without thereby ceasing to be sovereign. In Thomas Hobbes's *Leviathan* (1651) the ruler is also absolute in sovereignty and certainly would never allow Parliament to usurp the prerogative to declare war and command the army and navy. Thus, for the leading political thinkers of the time, a legislative assembly, much less an assembly that declared war, ceased to exist. It is not that Machiavelli, Bodin, or Hobbes argued against the estates but rather that they completely ignored them. Legislative assemblies simply had no function in their theories. Consequently, even without the diplomatic and conceptual changes that were taking place at the same time, by the end of the seventeenth century, there simply was no place in which to debate a declaration of war. Even in those countries that possessed an active parliament or assembly, kings no longer felt obliged to bring forward a declaration for consideration, as Charles V had in 1369.

Nonetheless, in the face of this triumph of absolutism, during the seventeenth century Grotius began his revival of the *jus gentium,* including the traditional belief in the necessity to declare war formally. Because of this Grotius marks the turning point, being simultaneously the apex of the antique tradition that held that formal declarations of war are always necessary and one of the principal sources for its disintegration. Ostensibly affirming the tradition, Grotius began his great work, *On the Law of War and Peace,* in the usual way by citing Cicero:

> Cicero defined war as a contending by force. A usage has gained currency, however, which designates by the word not a contest but a condition; thus war is the condition of those contending by force, viewed simply as such. This general definition includes all the classes of wars which it will hereafter be necessary to discuss. For I do not exclude private war, since in fact it is more ancient than public war and has, incontestably, the same nature as public war; wherefore both should be designated by one and the same term. (bk. I, ch. i, sec. 2)

Again in the usual way, he concluded that "declarations of war . . . were wont to be made publicly [*ex dicto*], with a statement of the cause, in order that the whole human race as it were might judge of the justness of it" (II, xxvi, 7).*

While he was affirming the tradition, however, Grotius was simultaneously undermining it, not intentionally, but most effectively nonetheless. His first mine was laid in his definition of war. By making explicit an ambiguity inherent in the word *war,* Grotius had drawn out a distinction that later generations would transform into an ill-considered bifurcation and then harden into an artificial difference, thereby oversimplifying and misrepresenting war greatly. Despite the demands of later jurists, war cannot be considered *either* a contest *or* a condition; rather, as Grotius saw, it must be seen as *both* a contest—often a violent one—*and* a social, psychological, economic, and legal condition. When the two components are allowed to rest conjoined, the distinction between them represents but a convenient academic abstraction that allows a jurist such as Grotius to focus upon the legal conditions of war and a military author such as Vegetius to focus upon the contest, without either author denying the value or relevance of the other's work. However, when later jurists recast this convenient abstraction as an empirical question—Is war a condition *or* a contest?— they created a bogus dilemma that inevitably produces a misbegotten response. Inevitably the contest will be seen as the only valid empirical reality, while the social, psychological, economic, and legal conditions will be viewed as derivative of and contingent upon the empirically more real contest.

---

* Grotius's final clause is striking in that it echoes so closely Jefferson's remark that "a decent Respect to the Opinions of Mankind requires that they should declare the causes which impel them to the Separation." One wonders whether Jefferson had Grotius in mind when he wrote his preamble.

But this first mine is a conceptual matter that was not set to explode until the eighteenth century. I therefore leave it undisturbed, hidden within Grotius's definition of war, and turn my attention to his second mine, which is found in his third book and constitutes an obvious departure from the traditional norms: in addition to the customary appeal to ancient custom, are there any reasons for always declaring war in due form? Yes, there are. According to Grotius, declarations are necessary so that "the fact might be established with certainty that war [is] being waged not by private initiative but by the will of each of the two peoples or of their heads" (III, iii, 11).

Grotius has not understood the ancient practices any better than Christine de Pisan understood them. He assumes without question that the declaring of war is an inherently executive function. This break with the ancients is signaled by the disjunct "*or* of their heads." The point is not that the ancients would have immediately recognized this as outright tyranny. The point is that, by accepting without comment what had indeed become common practice by the seventeenth century, Grotius was promoting the foreshortening and simplification of the political component of the complex negotiating strategy that had heretofore sustained the need for fully reasoned declarations of war. If public wars could now be lawfully declared by monarchs without public debate in governing forums, then declarations of war appeared to have lost half of their function and meaning.

More precisely, Grotius is caught in a cleft, straddling uncomfortably the ancient and the modern worlds. On the one side, he still believed in Cicero's ancient definition of war as a type of contending that peace and justice might thereafter prevail. Consequently, he still defended the need for declarations of war, recognizing the moral, if not the military, need for a formal, reasoned declaration that offered peace and justice to the enemy. On the other side, like any good modern, he saw no need whatsoever for extensive public debate in governing forums *before* declaring war. The only requirement was that *after* the monarch had decided for war, he should publish the reasons for doing so, "in order that the whole human race as it were might judge of the justness of it." In a word, Grotius accepted at face value the religious and legal arguments he found in the ancient texts while ignoring the political functions and practices that gave those arguments utility and meaning.

Needless to say, herein lies one of the taproots of the endless controversies that have surrounded the congressional war powers since 1789. The political component of declaring war has now been transformed from an inherently legislative function into a royal prerogative. No longer is it seen as a complex political process that encompasses a significant proportion of the citizenry. Neither Grotius nor anyone else—least of all nineteenth- or twentieth-century members of Congress—could imagine a decision for war being taken democratically in a public assembly after extensive debates such as those described by Thucydides. Now the number of participants would be extremely limited; the debates, secret; and the declaration, reduced to a press release by which sovereigns told their subjects what had been decided for them and what was expected of them.

This same failure of imagination also affected the diplomatic component of declaring war. No longer was a declaration seen as a crucial part in a complex negotiating strategy, such as Livy described. By approximately the time of Grotius's death in 1645, it had become merely the public announcement signaling the end of diplomacy and the beginning of war. For example, the last time a British sovereign made use of heralds was in 1557, when Mary Tudor sent a *roi d'armes* to Henry II of France. For the French, heralds were last employed in 1635, when Louis XIII sent them to Brussels to declare war against Spain with trumpets and all possible fanfare, while the last occurrence of this ancient tradition in Europe was in 1657, when Sweden declared war against Denmark. The final degeneration of declarations of war from international negotiating instruments to domestic propaganda was sealed by 1778, when the British made a mockery of the antique tradition by having a herald declare war against France without ever leaving London. Instead of traveling to the enemy and spending thirty-three days in negotiations, this last of the heralds made his declaration in the middle of his hometown and then went home to a warm dinner (de Louter 1920, 235). Soon, however, declarations of war lost even their value as propaganda. Without the heralds to sustain the formalities of this elaborate negotiating process—the job having been taken over by that new innovation in international relations, the permanently resident ambassador—the use of formal declarations of war soon became extinct for all practical purposes, as both Ward (1805) and Maurice (1883) demonstrated in their extensive studies of the question.

In sum, the substance of this five-thousand-year-old tradition died with the rise of absolutism and the decline of the heralds during the course of the seventeenth century. Yet perversely its spirit lingered on. For example, the political component of these ancient rites found expression in article 1, section 8, of the Constitution, whereas the diplomatic component eventually found expression in the words of convention 3 of the Second Hague Conference of 1907, Relative to the Opening of Hostilities. In addition, considerable effort can reveal fairly recent examples of both the political and diplomatic functions. For instance, the extensive media and congressional debates that preceded the Spanish-American War of 1898 were certainly democratic in character, if imperialistic in result. Likewise, the elaborate, if hypocritical, exchange of ultimatums, notes, and comments between the Austrians and the

Serbians in 1914 represents the sort of complex negotiating process between enemies that heralds traditionally undertook.*

But these are flawed examples and far too few in number. The tradition did not die with Grotius, but it soon became moribund, its heirs gradually diminishing in number and stature during the next three hundred years before all but disappearing by the end of the twentieth century. Consequently, the wonder of the last two centuries is how frequently the nations of the world, including the United States, have declared war, not how infrequently. In the face of an ever more powerful international consensus that formal declarations of war are archaic relics of the past and unable to discern any political, diplomatic, military, or moral reasons for formally declaring war, one must express surprise that Congress discharged its constitutional duty on even five occasions. Be that as it may, it is time to turn from the story of the forlorn defenders of the ancient tradition to the story of the triumphantly modern, instrumentally rational positivists who, intoxicated by the spirit of modern science and citing the undeniable facts of eighteenth-, nineteenth-, and twentieth-century diplomatic usage, have insisted that declarations of war, never necessary, are but outmoded relics.

By Force or Fraud

As the fifteenth century turned into the sixteenth, the first cracks in the traditional attitudes toward war appeared with a concatenation of three factors, each of which struck at the heart of the traditional conception of war as a forceful contending for the sake of peace and justice: first, a number of conspicuously cynical petty princes appeared on the scene; second, an author appeared who was prepared to break the taboos and shock the conventional piety of the age; and third, other authors subsequently took up the call, moving beyond shock to ridicule—satire being even more damaging than candor. For the soft spot in the antique tradition is the fact that the credibility of a fully reasoned declaration of war depends crucially upon honesty and sincerity. When a declaration is infected with the slightest cynicism, the effect is devastating: reasons turn into rationalizations and causes, into provocations.

Needless to say, during the fifteenth century, when princes "prefer[ed] to occupy themselves in the pursuits of war . . . rather than in the honorable activities of peace" (More 1965, 57), honesty and sincerity were commodities

---

* See Naval War College (1918) for the [Austrian] Ultimatum to Serbia, 22 July 1914 (38–41), [Austrian] Comments on Serbian reply to ultimatum, 27 July 1914 (42–49), [Austrian] Notice breaking Diplomatic relations with Serbia, 25 July 1914 (49), [Austrian] Declaration of war against Serbia, noon, 28 July 1914 (49).

in extremely short supply. Still, there had never been an oversupply of honest and sincere kings and princes, so this factor by itself was never a challenge to the prevailing conception of war for the sake of peace. More of a challenge, therefore, was the audacity of Machiavelli, who appeared willing not only to condone but even to encourage the natural cynicism of princes. Thus, at the same time that Thomas More was satirizing sovereigns for not practicing the arts of peace, Machiavelli was warning ominously, "It is seen that when princes have thought more of peace [*delicatezze*] than of arms, they have lost their states" (cited in Wright 1965, 427).

Machiavelli's words were stunning, shocking. They mark a clear break with the conventions that had governed previous authors. Clearly a new candor had been born. Before the fifteenth century princes were no more honest or sincere than during the fifteenth century. The difference was that before Machiavelli, few authors had dared to describe the practices of their princes so candidly. However, Machiavelli was perhaps less important for destroying the old conception of war than were others. Shocking as Machiavelli's words were, he still found war to be a necessary and noble pursuit of policy, the violence of war being of little or no concern to him. All he wished to do was to strip away the illusions of the idealists and the hypocrisy of the pious so as to look at war and politics as they "really" are, that is, to look at them instrumentally. Consequently, another group of writers was perhaps more important in changing attitudes toward war, for writers such as Erasmus, Thomas More, and John Colet not only wanted to look at war and politics as they really are, but more devastating, they used the lens of ridicule. As a result war was turned on its head. The hypocritical policies of cynical princes now became the barbs upon which a ruinous ridicule turned, exposing a senseless violence that no one could fail to mock.*

But these authors did not satirize only the hypocritical princes. They also took direct aim at the scholastic prelates who advised them and wrote the declarations of war. For example, when a prelate such as Honoré Bonet poses the question "IF A KNIGHT HAPPEN TO DIE IN BATTLE DO WE SAY THAT HIS SOUL IS SAVED?" and then answers it by saying yes, as long as the war is either ordained by the church or just "and [the knight] is not otherwise in

---

* The importance of Colet, More, and Erasmus in changing the attitudes of European intellectuals toward war is documented in Robert Adams's *Better Part of Valor: More, Erasmus, Colet and Vives on Humanism, War and Peace, 1496–1535* (1962). Although the coming of Luther and the early wars of the Reformation forced Erasmus to amend, if not recant, his antiwar views, this fact has done little to diminish the influence of his earlier writings against war. Indeed, most nineteenth- and twentieth-century pacifists trace their intellectual roots back to Erasmus and his biting ridicule of war.

mortal sin" (1949, IV, 52), Erasmus cannot resist such an easy target. Putting his tongue firmly in his cheek, he pens a colloquy during which Alastor tells Charon, the ferryman over the River Styx, about

> certain creatures [the friars, who] . . . never leave the courts of princes. They instill into their [the princes'] ears a love of war; . . . they proclaim in their evangelical sermons that war is just, holy, and right. And—to make you marvel more at the audacity of the fellows—they proclaim the very same thing on both sides. . . . [And] none of those who die in a just war come to you [Charon], I believe. For these, they [the friars] say, fly straight to heaven. (1957, 115, 117)

Thus began a sea change in our thinking about war. Erasmus in *Julius II* and other writings, Thomas More in *Utopia*, John Colet in his sermons, and a long succession of other writers mercilessly ridiculed such consummate cynics as Pope Julius II and Henry VIII who loudly proclaimed the justice of their obviously unjust wars. Attacks on the violence and idiocy of war were of course not unknown in the past. For example, Virgil could lament in the *Aeneid*, "War, I see, / Terrible War, and the river Tiber foaming / With streams of blood" (VI, 86–88), whereas Cicero could opine, when the occasion called for it, "I cease not to advocate peace; even though unjust it is better than the justest war" (1912, VII, esp. 14). Yet previously such laments had been almost perfunctory and in any case always balanced, if not overwhelmed, by the view that war is often justified in order "that peace and justice should afterwards prevail," to repeat Cicero's words.

Now, however, in the crucible of modernity, as innumerable senseless wars swirled around them, a small group of influential writers not only upended the balance but did so with a sustained, unrelenting, and devastating ridicule. As one of his *Adagia*, Erasmus repeated Cicero's antiwar sentiment—"The most disadvantageous peace is better than the most just war"—and left it at that. Thomas More, also echoing Cicero, repeated a common enough sentiment, that war is "an activity fit only for beasts and yet practiced by no kind of beast so constantly as by man" (1965, 199; cf. Erasmus 1986, 139, 306),* but now he left it dangling without counterpoise. The conception of war as senseless brutality was not new; the lack of balancing sentiment was. Still, this change had little immediate effect upon jurists. As I already mentioned, in the next century Grotius and his colleagues moved forward with their project to revive the *jus gentium* unaffected by the humanists' ridicule and still believing that the purpose of war is peace.

---

* More's pun, which cannot be translated, is "Bellum utpote rem plane beluinam, nec ulli tamen beluarum formae in tam assiduo, atque homini est usu" (1965, 198).

It was not until the dawn of the eighteenth century, therefore, that the full effects of Machiavelli's *raison d'état,* Erasmus's ridicule, and the savagery of the Thirty Years War penetrated the hushed chambers of the jurists and detonated the mine buried in Grotius's refinement of Cicero's definition of war. In 1737 Grotius's compatriot, Cornelius van Bynkershoek, published his *Quæstionum Juris Publici Libri Duo,* which he began by sharply criticizing Grotius's definition of war:

> When Cicero said that there are "two kinds of contests, one by means of discussion, the other by means of force," he had reference in the latter case to "war." However, he did not in this way intend to define war, as Grotius thought, for such a definition would be incomplete. . . . I add, a definition which, if I mistake not, embraces all the conditions of war: "War is a contest of independent persons carried on by force or fraud for the sake of asserting their rights." (I, i, 1)

Bynkershoek has made a stunning break with the then accepted conventions. None of the antique notion "that peace and justice should afterwards prevail" for him. He has even broken with Machiavelli's apparent cynicism. There is nothing devious or cunning about his approach. No, Bynkershoek is a thoroughly modern "positivist" and "realist." He looks at war with a cold empirical eye and tells exactly what he sees—a contest carried on by force or fraud to assert one's rights. Indeed, so modern is Bynkershoek's instrumental conception of war that he has no difficulty justifying what he calls "the war of extermination" (I, ii, 10) and what the twentieth century will come to call total war:

> But in war all social obligations are in a measure severed. We attempt therefore to subjugate the enemy and all that he has by seizing all the power that the sovereign has over the state, that is to say, by exercising complete dominion over all persons and all things contained in that state. Indeed war is by its very nature so general that it cannot be waged within set limits. . . . In defining war as a contest "by force," I did not say "lawful force"; for in my opinion every force is lawful in war. So true is this that we may destroy the enemy though he be unarmed, and for this purpose we may employ poison, an assassin, or incendiary bombs, though he is not provided with such things: in short everything is legitimate against the enemy. I know that Grotius is opposed to the use of poison. . . . But if we follow reason, who is the teacher of the law of nations, we must grant that everything is lawful against enemies as such. We make war because we think that our enemy, by the injury done us, has merited the destruction of himself and his people. As this is the object of our welfare, does it matter what means we employ to accomplish it? . . . I am not even willing to omit "fraud," since it is immaterial whether we employ strategy or courage

against the enemy. . . . I would permit every kind of deceit with the sole exception of perfidy, and I make this exception not because anything is illegitimate against an enemy, but because when an engagement has been made the enemy ceases to be an enemy as far as regards the engagement. (I, i, 2–4)

Bynkershoek was well aware of his audacity, and he had what might be called a "charming" way of explaining his cold-blooded instrumental conception:

And indeed, since the reason that justifies war justifies every method of destroying the enemy, I find but one way of explaining why so many authorities and precedents oppose the employment of deceit. This opposition is clearly due to the fact that writers, as well as military leaders, improperly confuse justice, which is the subject of our present inquiry, with *generosity,* a sentiment that often appears in warfare. Justice is indispensable in war, while generosity is wholly voluntary. The former permits the destruction of the enemy by whatsoever means, the latter grants to the enemy whatever we should like to claim for ourselves in our own misfortune, and it desires that wars be waged according to the rules of the duel which was formerly admissible in some states. (I, i, 4).

Justice, like war, knows no mercy. It is only the confusion of generosity with justice that has permitted the unenlightened to think that wars could and should be waged within limits. Any limits that might be set come not from the nature of war, which is violence pure and simple, or from reason, or from justice, but only from a prudential calculus of personal interest and advantage, as Bynkershoek explains in chapter 2, "Wars May Be Lawful Without A Formal Declaration":

My opinion, then, is that a declaration is not demanded by any exigency of reason, that while it is a thing which may properly be done, it cannot be required as a matter of right. War may begin by a declaration, but it may also begin by mutual hostilities. . . . However, nations and princes endowed with some pride are not generally willing to wage war without a previous declaration, for they wish by an open attack to render victory more honourable and glorious. But here I must repeat the distinction between generosity and justice. . . . The latter permits the use of force without a declaration of war, the former considers everything in a nobler manner, deems it far from glorious to overcome an unarmed and unprepared enemy, and considers it base to attack those who may have come to us in reliance upon public amity and to despoil them when such amity has suddenly been broken through no fault of theirs. (I, ii, 7–8)

No longer do the gods command formal, fully reasoned declarations of war; now the best argument that can be found is the vanity of rulers. Even more curious, however, is the strained rationality of Bynkershoek's instrumental "reasoning." He presents his argument in terms that sound as if they were simple prudential calculations: to "render victory more honourable and glorious," a noble and proud prince will issue declarations of war. Yet the very generosity that motivates this nobility partakes of a certain self-indulgent irrationality: glory and honor are all well and good, but to sacrifice victory to either is simply foolish.

Conceptually, the source of Bynkershoek's foolishness is his rejection of Grotius's definition of war as a condition. By marking out clearly the abstract distinction between condition and contest, Grotius opened up the topic of war, creating a space wherein jurists could legitimately claim a competence that was separate and distinct from the competence of tacticians and strategists: jurists were experts on the legal conditions of war; military authors, on the contest of war. Bynkershoek, by erasing this crucial, if abstract, distinction, inadvertently deprived jurists of all competence concerning war. If war is a contest carried on by force or fraud, then clearly jurists possess no competence. Being expert neither in the use of force nor in the use of fraud—at least not the types of fraud used in war—what could a jurist possibly say about war?

But let me defer my analysis of the conceptual flaws in Bynkershoek's reasoning for a moment so as to complete my story, so as to draw out the nonsense that Bynkershoek's completely modern conception of war inevitably produces. Accordingly, let me emphasize Bynkershoek's kinship with Erasmus and Machiavelli. Although the three are completely different in many other respects, what unites them is their devotion to overturning the pious prescriptions of the past in favor of a modern, realistic, and empirical view of the world. For Bynkershoek, this meant replacing custom with reason as the sole basis for the law of nations, as is seen most clearly in his continuing criticism of Grotius: "For he [Grotius] knew well that custom does not constitute the law of nations. Reason, I repeat, is therefore the soul of the law of nations, and if we refer to reason, we shall find no argument to support the need of a declaration, but many, which I have mentioned, to the contrary" (I, ii, 10; cf. 8 and 9). The modern world thus repudiates the ancient. The break with tradition and custom is made; an alternative conception of war is articulated. Enlightenment had been achieved. A combination of crippling cynicism, stinging ridicule, and a fatal rationality produces a modern "scientific" view of war as violence perpetrated by force or fraud.

However, and the point cannot be overemphasized, the modernity of an Erasmus or a Bynkershoek consists not in any novel discovery but rather in a failure to take the antique traditions seriously, a failure to seek out the political and diplomatic functions that had once animated declarations of war, which inevitably led to a loss of all balance. For what is new in Bynkershoek's gimlet-eyed conception of war is not his observation that wars are often fought with unrestrained force and fraud. That is hardly new. One has only to recall the fate of Troy or Melos or Carthage or the Deuteronomic command: "But of the cities of these people, which the Lord thy God doth give thee for an inheritance, thou shalt save alive nothing that breatheth: But thou shalt utterly destroy them" (Deut. 20:16–17). What was new was the one-sidedness, the lack of balance. Previously the empirical reality had been recognized by all as a given, as a steady-state background that needed no mention. The best of the ancient authors, those of the *Iliad,* the *Aeneid,* and the *Song of Roland,* for example, always depicted battle as brutal. But they also maintained that war is not merely brutality. It is not purposeless slaughter. War has, or at least should have, a purpose, and that purpose is peace and justice. Indeed, precisely because the purpose of war is not a given, it had to be insisted upon, which is why declarations of war are crucial—to articulate that purpose. In a word, the ancients seldom forgot the difference between Ares, the hateful and unrestrained god of battle, and Athena, the thoughtful goddess of war, wisdom, and the gentle arts and crafts of peace.

In contrast, by drawing the empirical reality of war out of the background and foregrounding it, Bynkershoek created the impression that war has no purpose except the destruction of the enemy by fair means or foul; indeed, war simply is that destruction. But if war has no purpose, then there is no need for a declaration of war to articulate its nonpurpose, which is precisely the conclusion Bynkershoek reached. Tellingly, Bynkershoek and those who followed him never considered the now-outmoded diplomatic and political functions of declarations of war. Nor did they ever consider that the primary function of a declaration of war might be to articulate grand strategy, the causes and goals of the war. For them, as for Erasmus, any such statement is but pure rhetoric, cynical posturing. Indeed, according to Bynkershoek, the primary function of a declaration of war had been to puff up the vanity of princes by increasing the glory and honor of their subsequent victories.

Consequently, Bynkershoek's "complete" definition of war creates the dilemma with which I will wrestle for the remainder of this chapter: formal declarations of war make sense only when one assumes (1) that war, like all other human activities, must have a purpose; (2) that this purpose can be articulated only through public debates; and (3) that once articulated, this purpose must be made public—indeed, carried to the enemy as the basis for ongoing negotiations. Under these circumstances a fully reasoned declaration of war becomes an essential and integral part of war, as the ancients maintained, their pseudoreligious explanations notwithstanding. In contrast, there is absolutely no need for a formal declaration of war of any sort when one assumes that war has no purpose but the destruction of the enemy by force or fraud, as Bynkershoek and other enlightened instrumental rationalists maintain.

For example, a hundred years after Bynkershoek, in 1836, the American jurist Henry Wheaton was willing to confirm Bynkershoek's conclusion that declarations of war are not necessary, but he did so for much more practical reasons. Wheaton thus developed a carefully nuanced view of declarations of war based upon changes in both form and function. With respect to form, Wheaton distinguished between a declaration of war *to the enemy,* which was no longer necessary, and a manifesto *to one's own people,* which, although not absolutely necessary, he saw as being most prudent as a practical matter: "A formal declaration of war to the enemy was once considered necessary to legalize hostilities. . . . The present usage is to publish a manifesto, within the territory of the State declaring war, announcing the existence of hostilities, and the motives for commencing them" (Wheaton 1936, IV, §297). With respect to function, Wheaton claimed that the domestically issued manifesto serves three down-to-earth purposes. First and foremost, a manifesto is recommended as a courtesy to merchants, so that they can protect their cargoes at sea and take suitable precautions to amend or cancel their various contracts. Manifestos also function as useful pedagogical instruments for one's own population: "This publication may be necessary for the instruction and direction of the subjects of the belligerent State in respect to their intercourse with the enemy, and regarding certain effects which the voluntary law of nations attributes to war in form" (IV, §297). Finally, they avoid unnecessary difficulties at subsequent peace conferences: "Without such a declaration, it might be difficult to distinguish in a treaty of peace those acts which are to be accounted lawful effects of war, from those which either nation may consider as naked wrongs, and for which they may, under certain circumstances, claim reparations" (IV, §297). In a word, Wheaton eschewed Bynkershoek's Dutch romanticism in favor of good solid New England pragmatism. Nevertheless, the results are the same: a conditional acceptance of the need for a declaration of war "in form."

By the end of the nineteenth century, however, even Wheaton looked romantic to those jurists schooled in the new instrumentalism. For example, William Edward Hall, writing in 1880, concluded that "an act of hostility, unless it be done in the urgency of self-preservation or by way of reprisal, is in itself a full declaration of intention; any sort of previous declaration therefore is an empty formality unless an enemy must be given time and opportunity to put himself in a state of defence, and it is needless to say that no one asserts such quixotism to be obligatory" (1924, 444). Obviously Victorian England was not one of those nations described by Bynkershoek as "endowed with some pride" and therefore "wish[ing] by an open attack to render victory more honourable and glorious." However, both Hall and Bynkershoek knew that custom, not reason, drove this "quixotic" desire for a formal declaration of war: "It may be suspected that the writers who in recent times have maintained the necessity of notification of some kind have been unconsciously influenced by the merely traditional force of ideas which belong to a period anterior to international law, and which are of little value under the conditions of modern war" (Hall 1924, 445). Moreover, Hall informed his readers, even in that anterior period the only significant function performed by a declaration of war was to fix the date at which lawyers switched from municipal law to the laws of nations. Yet, Hall asserted with great assurance, a formal declaration is not needed even for this purpose, because, "The date of the commencement of a war can be perfectly defined by the first act of hostility" (444).

Hall is wrong. The first act of hostility often defines the commencement of a war less than perfectly. For example, how does one determine which act of hostility is the *first* act? And just what is an act of *hostility*? A threatening diplomatic note? A sudden mobilization? Unexpected troop movements? An army crossing a frontier? Still, this is one of the less curious inconsistencies in his thinking. More curious still is that Hall, like Wheaton, insists that no declaration of war need be made to the enemy:

> Looking at the foregoing facts as a whole it is evident that it is not necessary to adopt the artificial doctrine that notice must be given to an enemy before entering upon war. . . . Since the middle of the eighteenth century it has had no sensible influence upon practice. In its bear [*sic*] form it meets now with little support. . . . In the form of an assertion that a manifesto must be published it is so enfeebled as to be meaningless. To regard a manifesto as the equivalent of a declaration is to be satisfied with a fiction. (451)

At the same time, however, he also asserts that "as a matter of courtesy it is due to the latter [neutrals] as friends that a belligerent shall not if possible allow them to find out incidentally and perhaps with uncertainty that war has commenced, but that they shall be individually informed of its existence. . . . Hence it is in part that it has long been a common practice to address a manifesto to neutral states, the date of which serves to fix the moment at which war begins" (689). But if a manifesto is due to neutrals as a matter of courtesy, then why should the same document not be addressed to the enemy? More to the point, since a manifesto is but a fictitious declaration, according to Hall, why should a belligerent not issue the "real" thing, addressing the whole world—neutrals, the enemy, and subjects—with a formal declaration of war? Would that not show an even greater courtesy toward neutrals, not to mention toward a state's own people, as Wheaton suggests?

But these are trivial inconsistencies for which there are no answers, and I pass over them so as to focus upon a much more important point. From my perspective, the most interesting aspect of Hall's exposition is an off-hand passage that appears as part of his attempt to discredit the traditional view that formal declarations of war are always necessary:

> Thus in the seventeenth century the theoretical assertion of the necessity of declaration was continuous and nearly universal; but the views and habits of men of action are better represented in a passage of Molloy than in the pages of Grotius or Pufendorf. "A general war," he says, "is either solemnly denounced or not solemnly denounced; the former is when war is solemnly declared or proclaimed by our king against another state. Such was the Dutch war, 1671. An unsolemn war is when two nations slip into a war without any solemnity; and ordinarily happeneth among us. Again, if a foreign prince invades our coasts, or sets upon the king's navy at sea, hereupon a real, though not solemn war may, and hath formerly, arisen. Such was the Spanish invasion in 1588. So that a state of war may be between two kingdoms without any proclamation or indication thereof, or other matter of record to prove it" [Molloy 1672, I, c, l]. The distinction which is here drawn between solemn and unsolemn war is indicative of the tenacity of life, which is shown by forms; and the history of the eighteenth century shows how powerless in this case they really were. (446–47)

Three comments are perhaps appropriate. First, Hall is mistaken. It is not "the merely traditional force of ideas" that divides "men of theory" and "men of action" on the necessity of a formal declaration of war. Rather, it is the ambiguity inherent in the word *war*. It is the failure to treat seriously Grotius's distinction between war as a condition and war as a contest. Second, as if to confirm Hall's belief in the unconscious influence of the merely traditional force of ideas, especially his own, it is instructive, if not ironic, to observe Philip Brown (1939, 539) approvingly citing Hall quoting Charles Molloy fifty years later, thereby propelling *this* traditional idea forward. Thus, whether secularized by speaking of "war in the legal sense" versus "war in the material sense" (Wright 1932, 362) or, after World War II, of formally declared wars versus undeclared armed conflicts, the merely traditional force of Molloy's solemn and unsolemn wars has continued down to the present.

Third, the most significant aspect of this passage is that the distinction between a solemn and an unsolemn declaration of war causes neither Molloy nor Hall any difficulties. Both assume that the expressions are but simple, perhaps more colorful, synonyms for declared and undeclared war. The reason no difficulties arise is that neither Molloy nor Hall could imagine an unsolemn war as being declared illegal. It would be incontestably a "real" war, and that is what matters. That the king has neglected to perform the customary solemnities is of no importance whatsoever, and certainly no cause to label the war illegitimate. Cicero would have disagreed, as would have Grotius, but by 1880, after more than two hundred years during which unsolemn wars had become the norm, not even the most fervent descendent of Grotius could plausibly label an undeclared war as illegal.

Herein lies the nub of the pseudoproblem that will eventually discredit the traditionalists' position entirely. In all logic, it is inconsistent for the descendants of Grotius to assert that a formal declaration of war is necessary but then to acknowledge that the failure to issue one does not produce any negative consequences. Unless the traditionalists can devise some way to stigmatize undeclared wars as not only unsolemn but also illegal, their position reduces to the making of a grand distinction where there is no real or practical difference. It is, indeed, to confirm the validity of the realists' most forceful argument: "Look," the instrumental rationalists say, "you insist that formal declarations are necessary, but what are the consequences when the king fails to make a formal declaration? None whatsoever. So what is the point of your assertion?"

In response, one should point out that from the legal perspective, declarations of war affect primarily the condition of war, not the contest, the declaration's specific juridical function being to establish the legal condition of war by voiding contracts and treaties, triggering the rights of neutrals, and activating the other provisions of the law of war. Only when one defines war as uniquely a contest do declarations of war loose their effects. In a word, the traditionalists should have thrown the argument back upon Bynkershoek's criticism of Grotius and fought it out there. However, with the triumph of empirical science, positivist jurisprudence, and instrumental rationalism by the end of the nineteenth century, any such a course was not possible.

Unable to argue that Grotius was right and Bynkershoek wrong, the traditionalists instead tried to make the strictures of the tradition look more like "real" laws. With the adoption of the Hague, Geneva, and a number of other conventions, the laws of war seemed to move beyond mere custom by creating the appearance of positive law and hence giving the impression of establishing firm criteria for determining whether any given war is legal or illegal. Of special interest here is the 1907 Hague convention 3, Relative to the Opening of Hostilities. This convention was one of the pet projects of the traditionalists in the Institut de Droit International. Their campaign to have it adopted was greatly assisted by the general perplexity and outrage that resulted from the excessively vague 1904 Japanese ultimatum to the Russians, which, it was argued, demonstrated the necessity for "legislation" on this matter. The incident unfolded as follows: At 4:00 P.M. on 6 February 1904, Mr. Kurino, the Japanese minister plenipotentiary, handed Count Lambsdorff, the Russian foreign minister, two notes. The shorter note severed diplomatic relations between the two countries, Mr. Kurino being ordered to leave St. Petersburg immediately. The longer note explained the reasons for severing relations:

> The obstinate rejections by the Russian Government, by means of amendments impossible of agreement, of Japan's proposals . . . have made it necessary for the Imperial Government seriously to consider what measures of self-defense they are called upon to take. . . . In adopting this course [of terminating the present futile negotiations], the Imperial Government reserves to themselves the right to take such independent action as they may deem best to consolidate and defend their menaced position, as well as to protect the acquired rights and legitimate interests of the Empire. (Asakawa 1904, 343–44)

Although both Japan and Russia subsequently issued formal declarations of war on 10 February 1904, in the eyes of many at the time, the ambiguity of the longer note amounted to an extremely sharp brand of diplomacy at best and downright deception at worst. For by the time the notes were delivered, the Japanese naval and military establishments had already deployed from their home bases, with the result that the first naval engagements took place during the day of 8 February, and Port Arthur was attacked during the night of 8–9 February 1904. Convention 3 was, consequently, seen as a remedy for such practices in the eyes of its promoters in the Institut de Droit International, although it provided no sanctions and applied only to those states that were party to it. Still, the assumption was that its mere adoption by the international community would codify the ancient custom and therefore provide a firm or at least firmer basis for stigmatizing undeclared wars as illegal in some sense.

Unfortunately, though, this effort was for naught, its inevitable outcome being only greater confusion and even stronger confirmation that the modern instrumentally rational jurists were correct all along. For once the traditionalists had codified in a manner of speaking the requirement to declare war, the next step was to flesh out convention 3 by specifying the forms and functions of legally adequate declarations, since obviously not every piece of paper that says "declaration of war" can qualify as a valid declaration of war. In an effort to do this, Clyde Eagleton wrote an intriguing article in 1938 optimistically entitled "The Form and Function of the Declaration of War." I say "optimistically" because in the end, despite his sincere efforts to support and

defend convention 3, Eagleton is forced to confess that declarations of war—
as he understood them, at least—possess neither form nor function.

Eagleton begins his analysis by putting forward two very inauspicious
ideas. First, he asserts that "the idea of the declaration of war seems to have
originated in the sportsmanlike belief that one should give fair warning in
advance of an attack to follow" (Eagleton 1938, 19–20; this assertion is repeated on 29). Clearly Eagleton lacked training as an anthropologist, or he would
have recognized this "fair-warning" rationale as the type of pseudoreason with
which ancient customs are usually clothed. It therefore did not occur to him
to look beneath the surface to see whether there might not exist substantial
political and diplomatic functions breathing life into the ancient custom of
declaring war. Second, he cautiously and without much conviction maintains
the lawlike character of the requirement to declare war: "Thus, adding recent
practice to the Hague Convention [3], it may be possible to aver that there is
a rule of customary international law to the effect that war must be declared.
What this signifies, it is difficult to say: whether war without a declaration is
illegal, or, since it is not declared, it is not war" (21). What this signifies is a
monstrous legal loophole, a Hydra-headed legal tangle, a constant and repeated incongruity that plagues both Eagleton's exposition and the traditional-
ist defense of declarations of war at every turn. He continues: "War has been
declared illegal, to a varying extent, in a number of modern treaties; it therefore becomes highly important to know what war is. If these prohibitions are
to apply only to declared wars (others not being wars under the convention
because not declared), they would have little effect upon war; for it would be
absurd for a state to declare war when by this mere failure to do so it would be
absolved from the guilt of having carried on illegal war" (21).

Needless to say, Eagleton can neither resolve nor avoid this legal tangle because he possesses no means to parse the ambiguity inherent in the word *war*.
He is unable to separate war from not war, legal wars from illegal wars, and war
from combat. He has accepted Bynkershoek's empirical definition of war as an
act of force, which erases all such distinctions. Eagleton was of course familiar
with Grotius's definition, having quoted it on page 258 of his 1933 article "The
Attempt to Define War," but he considered it as only part of the background
noise that left "one with a great deal of uncertainty as to the meaning of war"
(1933, 282). Still, had he recognized the importance of Grotius's distinction
between war as a condition and war as a contest, he would have possessed a tool
for coming to grips with the ambiguity of the word *war*. But several hundred
years have passed since anyone took Grotius's refinement of Cicero seriously.
In consequence, Eagleton's exposition repeatedly flounders.

For example, Eagleton begins his discussion of form by asserting that "a declaration of war is usually a formal proclamation issued on behalf of a state" (1938, 22). This "usual" form is not the only form, however. In addition, there are ultimatums (23); "other acts of a minatory or warning nature" (24); the rupture of diplomatic relations (24–25); "certain acts of a hostile nature," such as the U.S. ratification of the treaty annexing Texas (25); a proclamation of blockade (25); or a proclamation by a field commander (28)—all these can serve and have served as the functional equivalents of a formal declaration of war. Eagleton even speculates that, since a proclamation by a third-party government declaring its neutrality or a court in a third-party country ruling on some war-related case also establishes the existence of war, such a third-party proclamation might in some sense be viewed as functionally equivalent to a declaration of war, even though such a proclamation would not be binding upon the belligerents (26–27).

In a word, almost any announcement or action can be and probably has been taken as functionally equivalent to a declaration of war, which means that the declaration of war—at least as understood by Eagleton—has no form whatsoever, an observation that leads yet again directly to Eagleton's unresolvable difficulty: "Such acts may be interpreted, not as substitutes for declarations, but as evidence of a state of undeclared war. It nevertheless remains true that if certain announcements or acts may be regarded as preforming the same functions as a declaration, it would be very difficult to say which is a declared war and which is not. Any act of hostility accepted as creating the status of war could then be called a declaration" (25).

This same legal difficulty also plagues the first and most certain of the five functions that Eagleton identifies, namely, that "the declaration of war creates the legal status of war. This much seems sure, amid many uncertainties" (21). Eagleton, however, bases his confidence in this function upon four troubling characteristics:

1. It is not intended thereby to say that war can exist only after a declaration; the contrary undoubtedly is true. (21)
2. This [the legal status of war] may be accomplished by the declaration of one state alone. (21)
3. The magic of the declaration seems enough also to establish the legal status of war even in the absence of any actual exercise of physical power. (22)
4. The declaration of war may be issued after the war is ended and the treaty of peace signed. (29)

As the backing and filling of his four characteristics indicate, this first and most "certain" function possesses an aura of great uncertainty. Perhaps, however, we should let Eagleton summarize the confusion:

We may say, then, with confidence, only one thing: that a declaration establishes the legal status of war. It is not always clear what is to be regarded as a
declaration, nor what authority can issue it, nor when it is to be regarded as in
effect. Consequently, even though there has been what purported to be a declaration of war, the attacked state—and other states—may not realize that their
placid situation of peace has been shattered, or when it occurred, or whether
it was legitimately done. (29)

With such "confidence," is it any wonder that no one can see any need to issue formal declarations of war? Remember, Eagleton is writing a brief in defense of convention 3!

The sources of Eagleton's confusion are two. On the one hand, he has lost
all sight of Grotius's distinction between war as a condition and war as a contest. As a result, he is unable to sense the equivocation hiding within his odd
numbered characteristics. Yes, of course, the contest of war is not the only
means for establishing the condition of war. An alternative manner is to employ the "magic" of a declaration. And when one employs this magical alternative, the condition of war (especially, its legal conditions) can thereby be
established without ever triggering the contest of war. On the other hand,
Eagleton is so entrapped in the narrow juridical concerns of the tradition that
he cannot imagine that the first, foremost, and most certain functions of a
declaration of war might be military and moral, not juridical. As a result, what
strikes the reader most about Eagleton's most "certain" function is its irreali-
ty, its concern with the peripheral and omission of the essential. In defense
of Eagleton, it must be admitted that the legal status of war does touch on a
number of important matters, such as insurance claims, commercial contracts, tourism and other types of travel, and compliance with treaties. Nonetheless, although important, these matters are distinctly peripheral, hardly
matters that would compel one to think that formal declarations of war are
always required. Consequently, once again one is forced to conclude that if
establishing the legal status of a war so as to regulate these peripheral matters
constitutes the first and foremost function of declarations of war, then there
is not much to be said in the defense of formally declaring war.

But what of Eagleton's four other functions, the "less certain" ones? He
begins by asking again the seminal question: "What, then, is the function of
the declaration of war? The most obvious answer to this question is that it is
very important to establish a date upon which the metamorphosis from peace
to war takes place" (29). However, he immediately points out that "the cases
reveal no certainty whatever as to when war begins, even where a declaration
of war is issued" (29). Then, after demonstrating this point with numerous
cases, he ends his discussion of this second function by concluding, "On the

whole, then, it is difficult to maintain that the declaration of war serves the purpose of fixing the time at which war begins" (33).

The third possible function suggested by Eagleton concerns the need to distinguish between public and private war, a function that traces back to Grotius. Yet again, however, he is forced to conclude, "If this explanation of the declaration of war were ever justified, it is not so now, for the distinction between public and private war has been abandoned, and letters of marque and reprisal are no longer legitimate" (33).

The fourth possible function is to "serve internal purposes, such as calling citizens to arms, furnishing a guide for the courts, *et cetera*" (34). Unfortunately, though, Eagleton merely documents the fact that many recent declarations have had this internal purpose and does not elaborate or develop the idea any further.

Finally, Eagleton's fifth function is "to furnish a vehicle for the statement of the reasons why the war is being waged" (34). This function, of course, is the one specifically mentioned in the Hague convention 3, with its call for "reasoned declarations." Nonetheless, Eagleton observes that on the one hand, during World War I, "the ultimatum seems [to have been] more often used" to accomplish this function and that on the other hand, "if . . . this is the sole function of the declaration of war, it must be admitted that it has not much *raison d'être*" (34). I will forbear commenting upon this conclusion, except to note in passing that Eagleton has not only vitiated convention 3 but also torn out the heart of the military and moral functions of fully reasoned declarations of war.

In sum, Eagleton can find no compelling function that can justify a nation issuing declarations of war. He therefore concludes:

> It is unfortunately true that, from the viewpoint of the old international law, these functions are not served in a reliable and trustworthy fashion; and that, from the viewpoint of more recent international agreements dealing with the status of war, the situation has been so greatly changed that the declaration of war has become inadequate. . . . [Consequently,] the pressure of public opinion and of treaties condemning war makes it probable that undeclared wars, rather than declared wars, will be the rule [in the future]. (34, 35)

Indeed, Eagleton's final prediction was entirely correct. To "be absolved from the guilt of having carried on illegal war," nations have chosen the simple expedient of not declaring war at all. True, belligerents took the time to issue unreasoned declarations of war during World War II, but there has been only one case of declared war since 1945, the formal declarations that appear to have been made on 5 June 1967 by Algeria, Iraq, Kuwait, Sudan, and Syria against Israel. More precisely, since World War II, no one has been hardy enough to take up the challenge and attempt to flesh out convention 3, which is for all intents and purposes as dead a letter as are the congressional war powers. Eagleton's study of the forms and functions of the declaration of war remains definitive. Not surprisingly, then, the perceived irrelevance of declarations of war has now become crushing, as R. R. Baxter summarizes with an instrumental outlook that would have pleased Bynkershoek: "The declaration of war is in these days only of marginal importance. A state, whether in fact the aggressor or the victim of aggression, will seek to justify its resort to war as an act of self-defense. If war has been thrust upon one state by another, there is no need to declare war. If, on the other hand, a state is fatally bent on mischief, it will probably not pause to declare the war that it has [illegally] inflicted on another" (in Miller 1975, 20).*

Consequently, after World War II, attention turned from the seemingly hopeless task of trying to enhance the efficacy of convention 3 to the more sensible task of trying to mitigate or avoid its consequences. The most successful strategy has been to shift the burden from the adjectives to the nouns. No longer is it thought appropriate to speak of declared or undeclared, solemn or unsolemn, or perfect or imperfect wars, whereas *war in the legal sense* versus *war in the material sense* is much too cumbersome. Instead, it has become fashionable to distinguish war from armed conflict—the noun *war,* unencumbered by any adjectives, indicating specifically a formally declared war, preferably with a declaration that conforms to the requirements of the Hague convention 3, whereas *armed conflict* indicates more generally "any difference arising between two states and leading to the intervention of members of the armed forces," in the words of the Pictet Red Cross commentary on article 2, paragraphs 1 and 2, of the four 1949 Geneva Conventions (cited in Miller 1975, 20–21). For example, the Library of Congress and several other government agencies, following this new legal convention, never call the war in Vietnam a "war." Instead, they refer to it as the "Vietnamese Conflict" (Kimball 1990, 3).

At the level of practical enforcement, one must concede that this initiative has been successful. With the acceptance of armed conflict as the legal equivalent of undeclared war, the ability of the international community to enforce the Hague and Geneva Conventions has increased minutely. For example, the Bosnian Serbs were unable to frustrate the representatives of the

---

* The quotation deviates from that which appears on page 20 so as to correct a printing error. R. R. Baxter's manuscript read "illegally inflicted," not "legally inflicted," as appeared in the printed text (personal communication with the editor, Richard I. Miller, 17 January 1994).

International Red Cross seeking to inspect concentration camps by saying that the conventions did not apply because there was no formally declared war in Bosnia. There are numerous other ways to frustrate enforcement, but since 1949 no one has been able to use this excuse. The war in Bosnia was certainly an armed conflict, and so the conventions did apply.

At the level of theory, however, one must also concede that this initiative has solved nothing, as Eugene Rostow's following summary of the current situation illustrates:

> "Undeclared" (or "limited" or "imperfect") war is a category of public international law, used to denote hostilities on considerable scale conducted in time of "peace" rather than of "war," so far as international law is concerned. . . . The United States, like most other nations during the last two and a half centuries, has rarely chosen to invoke the international law of war by solemnly "declaring" that a state of war exists, signalling maximum hostilities, and implying the invasion or even the destruction of an enemy state. But a considerable number of our many "limited" or "undeclared" wars, like Vietnam itself, have been authorized by Congress as well as the President through procedures which have been approved in usage and in Supreme Court opinions since the first years of the nation under the Constitution of 1789. (1972, 834–35)

Although substituting *armed conflict* for *undeclared, limited,* or *imperfect war* will remove most of the cautionary quotation marks, it will not eliminate all of them. Most particularly, the newly fashionable noun phrase does nothing to improve the coherence of the passage. All the lose ends that became unknit when Bynkershoek challenged Grotius's definition of war continue to unravel.

In the first place, introducing *armed conflict* will not remove the cautionary quotation marks around *peace* and *war* and, consequently, the evasive absurdity of the relative clause remains: "Undeclared war/armed conflict is a category of international law, used to denote hostilities on considerable scale conducted in time of 'peace' rather than of 'war,' so far as international law is concerned." So far as international law is concerned, both war and peace are now formal categories, lacking substance and reality. When journalists report that war is ravaging Vietnam or Bosnia or Somalia or Nicaragua, the jurist must correct them by pointing out, first, that technically it is not war but an armed conflict that is ravaging the countryside and, second, that because there is no war, only an armed conflict, peace reigns in these countries—so far as international law is concerned, which is no doubt a great comfort to all concerned.

In the second place, how is one to sort out the relationships among formally declared war, war in general, and informally declared armed conflict? Is war the genus, which contains at least two species, (formally declared) war and (formally undeclared) armed conflict? Or is armed conflict the genus, which contains at least two species, (formally declared) war and (formally undeclared) war? Or is conflict the genus, which contains at least two species, unarmed conflict and armed conflict, which in turn subdivides into (formally declared) war and (formally undeclared) armed conflict? And just what is the relationship between armed conflict and peace? The relationship between armed conflict and "peace" is clear enough: an armed conflict is what we now call an imperfect, limited, undeclared war—that is, a war that occurs during times of "peace." But does the end of an armed conflict bring about a restoration of peace? Or does the term *armed conflict* contrast with *conflict,* such that the end of an armed conflict brings only an unarmed conflict, not peace? In other words, is the world truly Manichaean, composed of hot war and cold war only?

However one might sort out these insoluble questions, the fact of the matter is that the jurists have abandoned the search for a definition of war. They have stopped asking the difficult question "What is war?" and instead substituted the much simpler question "What is armed conflict?" The response to this question is that an armed conflict is a conflict that has somehow become armed. In addition, a conflict becomes armed whenever members of an armed forces intervene in the conflict. In other words, the jurists have substituted *who* for *what,* it always being easier to identify who is doing something than to define what they are doing.

But there was no reason for the jurists to abandon the search for a definition of war. All they had to do was to contest Bynkershoek, return to Grotius, and build upon that solid foundation. Returning to Grotius is no longer possible, however. Both he and international law have been too long irrelevant. Indeed, the only insight they can offer at this juncture on the cusp of the twentieth-first century is the observation that defining war in terms of who engages in war is tantamount to reducing war to combat, a position that even a junior operations officer finds difficult to accept. But if war cannot be reduced to combat, then what is war? I attempt to answer this question in the next chapter.

4

War: Perspective and Perversion

War is an exceedingly complex human activity. This complexity is necessarily reflected in the word itself, which struggles to encompass not only war but a long menu of vaguely similar activities, ranging from metaphorical expressions of maximal effort, such as a "war on poverty" or a "war on drugs," right through to expressions of maximal horror, such as nuclear war. Indeed, as a substantive, *war* fills over five pages of the *Oxford English Dictionary* (1989), to which must be added another column and a half explaining its usage as a verb, both transitive and intransitive. Even when the figurative and metaphorical uses of the word are excluded, the complexity of the concept remains.

The reason for this complexity is that the word is caught in a double ambiguity. The first ambiguity arises out of the great difficulty in achieving an appropriate perspective, because the relationship between war and combat is so clouded. Are the two terms synonymous, designating essentially the same thing, such that a war without combat or combat without war is inconceivable? Or are the two separable, designating essentially different things, such that combat without war and war without combat are not only quite possible but commonplace as well? The second ambiguity arises out of the uncertainty that surrounds the boundary between war and its perversions. The boundary between war and peace is reasonably clear, even when not formally declared, but even the existence of a boundary between war and its perversions is in doubt. Yet if no such boundary exists, then war is an unbounded phenomenon, the cliché that "all's fair in love and war" is literally true, and no horror or extreme of violence constitutes a perversion of war, which is improbable.

The first ambiguity has long been recognized. For example, Quincy Wright begins his monumental work *A Study of War* by alluding to the irreconcilable differences in perspective that color people's attitudes toward war: "To different people war may have very different meanings. To some it is a plague which ought to be eliminated. . . . On the other hand, there are some who take a more receptive attitude" (1965, 3). And indeed, the term *armed conflict* was introduced after World War II specifically to deal with this ambiguity. *Armed conflict* is itself ambiguous, however, mirroring the ambiguity it is supposed to clarify. It functions sometimes as a synonym for *combat* and at other times as a synonym for *war.* When used as a synonym for *combat,* as in the 1949 Geneva Conventions, it indicates that the rules enunciated are to apply to all instances of combat, even when that combat occurs outside formally declared wars in a so-called armed conflict. To be sure, a clearer remedy would have been to acknowledge that some provisions of the *jus gentium,* such as the law regarding neutrality or the Hague convention 3, Relative to the Opening of Hostilities, apply to the whole of war, whereas others, such as those governing the treatment of the wounded, of prisoners of war, and of noncombatants, apply only to combat, the violent fraction of war.

When used as a synonym for *war,* the term *armed conflict* reproduces the technical and legalistic distinction between wars that are formally declared and those that are not. Once one moves beyond this formal distinction and on to substance, however, all clarity is lost. For example, were Grotius to write his seminal work today, his title would have to read *The Laws of War, Peace, and Armed Conflict;* otherwise he would risk the charge of being out of date from reviewers such as Major James A. Burger, who complimented a new Air Force manual by noting that "even the title of the Air Force publication, 'The Conduct of Armed Conflict and Air Operations,' indicates that it is designed to take an up-to-date approach to the laws of war" (1978, 261). But why should an up-to-date approach to the laws of *war* consist in writing about the conduct of *armed conflict?*

The confusion caused by using *armed conflict* as a synonym for *war* is, however, only a symptom. The underlying cause is that both *war* and *armed conflict* imply that the phenomenon they designate is an unbounded activity. This is the case because both terms acknowledge only one limit to the phenomenon they name, namely, that which separates war from peace. The noun phrase *armed conflict* does this by creating a contrast with *unarmed conflict,* which is presumed to characterize a state of peace, whereas priests and jurists have asserted for millennia that the criterion for war is the declaration that announces the imminent transformation of peace into war. But this creates an impossible situation, for if there is only this one boundary, then war is an unbounded phenomenon, which is clearly impossible, since no human activity is without limits that can be transgressed.

To confront these two long-recognized ambiguities, my argument will develop over two stages. Initially it will examine the uncertainty that surrounds the relationship between combat and war. To determine whether combat and war are identical, my argument will address two issues. First it will consider the question of perspective—specifically, whether the perspective of those who experience combat as either combatants or noncombatants should be privileged above the perspective of others who do not. Although the experiences of those who were shot at can obviously tell us much of combat, can they tell us anything of war? Second, my argument will evaluate the relative positions of violence and policy. Which is central? Which is peripheral? The purpose of both arguments will be to make headway against the sublimity of the violence of combat, for combat, being sublime, enthralls. Its horror and glory touch upon the divine and engage all who look upon it to the exclusion of all else, including war and policy.

Next I will search for the boundary between war and its perversions. To locate this boundary, I pick up on Clyde Eagleton's claim that declarations of war "establish the legal status of war." This will send me back to the dispute between Grotius and Bynkershoek as to whether war is a condition or a contest and then forward to the conclusion that the primary function of a fully reasoned declaration of war is not to mark the boundary between peace and war, as we have been told for millennia, but rather to mark the boundary between war and its perversions. That is, I will return by a rather circuitous route to Clausewitz and his principal insight that "no one starts a war—or rather, no one in his senses ought to do so—without first being clear in his mind what he intends to achieve by that war and how he intends to conduct it" (1976, 579).

Resisting the Sublime Violence of Combat

Conceptually, one's attitude toward declarations of war depends upon one's conception of war: those who believe that *war* is synonymous with *combat* soon adopt the modern opinion that declarations of war are never required. In contrast, those who believe that war is policy cling to the ancient doctrine that a reasoned declaration is always required. The reasons for this contrast are no mystery. Conceiving of war as policy means that one also believes that war is a rational human activity, an activity in which the means used are calibrated to achieve the ends sought. As individuals engaged in a rational activity, decision makers not only can but must justify their decision, laying out the causes, defining the ends, and explaining how war is the appropriate means to achieving those ends, which is precisely what a fully reasoned declaration of war does. In contrast, conceiving of war as the violence of combat means that one also believes that war is profoundly irrational, the apparently pointless infliction of pain and suffering on others who have done one no harm. Being irrational, such war is profoundly inexplicable, any attempt to explain or justify its violence being merely an exercise in cynicism or worse. The brutal fact of the senseless carnage can perhaps be acknowledged officially with an unreasoned absolute declaration, such as Congress has always issued, but anything more is meaningless.

Conceptually, therefore, restoring faith in the need to write only reasoned declarations of war is contingent upon conceiving of war as policy, a human activity that rationally relates the military means to the political ends. This would be an easy task except that war often involves combat, sometimes extremely violent combat, which complicates the matter inordinately. In particular, it creates a tendency for the noun to usurp the adjective. That is, in the minds of many, conceding that war often involves violent combat is tantamount to defining war as violence. Logically, of course, this should not be done because it confuses the whole of war with one of its parts; it is like defining automobile driving as violence just because automobile accidents are often violent, on occasion extremely so.

Although the confusion of the visually most spectacular part of an activity with the whole of that activity is easily detected in the case of less sublime human activities such as automobile driving, coal mining, and the such like, in the case of war the same discrimination seldom occurs. Indeed, from many perspectives war *is* violence—not merely violent, but violence itself, violence incarnate, the essence of violence. For those who have experienced the horrors of combat directly, the proposition is usually beyond dispute; for those who have not, a short talk with a survivor of combat is usually sufficient. But one does not need to rely upon firsthand testimony. The media tell the same story. Be it still photographs, documentary films, or Hollywood productions, the evidence before one's eyes is incontestable. War *is* violence. Likewise, most written accounts offer the same perspective. Be they letters home, autobiographical accounts, or novels from Leo Tolstoy's sublime *War and Peace* to Joseph Heller's satirical *Catch 22,* their message is always the same. War *is* violence, indeed, senseless violence, nothing but killing and devastation. As Tolstoy summarized the situation in one of his more striking passages: "On the twelfth of June, 1812, the forces of Western Europe crossed the Russian frontier and war began, that is, an event took place opposed to human reason and to human nature" (1966, 667).

Part of the problem, therefore, is perspective. But why should the perspective of those who experience combat be privileged over that of those who do not? Just because General Dwight Eisenhower saw no combat during World War II, does that mean that he knew nothing of war? To be sure, we can readily agree that Eisenhower's personal experience tells us next to nothing about combat, about the specific modalities of getting shot at during World War II, but is it not precisely this fact that makes his perspective so valuable and informative concerning the war, the whole of the war, especially its policy and politics? Furthermore, does the existence of these two types of personal experiences not imply the existence of two different and separable phenomena as well? Some will experience combat; others, war, the noncombat components of war.

More precisely, one begins to lose sight of the violence of combat when one works in an operations section, as Clausewitz did. For the operations officer—the officer directly in charge of making a battle "happen"—war is an exceedingly abstract affair. The operations officer thinks in terms of units, not individuals. A platoon is ordered here, a company there, and where *are* the trucks to move them? This officer's job is all lines drawn on maps, orders received from above and drafted for those below, while, in between updating the map and drafting the orders, the officer writes reports, reports, and more reports. Seldom does violence intrude upon this paper world. Seldom does it shake the pencil loose from the officer's firm hand. Even the dead and wounded are transformed from bodies and buddies into numbers and acronyms: 3KIA, 5WIA, and 0MIA.

Likewise, for military or political historians, war is exceedingly abstract. Focusing upon such abstractions as "the infantry" attacking on the left while "the cavalry" charges on the right or the pomposity of diplomats and the hypocrisy of politicians, military and political histories present a dehumanized, some would say sanitized, perspective. As if to prove the point, even a tedious military history can be enlivened and become a best-seller when it changes its focus by privileging the experiences of those caught in the crossfire of combat, as John Keegan's popular book *The Face of Battle* (1976) does. In this ground-breaking book, Keegan sets out to "enlarge" the military historian's stock in trade, the "battle piece," by effacing strategy, not to mention policy, from war:

> I do not intend to write about generals or generalship . . . [or about] logistics or strategy and very little about tactics in the formal sense. And I do not intend to offer a two-sided picture of events. . . . On the other hand, I do intend to discuss wounds and their treatment, the mechanics of being taken prisoner, the nature of leadership at the most junior level, the role of compulsion in getting

men to stand their ground, the incidents of accidents as a cause of death in war and, above all, the dimensions of the danger which different varieties of weapons offer to the soldier on the battlefield. (78)

The irony of Keegan's intentions is quite startling. He plans to enlarge the battle piece by narrowing it. He plans to enlarge the reader's understanding by removing the significant context and dismissing precisely those elements of the story that situate, explain, and justify the battle. His battles will take place in a splendid isolation from history, politics, strategy, and logistics—but not, significantly, in isolation from technology, which is what Keegan means by "the dimensions of the danger which different varieties of weapons offer to the soldier on the battlefield," the different varieties of weapons being dependent upon the development of different varieties of technology as one moves from sticks and stones to bullets and bombs. His battles, therefore, focus instead upon the elements that absorb the individual soldier. Authorial intentions aside, what Keegan has done is to change perspective. Instead of viewing battle from the top, he wishes to view it from the bottom. Instead of seeing how policy guides and directs strategy down to the smallest operational detail, he wishes to see how individual experience and personal horror create the "human dimensions" of war. Yet this "enlarged" perspective has its limitations; when engulfed in the sublime violence of battle, one cannot see the war, or at any rate not the whole of it. With one's teeth in the dirt and that crisp crack rending the air above, it is impossible to see strategy, much less policy. And so, from this perspective, it is all but impossible not to conclude, as Keegan does, that "the central act of warfare" is killing (316).

But this conclusion follows only because of the chosen perspective. It cannot be sustained when a different perspective is taken. Insofar as the violence of combat is sublime, however, not privileging the experience of those who have seen combat is exceedingly difficult. Therefore, let me address the question directly. Which is more central to war, policy or violence? Since violence is but one of the possible outcomes of any human activity—including war—the alternatives can be reformulated as follows: which is more central to war, the purposes that motivate the war or one of its possible outcomes? Asked in this manner, it is clear that a war's purposes are more central. This is so, first, because the purposes that motivate any human activity are more important than any one of that activity's consequences taken in isolation, although not more important than all the activity's consequences taken together. Second, although a war's purposes can justify a certain amount of violence, the resulting violence can never justify any of the purposes. For example, the trauma caused by sticking a knife into someone's heart can never justify cutting open a human heart, whereas the hope of curing heart disease can easily justify the trauma caused by a surgeon's cutting into a patient's heart. Understanding the purpose of the resulting violence makes all the difference.

To argue the same point in a different way, consider the problem of victory. On his return from Korea in 1951, General Douglas MacArthur told a joint session of Congress, "There is no substitute for victory" (Brodie 1973, 4). Needless to say, this is a sentiment with which all can agree. After all the cheering and applause are finished, however, what does it mean? How does one know when victory has been secured? There are no objective measures. Victory does not boil at 100 degrees centigrade. It cannot be calculated at 3.1416. No level or extent of violence signals its arrival, as General Erich von Falkenhayn learned in the aftermath of Verdun during World War I.

In truth, victory is a purely relative phenomenon. It is the attainment of a previously fixed goal. Accordingly, to insist that there is no substitute for victory is to insist that there is no substitute for policy, no substitute for an official and authoritative declaration of the war's aims, indeed, for a fully reasoned declaration of war. Lacking a clearly articulated goal, victory is impossible, no matter what the level of violence. For example, consider the differences between the Revolutionary War and the Vietnam War. After 4 July 1776, but not before, both victory and defeat were possible, because the Second Continental Congress had articulated a clear goal—independence—that Commander-in-Chief Washington would either win or lose on the field of battle. In a very real sense, however, the United States could neither win nor lose its war in Vietnam because no one in a position of authority ever articulated the goal to be sought. To put matters more precisely, Hugh M. Arnold (1975) found twenty-two official rationales for U.S. intervention in Vietnam between 1949 and 1967. As a result, it is not surprising to learn that in a 1974 survey, Douglas Kinnard found "almost 70 percent of the Army generals who managed the war [in Vietnam] were uncertain of its objectives" (1977, 25). Inasmuch as no clear goal had been articulated, victory was literally unobtainable. The war could be neither won nor lost; it could only continue until we exhausted ourselves trying to reach a goal we refused to set for ourselves.

In fine, as a matter of simple logic, discussions of the weight of violence relative to that of policy in war always lead to the conclusion that the violence of combat is an accidental characteristic, not an essential or defining characteristic. As Hannah Arendt put the matter: "Violence is by nature instrumental; like all means, it always stands in need of guidance and justification through the ends it pursues. And what needs justification by something else cannot be the essence of anything" (Arendt 1972, 150). Still, the sublime power of the violence of combat is all but overwhelming, as can perhaps best be seen by examining the difficulties Clausewitz encountered in trying to overcome it.

The first sign of this difficulty is the fact that it was not until July 1827, toward the end of his life, that Clausewitz began emphasizing the centrality of policy over the violence of combat; before that he had focused upon the psychological and other technical aspects of battle. As a result of this late shift in emphasis, he was able to revise only the first chapter of book 1 of *On War* before his death in 1831. The result of this initial revision is far from satisfactory. Since Clausewitz is popularly known as a prophet of "total war," one can safely conclude that most readers are uncertain whether he took the violence of combat to be central or peripheral to war (see, e.g., Clausewitz 1976, 20; Mearsheimer 1988, 49; *Encyclopaedia Britannica,* 15th ed., s.v. "War, Theory of"). This confusion arises because Clausewitz tries to have it both ways in chapter 1 of book 1, defining war both as violence and as policy rather than separating combat from war. He is able to have it both ways because, instead of viewing the relationship between war and combat as that of a whole to one of its parts, he views it as the relationship of a Platonic idealization of war to the concrete historical reality of war. To flesh out this Platonic relationship, he constructs an idiosyncratic—some would say metaphysical—dialectic that contrasts an ideal, abstract world of absolute violence to the concrete world of historical wars.

To this end he begins his dialectic in section 2, "Definition," by asserting that ideally, in the abstract, "*War* [by which he surely means combat or battle] *is thus an act of force to compel our enemy to do our will*" (1976, 75). He next demonstrates in sections 3–5 that according to this "pure conception of war," war should be an absolute phenomenon, an act of extreme and unrestrained violence struck in a single devastating blow. Conceiving of war in this idealized, abstract manner is perverse and false, however, because no real war is ever absolutely violent; no real war ever strikes the enemy in a single blow. In reality all wars are discontinuous. They are fought in fits and starts, with inactivity and boredom, not violence, being the primary characteristics of all real war. The perverse abstract ideal of absolute violence is never reached for a number of reasons—chance, the frictions of war, and many others—that Clausewitz lists in sections 6–22 (see 217). In section 24 Clausewitz concludes that if no real war is ever absolutely violent, then all real wars must be "merely the continuation of policy by other means" (87).

Having moved his dialectic step by step from defining war as violence to defining war as policy, it should be clear that Clausewitz believed that policy is central to war and the violence of combat is peripheral. And it would be— except for one further ambiguity: what does he mean by "other means?" Since "other means" is usually interpreted as meaning "violent means," there seems to be little difference between the initial and the final poles of his dialectic. This circularity is perhaps best illustrated by the work of a group of academic strategists in the late 1950s and 1960s. Reacting to the unacceptable moral and intellectual consequences of a belief in war as violence, these neo-Clausewitzians turned to the Prussian staff officer as a way of restoring policy to its central position. For example, Bernard Brodie begins his *War and Politics* by admitting: "The central idea of this book I have borrowed from Clausewitz. . . . It is a simple idea, and the novice would justly imagine it to be a commonplace—that the question of *why* we fight must dominate any consideration of means. Yet this absurdly simple theme has been mostly ignored, and when not ignored usually denied" (1973, vii). He then goes on to describe the devastating results of ignoring Clausewitz, most tellingly in his chapters on World War I and the Vietnam War. Nonetheless, when asked to explain what is meant by the ambiguous phrase "by other means," these neo-Clausewitzians—for instance Raymond Aron in his *Clausewitz, Philosopher of War* (1985, 401)—turn to V. I. Lenin, a close student of *On War,* who explains: "'*War is simply the continuation of politics by other* [i.e., violent] *means.*' Such was the formula of Clausewitz, one of the greatest writers on the history of war, whose thinking was stimulated by Hegel. And it was always the standpoint of Marx and Engels, who regarded *any* war as the *continuation* of the politics of the powers concerned—and the *various classes* within these countries—in a definite period" (1964, 219; interpolation in the original).

But if the other means are simply violent means, then Clausewitz's dialectic is destroyed. Instead of moving progressively, step by step, argument by argument, from abstract ideal to historical reality, from war as the violence of combat to war as policy, Clausewitz's dialectic is transformed into a circle, a particularly murderous vicious circle, there now being no real difference between its beginning and its end.

In fine, it appears that even the "philosopher of war" is not immune to the sublime power of the violence of combat. Yet succumbing to it inexorably leads to tragedy. For those who believe war to be violence, there is little to prevent this belief from becoming a self-fulfilling prophecy—first by reducing war to a simple matter of technique, essentially to finding the biggest bomb, and then by authorizing technicians, such as General Curtis LeMay, to tell us what war is "really" like: "I'll tell you what war is all about—you've got to kill people, and when you've killed enough they stop fighting" (Powers 1984, 60).

But if war is the killing of enough people, then there is never a need for a declaration of war, and certainly never a need for a fully reasoned declaration. Why or how would anyone ever declare their reasons for killing "enough" people? Only those who believe that the central act of war is not about killing enough people but rather about achieving worthwhile policy objectives see the need for articulating those objectives, which of course is precisely what a fully reasoned declaration of war does. In other words, only when one adopts the perspective of those who are not caught up in the crossfire of combat is one able to elude the enthralling sublimity of combat and acknowledge that its violence is peripheral to war. Furthermore, substituting the violence of combat for policy, as Tolstoy did, means that it is impossible to even broach the moral and grand strategic dimensions of the war, because from this perspective they quite simply do not exist. As with open heart surgery, the violence that results from combat can never justify a war, although the purposes articulated in a fully reasoned declaration may.

Establishing the Condition of War

Clyde Eagleton asserted "with confidence . . . that a declaration establishes the legal status of war" (1938, 29). As I have shown, however, he was unable to support his confidence with any cogent reasoning. Nevertheless, since the assertion is obviously true, developing a cogent argument to restore confidence in it would be most useful. To do so, one must recognize that Eagleton failed to discover the form and function of the declaration of war for two reasons. In the first place, he failed to distinguish between reasoned and unreasoned declarations. As a result, he was not able to qualify or nuance his assertion in any useful way. Had he distinguished reasoned from unreasoned declarations, he then could have begun with the obvious fact that both reasoned and unreasoned declarations establish the legal status of war and immediately qualified that observation by pointing out that unreasoned declarations do so only in a technical, merely legal, sense. To put substance and meaning into a declaration, it must be fully reasoned, because only fully reasoned declarations possess substantive military and moral functions. In other words, Eagleton failed to distinguish between matters of formal logic and matters of substance.

In the second place, Eagleton got all tangled up in the ambiguity inherent in the word *war.* He failed to broaden and deepen his analysis by recognizing that the legal status of war is but a special case of Grotius's more general "condition" of war. Had Eagleton returned to Grotius, he then could have argued that what a declaration of war establishes is the social, psychological, economic, *and* legal conditions of war, not the contest, which is established by means of an actual clash of arms. Instead Eagleton accepted without reservation the modern conception of war as a contest, which led him into the usual absurdities: "War, by definition, is a contest between states; the term could not, therefore, apply to the use of armed force by the organized government of the community of nations [i.e., the League of Nations] against an offender" (1933, 282). Presumably an enforcement action by the league would be an armed conflict or perhaps a police action, although Eagleton fails to provide an alternative terminology for "the opprobrious term war."

With these preliminaries in place, Eagleton could next have rephrased his question more precisely by asking how or in what sense a fully reasoned declaration of war establishes the condition of war, or war in the legal sense. In response he could then have begun by recognizing that the question involves two subquestions. First, in what sense can a declaration of war be said to initiate or start a war and not simply to ignite combat? Second, in what sense does the condition of war in the legal sense differ from the contest of war in the material sense. Alternatively, do these phrases represent a distinction without any real difference, the contest of war being the only significant reality about which one needs to worry?

The two questions are linked, because conceiving of war as a contest inevitably reproduces Eagleton's unsatisfactory analysis. That is, when one believes war to be a contest, then war is quickly reduced to its violent fraction, to combat. It therefore follows that to initiate or start a war can mean only to initiate or start combat and hence that there is never a need to declare war. Who after all would be so ghoulish as to suggest that a solemn declaration of war in due form is needed to initiate large-scale killing? Large-scale killing is best initiated with bombs, not bombast.

In contrast, when one conceives of war as a condition, no longer is it necessary to view a declaration of war as a starting gun that immediately triggers combat. Now it is possible to see that a fully reasoned declaration of war, far from initiating combat, instead possesses an indispensable moral function. It denounces the necessities that have caused the conflict by articulating the grievances that have splintered the peace and suggesting remedies that will restore it. Clearly this letter of demands, this statement of causes and remedies, need not trigger combat, that is, the contest. As the negotiations unfold, combat may of course eventuate, but this is not a necessity. And it is precisely this lack of necessity that opens up the space for a fully reasoned declaration of war to establish the condition of war in the very real sense of initiating or starting the condition without at the same time igniting the contest.

In short, a fully reasoned declaration of war (or its functional equivalent) is what makes war whole. Without it, war is reduced to its violent fraction, to combat, and becomes an aimless, misshapen caricature of itself. At this point, however, I must recognize a deeper ambiguity, for I am attempting to speak of three states of affairs using only two terms. That is, I am trying to find a way to distinguish among *war with combat* (both the condition and the contest), *war without combat* (the condition without the contest), and most difficult of all, *com-*

bat without war (the contest without the condition). In other words, the problem is one of distinguishing among the whole, the whole minus its visually most striking part (i.e., its violent fraction), and the visually most striking part alone (i.e., the violent fraction alone).

To relaunch the argument, it is extremely difficult to distinguish among three states using but two terms—war and combat, condition and contest, war in the legal sense and war in the material sense, war and armed conflict, and so on. Significantly, the contest of war has always referred to the visible segment of war, principally to the violence of combat. By default, then, the condition of war refers to the invisible fraction of war, to the enmity that manifests itself in the changed social, psychological, economic, and legal relations that separate friend from foe. But crucially, enmity is not violence, at least not the violence of combat. Consequently, it is perfectly possible to divide war into two parts or types—the changed social, psychological, economic, and legal conditions that mark the enmity of war being conspicuously different from the violence of combat that marks the contest of war.

This difference between enmity and violence can be observed in a number of situations. For example, the imposition of economic sanctions seeks to inflict the social, psychological, legal, and economic costs of war upon a country while avoiding even the shadow of the violence of combat. A similar situation occurs when, after a considerable amount of fighting, both sides tire and stop fighting without ever signing a treaty of peace. Under these circumstances, the enmity of war continues unabated, even as the scars of the contest of war heal and are all but forgotten. The Korean War is an excellent example of this, the violence of combat having long since ceased without diminishing in the least the altered social, psychological, economic, and legal relations that separate North from South Korea. Israel is another case in point. It has suffered continuously from the enmity of the condition of war in the legal, economic, social, and psychological sense since its inception, but only intermittently from the violence of the contest of war in the material sense. Similarly, China and Taiwan have been foes in the legal sense since 1949, although their enmity has weakened in recent years. And Japan continues to restrict its relations with Russia artificially in the absence of a peace treaty.

Perhaps the best illustration of the condition of war existing without the contest is found in ancient Sparta. As soon as the Spartan ephors assumed office each year, they would immediately declare war against the Helots. According to Plutarch, Aristotle maintained that the purpose of this annual ritual was to invest the newly elected ephors with the right to kill the Helots with impunity, avoiding thereby the accusation of impiety that would normally be attached to murder (Plutarch 1948, vol. 1, xxviii, 4). This was no doubt a significant part of the Spartans' motivation. Nevertheless, by declaring war upon the Helots annually for over five hundred years, the Spartans did not just avoid a charge of impiety. They also changed the relationship between themselves and their subjugated peoples fundamentally. They created the social, psychological, economic, and legal basis for their state by establishing a constitution that transformed the Helots not into slaves or serfs but into enemies. If the Helots had been slaves or serfs, the Spartans would have been responsible for them in a personal and direct way, fully integrating them into Spartan society. Taking them as enemies, however, the Spartans were able to isolate themselves from the Helots psychologically, socially, legally, and even in terms of their microeconomic life, Spartan dependence upon the Helots in macroeconomic terms notwithstanding. In other words, because the two groups were legally enemies, the Spartans were under no legal obligation to show the Helots any amity, as would have been the case with slaves or serfs. This means that the Spartans were legally justified in doing all sorts of things that would have been unthinkable under any other constitutional regime. For example, the random, and not so random, assassination of Helots by specially trained "secret agents" (*krupteia*) was easily (perhaps too easily) justified under the laws of war, whereas the laws of peace would never have sanctioned such activities (Plutarch 1948, xxviii, 2–3; Thucydides 1982, IV, 80). In addition, the Helots were naturally drafted into Lacedæmonian military formations by the simple expedient of considering them as "defectors" from the enemy, whereas, had the Helots been slaves or serfs, this would have been extremely difficult for numerous legal, social, and psychological reasons. Serfs join armies only in desperation as acts of rebellion in times of social or religious upheaval, and slave armies are essentially a contradiction in terms, the Ottoman Janissary corps notwithstanding.

In summary, distinguishing between the enmity of war and the violence of combat makes it possible to distinguish among two of the three states of war: *war with combat* obtains whenever the enmity of the condition combines with the violence of the contest, whereas *war without combat* obtains whenever the condition exists without the contest, that is, whenever the enmity of war in the legal sense exists without going so far as provoking the violence of war in the material sense. For the sake of convenience, one would like to extend the schema by saying that *combat without war* (i.e., violence without purpose) obtains whenever the violence of the contest of war exists in the absence of the enmity of the social, psychological, economic, and legal conditions of war. Unfortunately, this is not possible, as Eagleton demonstrated in great detail to his chagrin.

The discomforting fact of the matter is that the violence of war in the material sense generates all the enmity of war in the legal sense willy-nilly, without there being any need to formally declare war, it being impossible to initiate combat without at the same time creating all the changed social, psychological, legal, and economic effects that a declaration of war entrains. We have clearly reached the limits of Grotius's distinction without having yet gotten to the heart of the matter. Dividing war into a condition and a contest opens up the space for a fully reasoned declaration of war to establish the condition of war, but opening up the space does not explain why a fully reasoned declaration is required to fill that space. In terms of establishing the condition of war, it is obvious that combat functions as well as, and perhaps even better than, a fully reasoned declaration.

To understand in what sense one may speak of *combat without war,* one needs to move beyond Grotius to something else. The simplest way to do this is to repeat Eagleton's question, not so much to answer it as to discover a yet deeper ambiguity: in what sense can a fully reasoned declaration of war be said to initiate or start a war?

To begin with, one must note that an unreasoned declaration of war is grossly defective precisely because it acts as a starting gun, doing nothing more than signaling the start of the contest. In contrast, a reasoned declaration initiates or starts a war in the sense that it informs the war, giving it purpose and design. Without a purpose, war is either aimless combat or purposeless enmity. This fact creates a strange situation. Both a fully reasoned declaration of war and combat entrain the condition of war, the enmity of war in the legal sense. The difference, to recall Cicero's distinction, is that combat does it by means of brute force (*vis*), allowing no time for the social, psychological, legal, and economic conditions of war to influence decision makers before the violence of combat erupts; a fully reasoned declaration of war, on the other hand, does it by means of reason (*disceptatio*), allowing decision makers to be influenced as negotiations unfold. Should the negotiations ultimately fail, however, a fully reasoned declaration of war possesses still other effects, shaping and controlling the violence of combat with a purpose. Hence it is the fully reasoned declaration of war—the way it informs war—that distinguishes between *war with combat* and *combat without war.*

Accordingly, a fully reasoned declaration of war initiates or starts a war not in the sense of initiating combat (an M-16 fired low in controlled bursts does that) or even in the sense of initiating the condition of war (both combat and an unreasoned declaration will do that) but rather in the sense of *informing* the war. It informs the condition of war by pinpointing the grievances that have transformed the social, psychological, economic, and legal relations between the two peoples from amity to enmity. It informs the contest of war, should there be one, by articulating grand strategy, the ends that will direct and control the means, and the remedies that will restore a shattered peace. Until and unless the war is so informed, in a very real sense there is no war. There may or may not be combat; there may or may not exist the enmity of the condition of war, but there is no war, just purposeless and aimless discord and violence.

Thus the word *war* has splintered yet again to reveal yet another level of ambiguity. When it is seen that a fully reasoned declaration of war initiates war by *informing* it, then not only can one explain in what sense it is possible to have *combat without war,* but one also realizes that there exists a fourth state of affairs, a mirror image, as it were, of *war without combat.* What this fourth state of affairs might be labeled is unclear—perhaps "sham war" or "cold war" or more simply, *enmity without war.* Whatever it might be labeled, acknowledging that a fully reasoned declaration of war initiates a war by informing it allows one to establish the boundary between war and its perversions: war, properly speaking, is separated from its perversions by a fully reasoned declaration of war. With a fully reasoned declaration, both the war and any combat that may occur are informed with purpose and direction. Without a fully reasoned declaration of war, however, one finds only the perversions of war—purposeless enmity or aimless combat.

Finally, having established the boundary between war and its perversions, one is forced to recognize that, beyond the perversions of war, there lies yet another boundary separating the perversions of war from atrocities, for whenever combat breaks out, especially the uninformed *combat without war,* a high likelihood exists that things will get out of hand and atrocities will occur, ranging from isolated brutalities through massacres, both large and small, on up to incomprehensible genocides. Crucially, though, the atrocities that characterize this fifth state of affairs are associated with war only by means of coincidence. Yes, they occur during a war, sometimes during combat broadly construed, but they are a part of neither.

Atrocities are not part of war first of all because war is a public phenomenon. Its goals and purposes, its victories and defeats, are all public knowledge, widely broadcast for the purpose of justifying and motivating the war. This is not the case with atrocities. Atrocities are usually committed in secret and covered up afterward, the perpetrators wishing their deeds never to be uncovered. Second, atrocities do not and cannot figure among either the purposes or the means of war. With respect to purposes, the committing of atrocities can never justify a resort to war, nor do they constitute a purpose from which a grand strategy can be developed. For example, even if some twisted logic led one to believe that the annihilation of the Jews justified Hitler's invasion of Czechoslovakia, Poland, and the other countries of Europe, no coherent grand strategy could be derived from this purpose, as Hitler's conduct of the war demonstrates.

With respect to means, atrocities are also not a part of combat, narrowly construed, because the committing of such outrages requires leisure, which simply is not available in combat. When the shooting starts, all one's attention and energy are focused upon the tactical situation. Before or after combat, there may be the leisure to commit atrocities, but not during combat itself. In addition, there also exists a technical reason that atrocities are not part of combat. As Clausewitz observed in "The Character of Strategic Defense," combat is always initiated by the defense, not the offense: "War [i.e., combat or battle] serves the purpose of the defense more than that of the aggressor. It is only aggression [i.e., an attack] that calls forth defense, and war along with it. The aggressor is always peace-loving (as Bonaparte always claimed to be); he would prefer to take over our country unopposed" (1976, 370). Clausewitz's point is that the attacker is always happy to avoid combat, which never serves its purposes. If at all possible, the aggressor hopes to achieve its objective without a fight. Combat begins, therefore, not when the offense attacks but rather when the defense resists. Until the defense resists, the attack proceeds unhindered and unimpeded toward its objective. This, in one sense, is the essence of combat—the defense resisting an attack. Atrocities, in sharp and brutal contrast, reverse this process. Unlike the situation in combat, it is the attacker, not the victim, who initiates the action. Indeed, an atrocity is heinous precisely because its victims are unable to resist effectively. Were they able to resist effectively, were they given a fighting chance, it would be not an atrocity but rather combat.

Therefore, beyond the boundary that separates war from its perversions, there exists yet another boundary that separates the perversions of war from atrocities committed under the cover of war. These atrocities, needless to say, contribute greatly to the ambiguity of the word *war*, appearing to many as part of a seamless process of ever-escalating violence: a war begins with high-spirited parades and visions of certain glory, is shocked by the relatively bloodless initial battles, and progresses battle by battle to ever greater levels of violence before degenerating into unrestrained inhumanity, no outrage or excess being too grotesque to inflict upon a despised enemy. The Civil War is perhaps the paradigmatic example. It began with picnickers driving their carriages out from Washington to view First Manassas and escalated to Sherman's march to the sea. Nevertheless, no matter how frequently this cycle of escalating violence is observed and documented, the underlying structure is not that of a seamless process but rather that of the transgressing of boundaries: peace becomes war; war is perverted into purposeless violence and then used as a cover for self-indulgent atrocities.

Now that I have marked out the boundaries that separate war from both its perversions and its atrocities, the sources of the ambiguity inherent within the word *war* and the location of the boundaries that clarify this ambiguity should now be clear. The word continually struggles to express not only itself, not only its perversions, but certain atrocities as well. It continually struggles to identify five states of affairs, only two of which are truly war:

1. War as an informed enmity:
   a. *War with combat* obtains whenever a well-articulated purpose informs both the condition of enmity and the combat that engages two peoples.
   b. *War without combat* obtains whenever a well-articulated purpose informs the condition of enmity that engages two peoples without initiating combat.
2. The perversions of war or war as an uninformed enmity:
   a. *Combat without war* obtains whenever neither the condition of enmity engendered by combat nor the combat itself is informed by a well-articulated purpose.
   b. *Enmity without war* obtains whenever the condition of enmity that engages two peoples is not informed by a well-articulated purpose and this uniformed enmity has not yet resulted in combat.
3. Atrocities committed under the cover of war.

The atrocities committed under the cover of war require no exemplification. Their mindless brutality sets them apart. Informed war and uninformed war, however, do require exemplification. The contrast between *war with combat* and its perversion, *combat without war,* may not be immediately apparent. The same is even more true for the noncombat forms of war, *war without combat* and its perversion, *enmity without war.* I will exemplify the first pair by comparing the war in Korea to the "war" in Vietnam and the second pair by comparing the Cuban Missile Crisis to the continuing U.S. reaction to Fidel Castro's accession to power in 1959.

War with Combat versus Combat without War

Before I begin this discussion, two preliminary problems need to be addressed—the existence of functional equivalents to formal declarations of war and the criteria for judging the quality of the reasoning contained in a declaration. As I have said, the difference between an informed war and an uninformed war is that only the former is shaped with purpose and point by a reasoned declaration of war. The point of confusion is that it is the quality of the analysis contained within the declaration that makes the difference, not whether the declaration is formally or informally denounced. Theoretically, therefore, the fact that the document is a functional equivalent of a formally denounced declaration does not affect the quality of the reasoning used. Practically, however, the proliferation of functional equivalents of reasoned declarations of war has become if not a problem at least an annoyance. That is, before the seventeenth century, when the nations of the world still made fully reasoned formal declarations of war, the analysis was straightforward and simple. One read the formal declaration and decided whether it contained solid reasons or hollow rationalizations. Since the seventeenth century, since nations stopped making formal declarations of war, the problem has grown somewhat more complex. Before making an evaluation concerning the quality of the analysis, one must often sift through a large number of speeches, messages, proclamations, and resolutions, all of which are functional equivalents of formal declarations of war, to isolate the "official" reasons for the resort to arms. Then, and only then, can one begin to evaluate the quality of the analysis.

This annoyance of not knowing which functional equivalent is the "real" declaration of war is a complicating factor in all the examples except the Cuban Missile Crisis. Still, the heart of the problem remains the quality of the text itself, the value of the analysis used to draft the "real" declaration of war, whatever it might be. In making this analysis, the ideal would be to apply all six of the criteria that I developed as a result of my analysis of the Second Continental Congress's 1776 Declaration of Independence in chapter 2. Using these six criteria, however, is neither practical nor useful. It is not practical because, again with the exception of the Cuban Missile Crisis, the declarations I will examine fall so far short of the standard set by the Declaration of Independence that the larger part of the analysis would be taken up with pointing out how each document fails to address four or five of the six criteria. It is not useful because my purposes here are extremely limited. I am interested not at all in the moral functions of a fully reasoned declaration and in the military functions only insofar as they will allow me to discriminate an informed war from an uninformed war. For this circumscribed purpose, an abbreviated set of criteria will be more useful. The criteria I will use are specificity and the ability to derive a coherent military strategy "down to the smallest operational detail." Needless to say, the ability to derive a viable military strategy depends crucially upon specificity. Without specificity, the declaration becomes a compendium of generalities such as "making the world safe for democracy," from which it is impossible to derive any military strategy whatsoever. Such crowd-pleasing generalities, however, are the heart and soul of any good public relations campaign to drum up support for a war. Hence, the difference between an informed war and an uninformed war can also be viewed as the difference between a serious document that fulfills the military and moral functions of a declaration of war and a public relations blurb.

The tension between public relations blurb and seriously reasoned declaration of war was conspicuous during the Korean War. It was conspicuous because America fought in Korea under dual auspices. Technically we fought under the auspices of the United Nations (see Fisher 1995). Actually, however, the United Nations was not the principal defender of South Korea; the United States was. Consequently, we also fought under our own auspices as South Korea's principal ally. In the absence of a formal declaration of war, a certain amount of confusion could easily have arisen concerning the source and the character of the policies that were to guide the war. Were the UN Security Council resolutions of 25 and 27 June 1950 and the UN General Assembly resolution of 7 October 1950 to guide military commanders in the field, since they were technically under United Nations command? Alternatively, were Commander-in-Chief Truman's principal speeches and addresses on Korea to guide military commanders in the field, since they were actually under his command?

That this potential conflict was minimized resulted from the fact that Truman systematically exploited the gap created by the dual auspices. First, he used the existence of the United Nations to segment his audience. Whenever he wished to address his domestic audience, he spoke in his own name. Whenever he wished to speak to his international audience—to the governments that constituted the United Nations—he addressed them via the UN, through its resolutions. Second, he used the UN resolutions as the basis for the military conduct of the war and his own speeches as the basis for the conduct of his public relations effort to drum up domestic support for the war. As a result, only the UN resolutions needed to be reasoned, to contain the specificity that military commanders require to develop a viable strategy. Relieved of the burden of specificity, Truman's own speeches were filled with the generalities important to a successful public relations campaign. (Incidentally, the Bush administration's conduct of the Persian Gulf War parallels the Truman administration's conduct of the Korean War in this respect and could have been used as an alternative example.)

To see how systematically serious grand strategic analysis was separated from public relations exercise, one need only compare the UN resolutions to

Commander-in-Chief Truman's speeches and addresses. The resolutions are models of brevity, specificity, and coherent analysis. Recalling that "the Republic of Korea is a lawfully established government having effective control and jurisdiction over" the southern half of Korea, the Security Council determined in its 25 June 1950 resolution that "the armed attack upon the Republic of Korea by forces from North Korea . . . constitutes a breach of the peace" and consequently called on "the authorities of North Korea (a) to cease hostilities forthwith; and (b) to withdraw their armed forces to the thirty-eighth parallel" (*Department of State Bulletin* 3 July 1950, 5). In other words, the grievance that had provoked the United Nations' entry into this war was the fact that an internationally recognized boundary had been violated and an internationally recognized country invaded. The political objective sought by the United Nations was a restoration of the *status quo ante bellum.* Two military strategies followed from that political objective. After stopping the momentum of the initial North Korean attack and stabilizing the front, commanders in the field could reasonably hope to restore the *status quo ante bellum* either by counterattacking along the length of the newly stabilized front and pushing the North Korean Army back across the Thirty-eighth Parallel or, because Korea is a peninsula, by making an amphibious assault in the vicinity of the Thirty-eighth Parallel, which if successful would cut the North Korean forces off from their sources of supply and force them to retreat across the Thirty-eighth Parallel. Needless to say, General Douglas MacArthur chose the amphibious option with spectacular results.

At this point the story becomes rather difficult. Briefly, in the wake of the 15 September 1950 landings at Inchon, which virtually destroyed the North Korean Army, the UN General Assembly passed a resolution on 7 October 1950 that in effect authorized General MacArthur to cross the Thirty-eighth Parallel and occupy North Korea. In retrospect this authorization was a mistake because it drew the Chinese into the war in November with disastrous results. In any event, whatever the flaws of this authorization at the level of policy, the resolution itself again provided field commanders with clear guidance. Again there were two options: commanders could either employ one or more amphibious operations to occupy the North in stages, or they could attack northward from the Thirty-eighth Parallel. This time General MacArthur chose a combination of both. The Eighth Army pushed northward along the western coast, while the marines of X Corps landed at Wonsan on the east coast before moving northward. With the North Korean Army shattered and Chinese intervention not anticipated, this plan could reasonably have been expected to accomplish the assigned objective. In the event, the Chinese did intervene, and the Eighth Army disintegrated before their onslaught.

What is most remarkable about the UN resolutions, therefore, is how clear and specific they were and how easily their political objectives translated into viable military operations. Because of this, one has no difficulty seeing how the resolutions informed the war, how they guided and directed operations "down to the smallest operational detail." Hence, because of the clarity of these resolutions, the Korean War is an example of *war with combat*. For my purposes, however, so as to introduce *combat without war,* the counterfactual case is also of great interest. Without the UN resolutions, the war in Korea could easily have degenerated into *combat without war* devoid of any informing analysis. This could have occurred because the alternative source for policy guidance was Commander-in-Chief Truman's speeches and addresses, all of which lacked the required specificity and relevance. For example, the most conspicuous characteristic of Truman's speeches is the way they completely ignore concrete circumstances on the Korean Peninsula. Kim Il-sung is never mentioned, and North Korea is mentioned in passing on only the rarest occasion. Instead of referring to the specifics of the Korean situation, Truman spoke of sound economic policies at home to prevent inflation while increasing both defense spending and economic production to meet the needs not only of the immediate war but the longer anticommunist struggle. He also spoke of the "lessons of Munich": the need to avoid all appeasement, to oppose all aggression, to uphold the rule of law, and to defend democracy around the world. First and foremost, however, and above all, he repeated over and over that the "Communist conspiracy" was the cause of the war and its defeat was the principal war aim. Inasmuch as anticommunist rhetoric was so persuasive during the cold war, this emphasis upon communist imperialism was no doubt useful in the public relations battle for domestic support. As Senator Arthur H. Vandenberg once told Truman, the best way to generate support was to "scare the hell out of the country" (cited in Kimball 1990, 8).

The substitution of the worldwide communist conspiracy for the specifics of the Korean Peninsula began with Truman's statement of 27 June 1950, two days after the start of the war. This short statement, which also represents one of the few times he mentions North Korea, begins in a rather peculiar way by implying that the South Korean government is the only government on the peninsula. Thus, after acknowledging that "in Korea the [South Korean] Government forces, which were armed to prevent border raids and to preserve internal security, were attacked by invading forces from North Korea," he goes on to declare, "The attack upon [South] Korea makes it plain beyond all doubt that communism has passed beyond the use of subversion to conquer independent nations and will now use armed invasion and war." He then moves on to other matters, announcing first, that he has ordered the Seventh Fleet "to prevent any attack on Formosa" and called "upon the Chinese Government on Formosa to cease all air and sea operations against the mainland [China]"; second, that he has "directed that United States Forces in the Philippines be strengthened and that military assistance to the Philippine Government be accelerated"; and finally, that he is also accelerating "military assistance to the forces of France and the Associated States in Indochina and the dispatch of a military mission to provide close working relations with those forces" (Truman 1965a, 492).

Although Truman's orders and directives with respect to Formosa, the Philippines, and French Indochina were arguably prudent given the specific circumstances in each of those areas, what strikes one most is their irrelevance to the two-day-old North Korean invasion of South Korea. This is especially true of his directives concerning Indochina and the Philippines. On reflection, can anyone suppose that the success or failure of either the Viet Minh insurgency in Indochina or the HUK insurgency in the Philippines would have had any impact upon the fighting in Korea? More to the point, though, this first statement by Commander-in-Chief Truman does not contain a grand strategic analysis of the situation in Korea from which military commanders could possibly have derived a coherent strategy. To say that communism has passed beyond subversion and that various points along the Asian littoral must be reinforced did not tell anyone what should be done in Korea, where the fighting was taking place. This same lack of a specific analysis of the situation in Korea characterizes Truman's other addresses. His radio and television address of 19 July 1950 (537–42), his radio and television address of 1 September 1950 (609–14), and his address of 15 December 1950 (741–46) are all filled with denunciations of communist imperialism, appeals to the "lesson of Munich," references to the rule of law, and similar generalities. Indeed, at the nadir of the war, ten months after it began, in his "Radio Report to the American People on Korea and on U.S. Policy in the Far East" of 11 April 1951, the day he relieved General Douglas MacArthur for publicly advocating a widening of the war by attacking China directly, Truman appeared even more confused than ever.

Ignoring the situation on the ground in Korea, Truman first raises the specter not only of a communist conquest but also of nuclear devastation, which is the technical meaning of the term *general war:* "The question we have had to face is whether the Communist plan of conquest can be stopped without a general war" (Truman 1965b, 225). Next he goes on to claim a modest victory, not in Korea, but rather in the rest of Asia—"Our resolute stand in Korea is helping the forces of freedom now fighting in Indochina and other countries in that part of the world. It has already slowed down the [Communist] timetable of conquest" (225)—before taking Senator Vandenberg's advice and really scaring the hell out of the country: "The dangers are great. Make no mistake about it. Behind the North Koreans and Chinese Communists in the front lines stand additional millions of Chinese soldiers. And behind the Chinese stand the tanks, the planes, the submarines, the soldiers, and the scheming rulers of the Soviet Union" (226). Most disturbing of all, he concludes by presenting a naïve and contradictory list of war aims:

> We are ready, at any time, to negotiate for a restoration of peace in the area. But we will not engage in appeasement. We are only interested in real peace.
> Real peace can be achieved through a settlement based on the following factors:
> One: The fighting must stop.
> Two: Concrete steps must be taken to insure that the fighting will not break out again.
> Three: There must be an end to aggression.
> A settlement founded upon these elements would open the way for the unification of Korea and the withdrawal of all foreign forces.
> In the meantime, I want to be clear about our military objective. We are fighting to resist an outrageous aggression in Korea. We are trying to keep the Korean conflict from spreading to other areas. But at the same time we must conduct our military activities so as to insure the security of our forces. This is essential if they are to continue to fight until the enemy abandons its attempts to destroy the Republic of Korea.
> That is our military objective—to repel attack and to restore peace. (226–27)

As a negotiating agenda, Truman's words are naïve both because his three enumerated points are redundant, all three reducing to the false proposition that peace is the absence of conflict, and because if his political objective was a unification of Korea and not a return to the *status quo ante bellum,* then it would have been virtually impossible to reach an accommodation with the North Koreans and the Chinese, especially the Chinese, who entered the war specifically to frustrate a unification of Korea. As a political analysis, his words are also naïve because he says he desires peace but "will not engage in appeasement," which may mean anything but probably means that he wants the fighting to stop but will not accede to any of the enemy's demands to achieve it. This is tantamount to demanding an unconditional surrender, which Truman was in no position to do. As a military analysis, his words amount to a list of four non sequiturs. He says that "our military objective" was "to resist outrageous aggression." Resisting outrageous aggression may or may not be a legitimate political objective, but it is certainly not a military objective. How long and to what purpose is the aggression to be resisted? He says, "We are trying to keep the Korean conflict from spreading," which again may or may not be a legitimate political objective, but it is certainly not a military objective. He says that we had to "insure the security of our forces" so that they could "continue to fight." Whatever this might have meant to Truman, for the dogfaces in the trenches along the Thirty-eighth Parallel, ensuring their security meant stopping the fighting, not continuing it. Finally, he says that our military objective was "to repel attack and to restore peace." Repelling an attack may be a tactical objective, but it can never be a strategic objective, whereas restoring peace is the traditional purpose of war, but this purpose is meaningless until it is fleshed out with specifics.

Notice, however, the underlying grand strategic contradiction that generates these non sequiturs. The occasion for Truman's address was his decision to relieve General MacArthur of command of the UN forces in Korea. General MacArthur was at the time publicly advocating the bombing of Chinese logistical facilities in Manchuria and making use of Nationalist Chinese forces from Formosa, possibly to launch an invasion of southern China. This certainly would have widened the war and might eventually have led to a general nuclear war. Wishing to avoid such a catastrophe, Commander-in-Chief Truman wanted the combat to remain confined to the Korean Peninsula, even if this meant a frustrating stalemate along the Thirty-eighth Parallel. The dispute was therefore framed as a technical matter concerning the scope of the combat. In Truman's words, "The question we have had to face is whether the Communist plan of conquest can be stopped without a general war." But the scope of combat is or at least should be determined by the purposes of the war. Consequently, if Truman's purpose was to avoid a general war by limiting the combat to the Korean Peninsula, then the appropriate way to have done that was to define limited war aims that focused exclusively upon the situation in Korea. The most obvious of these narrow purposes was the Security Council's goal of 25 June 1950 demanding a return to the *status quo ante bellum*. If, on the other hand, his purpose was to stop the communist plan of conquest because he saw the North Koreans as the front wave of a communist threat running back through the Chinese to the Soviet Union, then the logical military corollary was that the Chinese (or the Soviets) directing the conquest should be attacked, precisely as MacArthur was advocating. Hence, MacArthur's sin was not so much his public advocacy of a wider war but rather his failure to understand that he should pay no attention to Truman's speeches, which were part of the public relations campaign. When Lieutenant General Matthew B. Ridgway assumed command as MacArthur's replacement, he did not make the same mistake. He guided his efforts by the original Security Council mandate to restore the *status quo ante bellum,* which not incidentally ensured that the war was limited to the Korean Peninsula.

Such is the commotion that can occur when military commanders mistake the generalities of the public relations effort for the specifics of serious grand strategic analysis. In Korea, however, there existed an authoritative body—the United Nations—that was both willing and able to articulate the specifics of a serious grand strategy. Consequently, the war in Korea never degenerated into an example of *combat without war.* The same cannot be said for the war in Vietnam, which was not fought under the aegis of the United Nations. This meant that successive commanders-in-chief were unable to exploit the gap between the technicalities of UN sponsorship and the actualities of U.S. control, as Truman did in Korea. As a result, their speeches and addresses had to do double duty, providing the specificities required to guide military commanders in the field while simultaneously providing the generalities needed for the public relations campaign at home. In 1776 the Second Continental Congress had done precisely this by providing the philosophical generalities in the first part of the Declaration of Independence and the specificities in the latter half. But the art of writing fully reasoned declarations of war had long been lost by 1949, and without the UN resolutions to articulate the specifics needed by the military commanders in the field, successive commanders-in-chief found the burden too great. One searches in vain for a single document between 1949 and 1975 that by any stretch of the imagination could serve as the functional equivalent of a fully reasoned declaration of war. There is none; it does not exist. If none exists, however, then Clausewitz's principal insight is violated and transgressed in the most brutal and obvious way: "No one starts a war—or rather, no one in his senses ought to do so—without first being clear in his mind what he intends to achieve by that war and how he intends to conduct it" (1976, 579). Unless someone at some time articulates a war's purposes, its guiding aims and goals, then the war is uninformed, commanders in the field are unable to develop a viable strategy, and *combat without war* becomes all but certain, as happened in Vietnam.

That policymakers viewed Vietnam primarily as a public relations exercise is documented in a late 1964 report from Commander-in-Chief Johnson's National Security Council Working Group on South Viet-Nam/Southeast Asia: "Characterizing the use of force in the context of this alternative as a legitimate exercise of the right of individual or collective self-defense in response to an 'armed attack' from the North would be a major public relations effort" (cited in Arnold 1975, 42). However, the almost complete lack of grand strategic analysis can perhaps best be seen in Hugh M. Arnold's fascinating 1975 article, already referred to briefly, entitled "Official Justifications for America's

Role in Indochina, 1949–67." Arnold begins by identifying the problem, postulating a probable cause, and explaining his method:

> Vietnam was America's longest war and, despite many explanations by many people (or perhaps because of this), probably the least clearly understood. . . . This essay attempts to ascertain, through the technique of content analysis, the *official* justifications most often cited for America's involvement in Indochina from 1949 through 1967. Its purpose is simply to determine quantitatively the specific rationales cited for US policy during this time period, not to analyze their validity. The material examined comes entirely from the documents and statements of those actually in power and making decisions on Vietnam. (31)

After completing his content analysis, Arnold classifies the official rationales into twenty-three categories—twenty-two that appear with "some frequency in the official sources" plus, ominously, an "Others" category for those that do not appear frequently. Of the twenty-three categories, the communist threat was by far the most frequently cited rationale, constituting 1,141 references, or 57 percent of the total examined (35–36). This is not surprising. However, Arnold did find it surprising that the domino theory ranked only eighteenth at 8.9 percent, just below the category of "Other," which ranked seventeenth at 11.5 percent (36). Arnold then sorts the rationales by administration. For the Truman, Eisenhower, and Kennedy administrations, anticommunism was the leading rationale, earning 19.4 percent, 26.6 percent, and 20 percent, respectively (37–42; cf. Kimball 1990, 7). During the Johnson administration, however, anticommunism dropped to the fourth position (6.8 percent), whereas "simple response to aggression against an ally; self defense" became the number-one rationale (23.1 percent) (42–44). Next Arnold compares the rationales used in classified documents with those used in public: "The most striking point . . . is that the themes stressed in private were simply not the same ones offered to the public—with two exceptions. These were the [anti-]communist theme, and the specific threat of Communist China, both of which were prominently mentioned in both internal and external materials. Among the nine leading classified themes and the top nine public themes, they were the only two in common" (47). Arnold concludes, "If one single reason for the US involvement in Indochina can be derived from the analysis, it would be the perceived threat of communism" (48).

The first and most fascinating aspect of this study is that Arnold would have thought to do it at all. Under normal circumstances, when one wants to know the official justification for any governmental policy, one pulls out the appropriate document and reads it. This official justification will usually list a number of different reasons for the policy. Frequently the reasons given will be confused or wrongheaded, but the official justification itself will not be in doubt. For example, is there any doubt about the official justification for the Revolutionary War? Would a content analysis of the *Journals of the Second Continental Congress* tell us anything more or other than what we can learn from simply reading the Declaration of Independence? Amazingly, however, Arnold's content analysis is probably the only way to learn the official justifications behind the Vietnam War. Certainly one cannot discover them by reading any of the official documents produced between 1949 and 1975, since each document gives a different set of reasons.

The second fascinating aspect of Arnold's study is what can be learned from his results. Of minor interest is the changing rank of the twenty-three justifications. As one moves from one administration to the next and from private to public justifications, it is interesting to see how changing personalities and shifting domestic circumstances created pressures for a new and different public relations take on Vietnam. Of greater interest, though, is the conspicuous lack of specificity that characterizes all the official justifications. As Jeffrey Kimball noted, "[The official explanation] applies not only to Vietnam but to other cold war events and issues" (1990, 8). But if the twenty-three official justifications used in Vietnam are the same justifications used in Greece, Korea, Berlin, Cuba, and a large number of other places, then all specificity is lost. To assert that Vietnam is but one of a long string of events all of which possess the same cause and the same objective is simply to abdicate responsibility to provide the grand strategic analysis required to guide the entire strategic planning of military commanders.

However, it is not the anticommunist–cold war rhetoric per se that reduced Vietnam to *combat without war.* This rhetoric was, after all, but a transient fashion of the times. Rather, the difficulties spring from the vagueness, the obscurity, the ambiguity, the lack of specificity. Even when one filters out the greater part of the cold war rhetoric, the lack of specificity remains. For example, consider Commander-in-Chief Lyndon Johnson's 7 April 1965 "Address at Johns Hopkins University: 'Peace without Conquest,'" during which he asked:

> Why are we in South Viet-Nam?
> *We are there because we have a promise to keep. . . .*
> *We are also there to strengthen world order. . . .*
> *We are also there because there are great stakes in the balance. . . .*
> Our objective is the independence of South Viet-Nam, and its freedom from attack. We want nothing for ourselves—only that the people of South Viet-Nam be allowed to guide their own country in their own way.
> We will do everything necessary to reach that objective. And we will do only what is absolutely necessary. (Johnson 1966, 395)

As with the UN resolutions during the Korean War, anticommunism does not appear in this list of justifications. Moreover, the stated objective, "the independence of South Viet-Nam," appears to be both clear and specific, a paraphrase of the 25 June 1950 Security Council's objective in Korea. There are significant differences, though. Johnson calls for the independence of South Vietnam; the Security Council calls for "the authorities of North Korea (a) to cease hostilities forthwith; and (b) to withdraw their armed forces to the thirty-eighth parallel." The Security Council resolution is addressed directly to the North Korean authorities, who were in a position both to cease hostilities and to restore the *status quo ante bellum;* Johnson's speech is directed to the American people, who were not in a position to ensure the freedom of South Vietnam from attack. The Security Council resolution also identifies a specific action—the cessation of hostilities—and ties it to a specific geographical fact, the Thirty-eighth Parallel. Johnson's speech implies much but says little. Crucially for military commanders—because it defines the limits of the territory they must defend—the geographic character of independence is left undefined. The implication is that an independent South Vietnam would occupy the boundaries fixed by the 1954 Geneva Accords. But is this the case, or are the boundaries open for negotiation? Would a larger or smaller South Vietnam be acceptable to Johnson? If so, then the strategic problem changes radically.

More important still, fixing the political objective vaguely as the independence of South Vietnam fails to address the specific differences between Korea and Vietnam. Korea is a peninsula, and the combat was ignited by a sudden armored attack across the Thirty-eighth Parallel. Vietnam is not a peninsula, and infiltration along its western borders with Laos and Cambodia was the principal method of attack. Accordingly, although the political objective in Korea could be framed entirely in terms of the Korean Peninsula, the same could not be done in Vietnam. The occupation of eastern Laos and Cambodia by the North Vietnamese created an entirely different situation that required an entirely different political objective, an objective that took this occupation into account. Johnson's failure to include Laos and Cambodia in his statement of objectives is akin to Britain's sending its Expeditionary Force to defend France in 1914 without ever mentioning the German invasion and occupation of Belgium as one of the principal causes of its entry into World War I and the German evacuation of Belgium as one of its principal objectives. To do anything less is to abdicate responsibility to do the grand strategic analysis upon which commanders in the field depend to formulate a viable strategy.

To deal with this situation, Commander-in-Chief Johnson had two options in his 7 April 1965 address. First, he could have described the situation on the ground—the scope of the North Vietnamese invasions; the extreme difficulties of the terrain; the widespread corruption of the South Vietnamese, Cambodian, and Laotian governments; and so on—and concluded that, realistically, the United States did not possess the resources to defend all three countries. One or two perhaps, but not all three. This line of reasoning would have led him to order the withdrawal of most of the U.S. forces already committed. Alternatively, he could have stated that the North Vietnamese invasion and occupation of all three countries was unacceptable, that aggression ought not to be rewarded, that the independence of sovereign nations must be upheld, and consequently, that the independence of all three was our objective. This being the case, he was ordering his commanders in the field to prepare a plan to defend all three countries. It is true that, at this late date, to have publicly widened the war in this manner would have created considerable political difficulties at home, but that is only to acknowledge that the preceding commanders-in-chief had been negligent, for not to include Laos and Cambodia explicitly among the war's objectives was to cripple field commanders by failing to make the grand strategic decisions upon which they depended.

The irony in this is that the importance of the North Vietnamese occupation of the Annam Cordillera had been fully recognized by successive commanders-in-chief. Unfortunately, though, instead of dealing with it in an explicit and public way, the response was to obfuscate, to wage a "secret war" by arming the montagnards in Laos; by deploying Special Forces along the western border of South Vietnam; by conducting secret operations across that border; and by bombing, bombing, bombing. But subterfuge is no substitute for policy, a fact demonstrated by Douglas Kinnard in the previously noted 1974 survey:

> Apparently, translating the overall United States objectives into something understandable to the general officers of the war was not successfully accomplished by policy makers. It is possible for lower-level soldiers and officials to fight a war without being sure of their objectives, but that almost 70 percent of the Army generals who managed the war were uncertain of its objectives mirrors a deep-seated strategic failure: the inability of policy makers to frame tangible, obtainable goals. (1977, 25; cf. Herring 1994, 181)

In fine, whenever the generals waging a war are uncertain of its objective, the war is by definition uninformed. It lacks purpose, aims, or goals, which is tantamount to saying that it is *combat without war,* as the "war" in Vietnam was.

Strangely then, without the support the United Nations, successive commanders-in-chief were unable to produce the functional equivalent of a fully reasoned declaration of war. Why they allowed the public relations effort to supplant grand strategic analysis is a matter of speculation. There were no doubt several reasons. For my purposes, however, the more fruitful approach is to focus upon the United Nations' successes and not on the United States' failures. Why was the UN able to do in Korea what successive commanders-in-chief were unable to do in Vietnam? There appear to be two principal reasons. First, the UN is cosmopolitan. Whatever the issue may be, all sides are represented; all sides have a voice, and all sides have to be satisfied to some degree. As a result, the rhetorical extremes that are commonly effective at home must be toned down or abandoned altogether. In the case of Korea, this meant that the anticommunist rhetoric that dominated Truman's speeches at home was simply inadmissible. To take an extreme example, whereas it was perfectly acceptable for Truman to say in a speech for domestic consumption that "'liberation' in 'commie' language means conquest" (Truman 1965b, 224), a more neutral rhetoric was required in the UN resolutions. Deprived of the easy clichés of domestic politics, the drafters of UN resolutions were forced to focus upon the specificities of the situation, indeed, upon the least controversial specificities, which are often the most important.

Second, UN resolutions are debated and voted upon, whereas speeches are not. Speeches are written with an eye toward newspaper headlines and television coverage. Their purpose is to shape public opinion. Resolutions are written with an eye to garnering votes. After they pass, they will be used to shape public opinion, but before that their purpose is to articulate a position for which a majority of the delegates can vote. As part of this process, resolutions are debated. Embarrassing questions are raised and must be addressed because those who raise them are active voters. Speeches may raise the same embarrassing questions, but these questions do not have to be addressed because the listeners are relatively passive spectators. Their questions can be ignored or deflected in ways that are impossible with the questions raised in a debate leading to a vote.

In fine, the vote at the end of a debate imposes a discipline upon the UN resolutions that speeches escape. As the Korean War resolutions demonstrate, this discipline, when combined with the need to avoid ideological clichés, tends to focus delegates upon the specifics of the situation, producing the functional equivalent of a reasoned declaration of war, which is precisely what military commanders require to develop a viable strategy. As the Vietnam speeches and addresses of successive commanders-in-chief demonstrate, embarrassing questions are too often ignored when policymakers are released from this discipline, and speeches that should function as the equivalents of reasoned declarations of war, providing commanders with the grand strategic analysis upon which they depend, become little more than public relations blurbs, compendia of clichés that are of no help to commanders in developing a viable strategy. The former produces an informed war, *war with combat;* the latter, an uninformed "war," *combat without war.*

There is, however, considerable irony in these conclusions. Debate leading to a vote is one of the principal hallmarks of democracy, but no one has ever accused the United Nations of being a bastion of democracy. It resembles a medieval council of great barons more than it does a modern representative assembly. Therefore, to observe that the UN resolutions function well as equivalents to reasoned declarations of war in part because of the discipline imposed by a debate leading to a vote is more than a little troubling. Could this mean that, with respect to the declaring of war, "democratic" debate works only in undemocratic councils such as the Security Council? That in democracies the generalities of the public relations battle are more important and more effective than the specificities of grand strategic analysis? That sooner or later democratic assemblies succumb to the fatal attractions of rhetorical generalities, as the Athenian Assembly did before the Sicilian expedition? Or could it simply mean that modern representative assemblies have no experience in debating fully reasoned declarations of war, having always left these decisions to the executive? That, with suitable training, even a representative assembly, such as Congress, could learn to produce fully reasoned declarations of war of sufficient specificity to provide useful guidance to commanders in the field?

War without Combat versus Enmity without War

It is to be hoped that Congress and other such representative assemblies would learn to produce fully reasoned declarations of war. Unfortunately, though, there is no evidence to support such a hope and considerable evidence to quash it. Whatever the case may be, it is time to exemplify the forms of war that do not involve combat: *war without combat* and its perversion, *enmity without war.* Like the forms that involve combat, the difference between the two is that the former is informed with a well-reasoned formal declaration of war (or its functional equivalent), whereas the latter is not, with the result that it soon degenerates into a rather pointless expression of ill will. Unlike the forms that do involve combat, finding suitable examples represents a considerable challenge. The difficulty lies not in finding possible candidates, which is not a problem because both economic sanctions and military demonstrations of force are common enough. Rather, the challenge lies in finding examples that are initiated with a document that might be considered the functional equivalent of a well-reasoned declaration of war.

Even rarer, but for my purposes of greater interest, are well-motivated examples that were initiated by Congress, not by the commander-in-chief. Just how rare these are may be judged by the fact that there exist no cases of a congressionally initiated show of force and but few of a congressionally initiated episode of economic sanctions. Still rarer are examples of economic sanctions initiated by Congress with what can be or at least might be considered to be a reasoned declaration of war. Indeed, there exists but one: the Comprehensive Anti-Apartheid Act of 1986, imposing sanctions against South Africa. As the reservations and qualifications of the preceding sentences indicate, the Comprehensive Anti-Apartheid Act of 1986 represents a less than ideal example of *war without combat,* although it is the best available for my purposes. Therefore, instead of trying to deal with all its ambiguities at the present time, I will forgo examining this sole example of congressionally initiated economic sanctions. Instead of examining an example of economic sanctions, then, I will explore an example of a show of force—the Cuban Missile Crisis—which possesses the additional virtue of tying in nicely with the example of *enmity without war* that I will examine, the U.S. embargo of all trade with Cuba.

For the U.S. public, the Cuban Missile Crisis began at 7:00 P.M. on 22 October 1962, when Commander-in-Chief John F. Kennedy made his "Radio and Television Report to the American People on the Soviet Arms Buildup in Cuba." For several months prior to that time, there had been a steady stream of rumors and allegations of a Soviet military buildup, possibly including missiles, but these rumors had been denied all around, by the Soviets, by the Cubans, and not least by Kennedy. However, as the photoreconnaissance data gathered the week before demonstrated, the rumors were not just rumors. Soviet missiles were being deployed to Cuba. Acting upon this certain knowledge, Kennedy spoke to the nation, delivering the functional equivalent of a fully reasoned absolute declaration of war that is a model of specificity.

The first sign of this specificity is that the word "Communist" appears but once in the entire address: "But this secret, swift, and extraordinary buildup of Communist missiles . . ." (Kennedy 1963, 807). Otherwise Kennedy makes it abundantly clear that this is a "Soviet military buildup on the island of Cuba" (806), that "this Nation is prepared to present its case [in any forum] against the Soviet threat to peace" (808). The unhelpful clichés and generalities of cold war rhetoric played no part in this address, although these generalities were conspicuous among the "whereas" clauses of Proclamation 3504: Interdiction of the Delivery of Offensive Weapons to Cuba, which Kennedy signed the following day. A second sign is that Kennedy names names: "Soviet Foreign Minister Gromyko told me in my office that . . . Soviet assistance to Cuba, and I quote, 'pursued solely the purpose of contributing to the defense capabilities of Cuba.' . . . That statement was also false." (806–7). Likewise, Kennedy appealed personally to "Chairman Khrushchev to halt and eliminate this clandestine, reckless, and provocative threat to world peace" (808). A third sign is that, although Kennedy named two Soviet leaders, he did not name any Cuban leaders; most especially, he failed to name Fidel Castro. Clearly the Cuban Missile Crisis was a dispute between the Soviet Union and the United States; it had little or nothing to do either with Sino-Soviet communism or with Cuba, although he did digress slightly "to say a few words to the captive people of Cuba" in the penultimate section of his address (809).

In addition to avoiding anticommunist clichés and identifying the antagonists unambiguously, Kennedy also articulates the two sources of the crisis with exceptional clarity: the crisis arises both from the Soviets' attempt to deploy missiles to Cuba and even more important, from their brazen attempt to deny that they were doing so. More important still, Kennedy goes on to flesh out these two charges with a wealth of detail: the missiles are of two types, a medium-range ballistic missile capable of reaching targets from Washington, D.C., to the Panama Canal to Mexico City and an intermediate-range ballistic missile capable of reaching targets from Hudson Bay, Canada, to Lima, Peru. Their deployment violates the Monroe Doctrine, the Rio Pact of 1947, the Charter of the United Nations, a joint resolution of the Eighty-seventh Congress (which I examine later), and his own public warnings of 4 and 13 September 1962. The attempted denials were made in a statement of 11 September, from which Kennedy quotes, and on the previous Thursday during Foreign Minister Andrey Gromyko's visit in Kennedy's office. Supported by this detailed information, Kennedy concludes that "neither the United States of America nor the world community of nations can tolerate deliberate deception and offensive threats on the part of any nation, large or small" (807). This conclusion in turn is fleshed out by a short discussion of how the mere existence of nuclear explosives threatens peace, of how the "cloak of secrecy and deception" unacceptably increases this threat to world peace, and finally, of how "the 1930's taught us a clear lesson: aggressive conduct, if allowed to go unchecked and unchallenged, ultimately leads to war" (807).

Having examined and detailed the sources of the crisis, Commander-in-Chief Kennedy next articulates his objectives: "Our unswerving objective, therefore, must be to prevent the use of these missiles against this or any other country, and to secure their withdrawal or elimination from the Western Hemisphere" (807). To achieve these objectives, Kennedy next proposes an eight-point plan consisting of three military actions (a naval blockade, increased surveillance, and military preparation for "any eventualities"), an explicit threat to retaliate directly against the Soviet Union should any missiles be fired from Cuba, an administrative matter (the evacuation of dependents from the Guantanamo base), and three diplomatic initiatives (convening the Organization of American States, calling a special session of the Security Council, and appealing personally to Chairman Nikita Khrushchev).

Journalists and others have always paid the greatest attention to point three, Kennedy's threat: "*Third:* It shall be the policy of this Nation to regard any nuclear missile launched from Cuba against any nation in the Western Hemisphere as an attack by the Soviet Union on the United States, requiring a full retaliatory response upon the Soviet Union" (808). Indeed, his threat of retaliation in kind is dramatic. Moreover, it is just the type of double hypothetical that makes for facile speculation: if at some point in the not too distant future the Soviet missiles should become operational, and if at some point in the more distant future any of those missiles should be launched for some unimaginable reason, then dire consequences would follow. Although dramatic, such speculations should not be taken too seriously. On the one hand, it appears that there was only the remotest possibility that Kennedy would have to carry out his threat. According to General Curtis E. LeMay, chief of staff of the U.S. Air Force at the time, "During that very critical time [October 1962], in my mind there wasn't a chance that we would have gone to war with Russia because we had overwhelming strategic capability and the Russians knew it" (in Kohn and Harahan 1988, 94). Just how well the Russians knew it was explained by General David A. Burchinal, USAF, a senior staff officer with the Joint Chiefs of Staff in 1962, who was also present at the oral history interview at which LeMay made his remarks:

> It has since always worried me that publications about the Cuban missile crisis all claim that we were so close to nuclear war; ninety-nine percent of the people who write about it don't understand the truth. . . . The Russians were . . . thoroughly stood down, and we knew it. They didn't make any move. They did not increase their alert; they did not increase any flights, or their air defense posture. They didn't do a thing, they froze in place. We were never further from a nuclear war than at the time of Cuba, never further. (95)

On the other hand, all the journalistic speculations that worried General Burchinal neglected or ignored the fact that Kennedy had a plan to ensure that the Soviet missiles would never become operational—and if the Soviet missiles never became operational, Kennedy's threat would never be tested. Not only did he have a plan, however; he had an unusually good plan. Indeed, taking Kennedy's plan as an integrated package of military and diplomatic initiatives, it is difficult to imagine a better one. As it happened, the package proved successful in forcing the Soviets to remove their missiles from Cuba. For my purposes, however, the most interesting aspect of Kennedy's address to the nation is how it informed the crisis, providing us with an excellent example of *war without combat.* I say *war without combat* because combat was the only element of war that was missing. In every other respect, the crisis sounded like, looked like, and felt like war. More precisely, it was a show of force coupled with a naval blockade. Thus, the first step in securing the withdrawal or elimination of the Soviet missiles was to ensure that no more of them arrived in Cuba. This implied a naval blockade. The second step was to monitor the situation in Cuba to ensure that the missiles already there did not become operational. This implied increased surveillance, a stepped-up schedule of aerial reconnaissance. The third step was to deploy sufficient forces, particularly air forces, to the area around Cuba so as to be prepared for "any eventualities." Should the various diplomatic initiatives have failed, these eventualities obviously would have entailed either a series of air strikes or, less likely, commando raids to eliminate the missiles already in Cuba. As a result, even if this example of *war without combat* should have taken a turn for the worse and become an example of *war with combat,* the stated political objectives would still have directed and guided military activities "down to the smallest operational detail." Eliminating the Soviet missiles did not imply the same kind of an open-ended military commitment that created the quagmire of Vietnam; instead, Kennedy's political objectives dictated a relatively restricted number of sorties against a relatively few clearly defined targets—this radar van or that missile launcher.

Therefore, like the United Nations resolutions during the Korean War, Commander-in-Chief Kennedy's 22 October 1962 address during the Cuban Missile Crisis possesses the specificity that makes for the type of well-reasoned declaration that informs a war, be it with or without combat. Had his address lacked this specificity, as Commander-in-Chief's Truman's addresses did during the Korean War, the crisis would have been uninformed, sowing confusion and distress all around and reducing greatly the chances for a successful resolution. Whereas the Cuban Missile Crisis is an excellent example of informed *war without combat,* however, the U.S. reaction to Fidel Castro's accession to power in January 1959 is an equally fine example of its perversion, *enmity without war.* Not only does it exemplify how vague generalities render a policy uninformed, but it also raises the question of how long one should persist in obviously failed policies. I was able to avoid this perplexing question during my discussion of the infinitely more complex case of Vietnam. In the simpler Cuban case, it cannot be ignored or avoided. More particularly, in tracing the U.S. reaction to Fidel Castro, I face three different tasks. First, I must identify at least some of the documents that could have or should have informed U.S. enmity toward Cuba. Second, I need to show how they lack the specificity required to inform U.S. policy toward Cuba. Finally, I need to identify how Castro was able to thwart the sanctions imposed upon him and, given his success in doing so, to ask whether different policies were not required.

Initially Castro was greeted as a liberator in both Cuba and the United States for overthrowing the discredited dictatorship of Fulgencio Batista. This initial euphoria, however, soon gave way to growing concerns as Castro expropriated U.S. holdings in Cuba, converted large private farms into state farms, and began espousing communist policies and doctrines. In response Commander-in-Chief Eisenhower canceled the Cuban sugar quota on 16 December 1960, marking a decided shift from amity to enmity. The next step in this building enmity occurred on 3 January 1961 when Eisenhower severed diplomatic relations with Cuba in response to a Cuban order to reduce drastically the size of the U.S. diplomatic mission in Havana. The increasing enmity boiled over for an instant into *combat without war* on 17 April 1961 when a CIA-trained force of Cuban exiles attempted to land at the Bay of Pigs, a fiasco that greatly embarrassed Kennedy during the first months of his administration.

In the wake of this embarrassing fiasco, as expressions of good will became more and more difficult to find, the Eighty-seventh Congress moved in September 1961 to further increase the enmity. It did this not directly but rather in a crablike, indirect manner by appending to section 620 (a) of the Foreign Assistance Act of 1961 an additional sentence: "(a) No assistance shall be furnished under this Act to the present government of Cuba. As an additional means of implementing and carrying into effect the policy of the preceding sentence, the President is authorized to establish and maintain a total embargo upon all trade between the United States and Cuba" (Pub. L. No. 87-195, 75 Stat. 444-5). First, to put subsection (a) into perspective, it must be emphasized that the Eighty-seventh Congress did not impose an embargo upon Cuba. Instead, it merely authorized Commander-in-Chief Kennedy to do so when and if he should feel it necessary. The Eighty-seventh Congress was not about to disturb the traditional subordination of Congress to the commander-in-chief in matters of war and peace. Second, to highlight how uninformed U.S. policy toward Cuba was from the beginning, the internal inconsistency of the subsection must be noted. Which policy is the embargo designed to facilitate? Nominally, it is "the policy of the preceding sentence." But the policy of the preceding sentence—to deny all foreign aid to Cuba—is effected by not sending any foreign aid to Cuba. Instead of being "an additional means of implementing" the denial of foreign aid, an embargo represents a significant escalation of enmity between the two countries. Third, and most important of all, subsection (a) identifies neither the causes that would justify the establishment of an embargo nor the remedies that would lead to the embargo's being lifted. Still, the congressional motives are not hard to divine from the two succeeding subsections, which, although applying to the administration of U.S. foreign aid in general, obviously also apply to Cuba. Subsection (b) rules: "No assistance shall be furnished under this Act to the government of any country unless the President determines that such country is not dominated or controlled by the international Communist movement" (ibid.), whereas subsection (c) denies foreign aid to any country that has expropriated U.S. property without compensation.

It therefore appears that at this early stage, the United States entertains two grievances against Castro: first, he is "dominated or controlled by the international Communist movement," and second, he has expropriated U.S. investments. Assuming that these are indeed the U.S. grievances, the first observation to be made is that neither grievance lends itself to the type of military operations that characterizes an informed *war with combat.* This is the case because neither can be translated into precise geographic objectives. With respect to the first grievance, its excessive generality precludes military commanders from devising a viable strategy. With respect to the second grievance, it is certainly specific, but still it resists a viable military solution, it being unclear what geographic objective could have served as the military objective since the expropriated properties were dispersed more of less evenly across the entire island. In addition, combat operations to recover the expropriated properties would have risked destroying many of the properties during the course of the operations. This would have rendered many of the recovered properties worthless. Having said this, it must be admitted that there is always a military option for removing a government that is dominated and controlled by unfriendly powers or has expropriated properties—a massive invasion and an extended antiguerrilla campaign to install a new and more friendly government. However, whether this option would have represented a truly viable strategy in the case of Cuba during the early 1960s is a matter of considerable doubt. In fine, the character of the grievances means that any military operations against Cuba would probably have degenerated into a pointless *combat without war,* an unsettling thought suggesting the possibility that Cuba, instead of Vietnam, could have become the quagmire into which the United States was soon to sink.

The second observation to be made is that only the second grievance lends itself to the type of nonmilitary operations that characterize an informed *war without combat.* This is the case because not only did the expropriations concern U.S. interests directly and particularly, but their value could be calculated down to the penny. This specificity means, first, that they constituted a viable subject for negotiations between the two governments and, second, that those negotiations could have been be influenced by the types of diplomatic, economic, and legal pressures that *war without combat* generates, the imposition or lifting of various sanctions constituting a quid pro quo for Cuba's compensation of the owners of expropriated properties. In contrast, the first grievance does not lend itself to the type of nonmilitary operations that characterizes an informed *war without combat.* This is the case because who dominates and controls Cuba (or any other country) is a broad philosophical topic that can be argued endlessly among individuals but does not constitute the type of issue that is subject to intergovernmental negotiations. Intergovernmental negotiations require much greater specificity. If negotiations between the two governments are highly improbable on this issue, then it is also highly improbable that the types of diplomatic, economic, and legal pressures that *war without combat* generates would be effective, it being tautological to observe that nonexistent negotiations cannot be influenced.

At this early stage of the dispute, therefore, the range of possible options can be identified. If an equitable settlement of the expropriations had become the centerpiece of U.S. policy, the enmity between the two countries would have been informed by a reasonable grievance and an attainable goal. With the issue awaiting resolution, any sanctions imposed in response to the expropriations could be characterized as *war without combat.* Alternatively, if the replacement of the Castro government with a more friendly government not "dominated or controlled by the international Communist movement" had become the centerpiece of U.S. policy, any sanctions imposed upon Cuba would have been uninformed and would soon have degenerated into *enmity without war.* Hence the crucial question in the fall of 1961 was which of these two grievances was going to become the centerpiece of U.S. policy toward Cuba.

The answer was not immediately forthcoming. Having received congressional authorization, Commander-in-Chief Kennedy chose not to exercise it until five months later. Then, on 3 February 1962, following the Pan-American Foreign Ministers meeting at Punta del Este, Uruguay, he issued Proclamation 3447, which imposed an embargo on all trade with Cuba. Congressional authorization having finally been transformed into presidential action, the escalating enmity now acquired virtually all the characteristics of war—except combat. Diplomatically, economically, and legally, the condition of relations between Cuba and the United States was now indistinguishable from war, the enmity having increased steadily from a revocation of the Cuban sugar quota on 16 December 1960 to the breaking of diplomatic relations on 3 January 1961 to the Bay of Pigs invasion on 17 April 1961 to the congressional authorization of an embargo in September of 1961 to the actual imposition of a total embargo on 3 February 1962. Unfortunately, though, this enmity was uninformed, the expropriations having been dropped from the official grievances:

> WHEREAS the Eighth Meeting of Consultation of Ministers of Foreign Affairs, Serving as Organ of Consultation in Application of the Inter-American Treaty of Reciprocal Assistance, in its Final Act resolved that the present Government of Cuba is incompatible with the principles and objectives of the Inter-American system; and, in light of the subversive offensive of Sino-Soviet Communism with which the Government of Cuba is publicly aligned, urged the member states to take those steps that they may consider appropriate for their individual and collective self-defense; . . .
>
> WHEREAS the United States, in accordance with its international obligations, is prepared to take all necessary actions to promote national and hemispheric security by isolating the present Government of Cuba and thereby reducing the threat posed by its alignment with the communist powers:
>
> NOW, THEREFORE, I, JOHN F. KENNEDY, President of the United States of America, acting under the authority of Section 620 (a) of the Foreign Assistance Act of 1961 (75 Stat. 445), as amended, do
>
> 1. Hereby proclaim an embargo upon trade between the United States and Cuba.

Proclamation 3447 makes it abundantly clear that Castro's "alignment with the communist powers," and not his expropriations of U.S. investments, was to be the official justification for the United States' enmity toward Cuba. Confirmation of this choice came in October 1962, when the Eighty-seventh Congress passed the "Joint Resolution Expressing the Determination of the United States with Respect to the Situation in Cuba." As its title suggests, the resolution is little more than an expression of frustration. It offers neither analysis of nor remedy for the deteriorating relations between the two countries. This fact makes it one of the more curious congressional policy-support resolutions because, as a 1970 background report for the House Committee on Foreign Affairs noted, "The resolution contains no clause 'authorizing' the President to do anything, and the President took the position that he needed no authorization, although he welcomed an appropriate endorsement" (Committee on Foreign Affairs 1970, 35–6). Beyond expressing a frustrated determination to do something—anything—its four "whereas" clauses and three "resolves" are significant only as expression of the anticommunist fears of the Eighty-seventh Congress. The first "whereas" clause sets the stage for these fears by quoting relevant passages from the 1823 Monroe Doctrine. The second clause suggests the possible legal basis for some undefined future action by citing the 1947 Rio Treaty for mutual defense and article 51 of the United Nations charter concerning the right to individual and collective self-defense. The third clause demonstrates international recognition of the congressional fears by repeating the finding from the final act of the January 1962 foreign ministers meeting at Punta del Este cited in Proclamation 3447 concerning Cuba's identification with the principles of Marxist-Leninist ideology, an identification that was clearly unacceptable, as is clear from the fourth clause: "Whereas the international Communist movement has increasingly extended into Cuba its political, economic, and military sphere of influence." Based upon these "grievances," the Eighty-seventh Congress resolved

> that the United States is determined—
> (a) to prevent by whatever means may be necessary, including the use of arms, the Marxist-Leninist regime in Cuba from extending, by force or the threat of force, its aggressive or subversive activities to any part of this hemisphere;
> (b) to prevent in Cuba the creation or use of an externally supported military capability endangering the security of the United States; and
> (c) to work with the Organization of American States and with freedom-loving Cubans to support the aspirations of the Cuban people for self-determination. (Pub. L. No. 87–733, 76 Stat. 697)

In fine, the three documents cited trace the evolution of U.S. policy toward Castro. They illustrate the inverse relationship between enmity and specificity. As the enmity increased, the specificity of both the grievances and the possible remedies decreased. Instead of informing the U.S. enmity with purpose and point, the documents progressively dissipate what specificity the situation possessed, substituting instead a gathering obscurity of generalities. To recall Jeffrey Kimball's observation in regard to U.S. policy toward Vietnam, since the generalities of anticommunism apply not only to Cuba but to other cold war events and issues as well, they contribute little to either the analysis or the solution of any specific situation.

Still, despite the excessive generality of the documents that motivated the embargo, one must acknowledge that this lack of specificity did not guarantee that the embargo would fail to topple Castro. Such an outcome, although highly improbable insofar as the enmity was uninformed, was certainly not impossible, for if any country was ever vulnerable to economic sanctions, Cuba was certainly one of them. The Cuban economy in 1962 was all but totally dependent upon U.S. trade and investment. It was not, therefore, unreasonable to assume, as Commander-in-Chief Kennedy did when he proclaimed the embargo on 3 February 1962, that any break with the United States was bound to be devastating: "The President pointed out that the embargo will deprive the Government of Cuba of the dollar exchange it has been deriving from sales of its products in the United States. The loss of this income will reduce the capacity of the Castro regime, intimately linked with the Sino-Soviet bloc, to engage in acts of aggression, subversion, or other activities endangering the security of the United States and other nations of the hemisphere" (Kennedy 1963, 106). However, at the same time that Kennedy identified the way in which the sanctions should work, he also identified the way in which they could be frustrated. If the deprivation of dollar exchange would reduce the capacity of the Castro regime to engage in acts of aggression, the replacement of that dollar exchange with something else—a ruble exchange, for example—would sustain that capacity and render the U.S. sanctions ineffective. Despite enormous costs, Castro was successful in switching from a dollar to a ruble economy, which meant that the sanctions soon lost all point and purpose.

Castro's success in replacing U.S. investment with Soviet subsidies suggested strongly that the sanctions would fail to achieve their stated objective and that the policy would have to be changed. During the 1960s, however, the situation was somewhat ambiguous. On the negative side, Canada and the other major industrial powers refused to go along. Beginning in 1964, when the British government encouraged the sale of Leyland buses to Havana, the world's major industrial nations—the United States' closest allies—did not miss an opportunity to trade with Cuba, although it must be admitted that such opportunities were few and far between as long as the Soviets continued to dominate and subsidize the Cuban economy. On the positive side, the United States was able to get twenty-one of the twenty-two members of the Organization of American States (OAS) to impose sanctions against Cuba in 1964. In the end, though, this vote in the OAS proved to be little more than a gesture. In terms of increasing the economic pressure on Cuba, these counties conducted so little trade with Cuba that its loss affected little. In terms of diplomatic pressure, the sanctions were of some consequence when first applied in 1964, but they soon lost potency as the Latin American countries reestablished relations with Cuba one by one. This led the OAS to reconsider its earlier endorsement of the sanctions in July 1975, at which time it voted to end its endorsement of the sanctions altogether.

Thus, by the mid-1970s it was clear that the sanctions had failed. Citing Secretary of State Cyrus Vance's opinion that the embargo against Cuba was a "failure," Donald Losman concluded that "sanctions, then, have been economically effective [i.e., enormously costly to Cuba], yet politically unsuccessful," observing further that "the absolute refusal to trade with Cuba literally forced and cemented almost permanent relations with the Communist world" (1979, 44, 46). Sheer power proved to be a poor substitute for hardheaded analysis and coherent policy goals. Having failed so completely, the sanctions became little more than an expression of a continuing but vague and uninformed enmity between the two countries, that is, an example of *enmity without war*. Had equitable compensation for the expropriated investments been the goal of the sanctions, one might speculate that the sanctions could have been successful, not in toppling Castro, but in establishing some mutually agreeable formula for compensation, the specificity of the goal providing hope for a resolution to the grievance.

Still, acknowledgment by Secretary Vance and others that the sanctions had failed did not lead to any change in the basic policy, as one might expect. Thwarted by Soviet subsidies, unsupported by the United States' closest allies, this ineffective "total" embargo nonetheless remained in place. The reasons for this failure to change, which lie outside the scope of my study, arise out of simple inertia and the need to placate various domestic constituencies, particularly the Cuban-American community. Although the policy did not change, however, the world did, leading to an even more incoherent policy toward Cuba.

In 1989 the Berlin Wall came crashing down, affecting both the economic assumptions and the ideological basis of the Cuban embargo. In a move affecting the economic assumptions, Mikhail Gorbachev announced in September 1991 that the Soviet Union could no longer continue to subsidize the Cuban economy. After a short transition period, the Cubans would have to pay for Soviet oil and other goods at market prices in dollars. Since Cuba had been able to thwart the U.S. sanctions by converting from a dollar to a ruble economy, this sudden reversion to the dollar would not only be devastating but offered some hope that Commander-in-Chief Kennedy's 1962 predictions would finally come true. Greatly diminishing these hopes, however, was the fact that few other countries were willing to support the continued U.S. sanctions, which had become a great embarrassment to the United States' closest allies. Hence, while trade and investment were not available from the United States, they were available from Canada, Spain, and the other countries of Europe and Latin America. With alternative sources of trade and investment available to Cuba, it was extremely unlikely that the sanctions would be any more successful over the next thirty years than they had been over the preceding thirty years. Indeed, as Lisa Martin (1992) has argued persuasively, economic sanctions must be credible to be successful, and their credibility depends crucially upon the "sender" country's convincing other countries to join in. Without this "coercive cooperation," the sanctions will fail.

As for the ideological basis of the sanctions, obviously they could no long-er be justified by reference to Castro's alignment with the Sino-Soviet, Marx-ist-Leninist communist powers. With the demise of these powers, the align-ment ceased to exist. Stepping into this ideological void, Representative Robert G. Torricelli, Democrat of New Jersey and chair of the House Subcommittee on Western Hemisphere Affairs, sponsored the Cuban Democracy Act of 1992, which was enacted as title 17 of the National Defense Authorization Act for Fiscal Year 1993 (Pub. L. No. 102-484, 106 Stat. 2575). The Cuban Democracy Act attempts to address three concerns: First, it tightens the sanctions some-what. Second, it attempts to fill the ideological void. Third, and most impor-tant, it attempts to deal with the fact that few other countries are supporting the sanctions. Section 1706 of the act tightens sanctions in several ways, but the two most important are new restrictions upon remittances from Cuban-Americans to their families and relatives in Cuba and a rule that prohibits ships that have entered Cuban ports from entering U.S. ports for 180 days. These measures will obviously have some marginal, but not decisive, effect upon the economic situation in Cuba.

The ideological void is filled, in a manner of speaking, by sections 1702, 1703, 1707, and 1708. Section 1702 consists of eight "findings," all of which add up to the charge that "the government of Fidel Castro has demonstrated consistent disregard for internationally accepted standards of human rights and for democratic values." Instead of being his alignment with the commu-nist powers, the United States' grievance against Castro is now that he abuses human rights and lacks democratic values. Although the charges are no doubt true, for my present purposes, it must be noted that there has been no increase in the level of specificity. Abusing human rights and frustrating the democrat-ic impulses of the Cuban people are no less vague than complicity with Sino-Soviet Communism. The enmity between the two countries remains strong but uninformed. In the light of these new grievances, the act proposes reme-dies in section 1703, supplemented by sections 1707 and 1708. Section 1703 consists of ten "statements of policy," the intent of which is captured in state-ment 6, "to maintain sanctions on the Castro regime so long as it continues to refuse to move toward democratization and greater respect for human rights." This overall objective is supplemented by section 1707, "Policy toward a Transitional Cuban Government," and section 1708, "Policy toward a Dem-ocratic Cuban Government," both of which offer a variety of financial and diplomatic assistance to a post-Castro government. Although the assistance listed in sections 1707 and 1708 is specific enough, the overall goal of realign-ing the Cuban government toward democracy suffers from the same sort of vague generality that plagued the old goal of realigning the Cuban government away from Marxist-Leninist communism. In terms of the specificity that could inform the United State's enmity toward Cuba, there has been no change or improvement. Both the officially articulated grievances and the officially articulated remedies render that enmity uninformed.

But I have been discussing superficialities. I have not yet reached the heart of the Cuban Democracy Act of 1992. In 1992, twenty-nine years after Commander-in-Chief Kennedy imposed a total embargo upon Cuba, in the year the Soviet Union ended its enormous subsidies, the key to success for proponents of the sanctions was to be found in forcing the other governments of the world to join. As noted previously, the end of Soviet subsidies did not leave Cuba without other resources, because it was able to conduct business with other countries. These other countries provided nothing like the subsidy that the Soviet Union had provided. Still, this alternative trade meant that Cuba was not totally without resources. It followed, therefore, that if this alternative trade could be cut off, Cuba would finally be totally without resources and Castro would soon fall. As a result virtually every section of the Cuban Democracy Act of 1992 contains a veiled or not so veiled threat against any country that does not impose sanctions against Cuba. For example, section 1703 (3) seeks "to make clear to other countries that, in determining its relations with them, the United States will take into account their willingness to cooperate in such a policy [of sanctions]," whereas section 1704, entitled ironically "International Cooperation," begins softly enough:

> (a) Cuban Trading Partners.—The President should encourage the governments of countries that conduct trade with Cuba to restrict their trade and credit relations with Cuba in a manner consistent with the purposes of this title.

But lest anyone miss the point, it immediately goes on to threaten consequences for noncooperation:

> (b) Sanctions Against Countries Assisting Cuba.—
> (1) Sanctions.—The President may apply the following sanctions to any country that provides assistance to Cuba:
> (A) The government of such country shall not be eligible for assistance under the Foreign Assistance Act of 1961 or assistance or sales under the Arms Export Control Act.
> (B) Such country shall not be eligible, under any program for forgiveness or reduction of debt owed to the United States Government.

In effect, then, the unilateral U.S. sanctions against Cuba having failed to elicit "coercive cooperation" from the other countries of the world, the 102d Congress, in its wisdom, has decided to declare war on any country that assists Cuba, which includes most of the United States' closest allies. Countries, corporations, and vessels that trade with or assist Cuba will be penalized under this act in one way or another.

As one might expect, this congressional declaration of war, this extraterritorial application of U.S. law to the other countries of the world, did not go unnoticed. The act was approved by Commander-in-Chief Bush on 23 October 1992, and a month later, on Tuesday, 24 November 1992, the UN General Assembly passed a Cuban-sponsored resolution calling for an end to the thirty-year-old U.S. embargo against Cuba. The vote was an embarrassing fifty-nine in favor, seventy-nine abstentions, and three against. The three against were the United States, Israel, and Rumania. The *New York Times* reported, "Most of the allies declining to come to Washington's support made it clear that they were using the nonbinding vote to signal their anger at a new American law that . . . extends American jurisdiction beyond the boundaries of the United States to cover foreign subsidies of American companies" (25 November 1992, A1). The *New York Times* also reported that Representative Torricelli insisted that the Cuban Democracy Act did not apply to foreign countries (A10), but even a casual reading of the act does not support this view. When the Cuban delegation introduced the same resolution again in 1993, eighty-eight nations voted in favor, and only fifty-seven abstained. In 1994 the trend continued, 101 countries voting in favor, forty-eight abstaining, and even Rumania failing to hold fast; only Israel and the United States voted against the resolution.

Theoretically, then, at some abstract level of legal technicality, the Cuban Democracy Act not only reconfirms the United States' thirty-year-old commitment to economic sanctions against Cuba but declares war against any country that trades or assists Cuba as well. At a more practical level, however, since no one, including Representative Torricelli, believes that the United States would ever actually impose sanctions against a country that assisted Cuba, the current policy toward Cuba is pretty much a dead letter. It does little more than express a continuing enmity toward Castro without any real hope of accomplishing its stated objective of toppling him. Still, for my purposes, the incoherence that the act introduces into U.S. policy toward Cuba is the least interesting aspect of the Cuban Democracy Act. Of greater interest is the way other countries reacted to it in the United Nations. They obviously find it neither very persuasive nor very helpful. Their reaction leads to speculation about what would have happened if the Security Council, and not the 102d Congress, had debated the question of Cuban-American relations after the fall of Soviet Communism.

As noted in my discussion of the UN resolutions during the Korean War, the cosmopolitan composition of the UN means that the easy generalities of the domestic debate must be either abandoned or toned down considerably. In this more rigorous atmosphere, the extraterritorial provisions of Representative Torricelli's act would never have been mentioned, much less proposed. In addition, the UN would never have entertained a proposal to topple Castro. The membership of the UN is almost uniformly opposed to the undermining of existing governments, no matter what their crimes and misdemeanors may be. Nonetheless, one might speculate that the Security Council could well have entertained a resolution calling for economic sanctions against Cuba for the purpose of encouraging Cuba to negotiate in good faith toward an equitable compensation for the properties it had earlier expropriated. Since the U.S. expropriation claims are ultimately going to be the final obstacle in a return to normal relations between the two countries, and since this issue possesses the specificity that lends itself to negotiations between two governments, it might have been possible for the UN to endorse wider sanctions to achieve this narrow purpose. Thus, again, one is drawn to the troubling conclusion that, with respect to the declaring of war, the democratic mechanisms of open debate leading to a vote work best in undemocratic assemblies.

PART 3

Speculating on Solutions

5

The Military, the Public, and Congress

Before Congress could begin to discharge its constitutional duty to declare war, dramatic and substantive changes would have to occur in three different groups: Congress, the general public, and the professional military. With respect to the complexity and scope of these changes, Congress would have to undergo the most thoroughgoing change and the professional military the least, with the general public somewhere in between. With respect to the politics of instituting such changes, the general public is crucial, the professional military is largely irrelevant, and Congress is impotent. The moment the general public insists that Congress discharge its constitutional responsibilities to write and vote fully reasoned declarations of war, Congress will dutifully do as it is told, just as it has always dutifully done whatever the commander-in-chief has told it to do. However, it is neither indolence nor inertia that prevents Congress from reforming itself; without the active support of the general public, any attempt to force a congressionally drafted declaration of war upon the commander-in-chief would surely fail, for the political power of the commander-in-chief coupled with over two hundred years of precedent and tradition would ensure an ignominious defeat for any purely congressional initiative.

Since the politics of these changes are both obvious and uninteresting, this chapter will ignore them, focusing instead on the issues of complexity. To this end, the simple changes affecting the professional military will be explored first, followed by the more complex changes affecting the general public and finally by the numerous unprecedented changes affecting Congress.

The Professional Military: "The Instrument of His Army's Downfall"

Only an extremely limited segment of the professional military would be directly affected by the advent of fully reasoned congressional declarations of war. It would consist exclusively of general officers, most particularly the Joint Chiefs of Staff and the commanders of Unified Commands. That is, any changes in this area would concern principally those officers whose duties place them at the intersection of military operations and domestic politics. At first glance, a formal congressional declaration of war would appear to have little impact upon this group of "political" officers. They have always looked to the commander-in-chief for the articulation of grand strategy; the substitution of Congress for the commander-in-chief would represent only a minor change. A further minor adjustment would be a slight shift in whom they advise. At present, whenever a commander-in-chief contemplates making an informal declaration of war that might include combat, the Joint Chiefs of Staff and other relevant commanders are consulted. In the future Congress would obviously want to avail itself of this same advice before it began drafting a declaration of war. Some of these consultations would be public, in congressional hearings, in the newspapers, and such like. Nicias's speech to the Athenian Assembly just before the Sicilian expedition should serve as a model for these public consultations (Thucydides 1982, VI, 9–14). Other consultations would be private and confidential, the nature of the military topics being discussed demanding no less. But again, this is a minor adjustment, a simple substitution of Congress for the commander-in-chief.

A closer look, however, reveals that the greatest impact of fully reasoned congressional declarations of war upon these highest-ranking officers would come not before but after the declaration had been voted by Congress and approved by the commander-in-chief. At this point in the process, the professional military would be called to assume the much less familiar role of ensuring the relevance and correctness of the grand strategic analysis that motivated the congressional declaration. To be sure, the military has always possessed this function, but in a truly representative democracy, with the people's representatives discharging their responsibility to articulate grand strategy, this long-neglected role would assume a much greater importance. Democratic procedures do not ensure infallible results, as the Sicilian expedition demonstrates. Therefore, one can assume that the grand strategic analysis motivating at least some of the congressional declarations would be irrelevant and wrong. In these cases, whenever the war included combat, the military would be the first to feel its untoward effects. Being the first, it would have a special responsibility to bring these errors to the attention of Congress, so that Congress could revise its war aims accordingly.

This too-often-neglected duty is illustrated most poignantly in Colonel Harry G. Summers's *On Strategy: A Critical Analysis of the Vietnam War*. The relevant passage begins with the absolutely damning observation that "our military leaders evidently did not feel so strongly about their strategic concepts that they were willing to 'fall on their swords' if they were not adopted" (1982, 120). The passage then continues by quoting General William Westmoreland quoting a Napoleonic maxim that Westmoreland had kept under a panel of glass on his desk in Saigon:

> A commander-in-chief cannot take as an excuse for his mistakes in warfare an order given by his sovereign or his minister, when the person giving the order is absent from the field of operations and is imperfectly aware or wholly unaware of the latest state of affairs. It follows that any commander-in-chief who undertakes to carry out a plan which he considers defective is at fault; he must put forward his reasons, insist on the plan being changed, and finally tender his resignation rather than be the instrument of his army's downfall. (ibid.)

General Westmoreland then explains, "I suffered my problems in Vietnam because I believed that success eventually would be ours despite them, that they were not to be, as Napoleon put it, instruments of my army's downfall" (in ibid.). Colonel Summers's point is not that one commander in Vietnam misjudged the situation but rather that none of the many general officers who disagreed with the way the war was being conducted possessed the courage of their convictions. None of them put their careers at risk. None of them resigned in protest. All of them stepped back from the precipice and kept silent, to the great regret of all.

The need for senior commanders to protest and then to resign in order not to be the instrument of their army's downfall is not grounded solely in tragic experience or Napoleonic maxims. It is embedded deeply in the logic of war. As articulated by Clausewitz, the logic of war is organic. It begins with the articulation of a political purpose. This purpose, then, controls the operational objectives, which in turn determine the conduct of the war "down to the smallest operational detail" (Clausewitz 1976, 579). The energy that drives this organism is a correct and appropriate grand strategic analysis. When the grand strategic analysis is correct, the political purpose of the war will be identified with relatively little difficulty, which means that the operational objectives will also be relatively easily identified, which in turn means that the operational details will fall into place more or less naturally. In fine, in wars with combat, the correctness and appropriateness of the grand strategic analysis articulated in a fully reasoned declaration of war find their definitive empirical test in the coherence of the smallest operational details.

Inasmuch as this empirical test is the irrefutable proof of inappropriate declarations of war, it is the professional military who, in the last resort, must warn both Congress and the general public of the errors that have been made. The hazards and dangers of this enterprise to the careers of these highest-ranking officers are great, however. Thus, the officers who raise the alarm must possess an exceptional degree of moral courage and a willingness to sacrifice their own careers to preserve the lives of their men. They must also be exceptionally competent, able to separate insubordination from justified frustration, to distinguish a temporary military setback from the reversals that a fundamentally flawed grand strategy engenders, and finally, to differentiate the incompetence and bungling at the tactical level that are but one of the frictions of war from the missteps incumbent upon a deeply flawed declaration of war. Moreover, since the ultimate weapon in this battle is the resignation, only the most senior officers are in a position to raise the alarm. The protests and resignations of company- and field-grade officers signal discontent at best and cowardice at worst; the protests and resignations of senior commanders signal serious defects in the grand strategic analysis.

This being the case, one can imagine the following process percolating up from the bottom of the military hierarchy. On visits to regimental commanders, a division commander hears increasing complaints of frustrations. The regimental commanders point out that the congressional declaration of war has fixed such and so as the war aims and that the theater commander has translated these aims into a local strategy that in turn has been broken down by the division commander into a set of regimental objectives. Having conducted operations of this, that, and every other kind, however, not only has the regiment not attained its assigned objectives, but it will not be able to attain them in the foreseeable future. Having been assured of the competence of the regimental commanders and the reality of their frustration, the division commander investigates among the other division commanders in the area to find out whether it is just the one division or whether these frustrations are widespread. Should the frustrations prove widespread, the division commanders order their regimental commanders to conduct operations with an eye to minimizing casualties and bring the matter to the attention of their corps commander. The corps commander, having in turn obtained assurance of the division commanders' competence and the reality of their frustration, begins inquiries among the other corps commanders. If the other corps commanders confirm the frustrations, they bring them to the attention of the theater commander. In this way, the frustrations of the regimental commanders quickly come to the attention of the Joint Chiefs of Staff and the commander-in-chief, who are in a position to bring them to the attention of Congress and the general public.

At this point, Napoleon's chain of protest comes into play. The commander-in-chief and the Joint Chiefs of Staff put forward their reasons for thinking that the grand strategic analysis motivating the congressional declaration of war is wrong; they insist on the analysis being changed, and if Congress refuses to change it, the Joint Chiefs of Staff resign and lead the opposition to the war. Because the commander-in-chief is also president, that individual is not in a position to resign. The commander-in-chief's role is to lead the opposition from inside the government as a check upon Congress. Only the Joint Chiefs of Staff and the commanders of Unified Commands are in a position to resign, and they must do so, as General Westmoreland reminded himself daily, in order that they may not be the instrument of their army's downfall.

In summary, then, should Congress ever begin to discharge its constitutional duty to make fully reasoned declarations of war, the principal effect upon the professional military would be to increase its importance as a bulwark against faulty grand strategic analyses. Ironically, in the past, precisely because Congress shirked its constitutional responsibilities in this area, it was in a position to act as a defense of last resort against the inappropriate grand strategic analyses of the commander-in-chief, as was demonstrated toward the end of the Vietnam War. Once it takes up its constitutional responsibilities, however, Congress will no longer be able to play this role. In its stead, the professional military will become the defense of last resort.

More fully, the first defense against bad declarations of war would be Congress itself. It is to be hoped that vigorous and open debate would make it difficult for faulty analyses to survive. Nonetheless, some bad declarations would undoubtedly pass Congress. Hence, the second line of defense would be the commander-in-chief's veto, it being incumbent upon that office not to approve poorly motivated declarations of war. But again, driven by the emotions of the moment, some bad declarations would inevitably pass through this defense also. Consequently, the last line of defense against inappropriate grand strategic analyses in wars with combat would be the professional military, the coherence of the smallest operational details providing the irrefutable empirical test for the congressional theories that motivated the declaration in the first place. In anticipation of this, doctrine should be developed that clearly requires division commanders and their superiors to evaluate continually the coherence of the smallest operational details. Then they should be trained to act appropriately whenever these details become incoherent, as they did in Vietnam, conducting operations in a manner so as to minimize casualties and then protesting—putting forward their reasons, insisting that the analysis be changed, and finally, tendering their resignations rather than being the instrument of their army's downfall.

Committees of Correspondence: Creating an Informed Public

As noted previously, in terms of politics, the general public is the key to forcing Congress to assume its constitutional responsibility to declare war. As soon as the public demands that Congress discharge its responsibilities in this area, Congress will dutifully comply. Therefore, the political problem reduces to one of moving public opinion in this direction strongly enough that neither Congress nor the commander-in-chief will be able to resist it. More specifically, there are two related political problems. Initially public opinion must be marshaled to demand that commanders-in-chief stop declaring war informally on their own authority, as kings have always done, and that Congress instead begin debating fully reasoned formal declarations of war, as representative democracy demands. That having been accomplished, the next step is to find a mechanism to ensure continued compliance by Congress, to ensure that Congress does not lapse back into its old ways and allow the commander-in-chief to declare war informally.

The solution to both problems is the development of an informed public, that is, the development of a cadre of citizens trained in the art of grand strategic analysis around whom the larger public could coalesce to pressure Congress. To develop this cadre, a nonprofit foundation should be established. This private foundation would possess three functions: research, training, and organizational support for local chapters. The research function would support research into questions of war and peace with a special emphasis on grand strategic analysis and its relationship to the drafting of fully reasoned declarations of war. An additional focus would be the relationship of grand strategy to strategy and tactics—that is, to the smallest operational details. The training function would support the development of materials and curricula for Congress (I will say more about this in the following section), the local chapters, and schools and colleges.

Both the research and training functions would be important but secondary support functions. The first and foremost function of the foundation would be to support the local chapters, the members of which would form the cadre around which an informed public opinion would crystallize. With respect to a name, because of their revolutionary purpose and their local organization, an appropriate name would be "Committees of Correspondence," a name that recalls Samuel Adams's Revolutionary Committees of Correspondence. Like the colonial committees that did so much to shape public opinion just before and during the Revolutionary War, these modern-day committees would inform and shape public opinion on the crucial issues of the day. Given this colonial association, an appropriate symbol or logo for the modern Committees of Correspondence would be a quill pen, a small gold lapel pin serving to identify members.

With respect to membership, the Committees of Correspondence would be an amalgam of a civic organization, the Council on Foreign Relations, and the Légion d'honneur, with an added academic entrance requirement. The committees would be like civic organizations in that membership would be voluntary and the members would be organized into numerous local chapters, like the Lions Club or the Rotary. They would be like the Council on Foreign Relations in that their principal, but not exclusive, focus would be foreign affairs, especially those affairs that might lead to war. The committees would be like the Légion d'honneur in that membership would constitute a high civic honor, recognizing distinguished service to the community, as a knighthood does in Britain and the rosette of the Légion d'honneur does in France. To underscore the importance of distinguished service to the community, the minimum age for membership would be forty-five years of age, ten more than the minimum age for the presidency.

Unlike induction into British knighthood or the Légion d'honneur, however, membership in the Committees of Correspondence would be contingent upon the applicants' first passing a prescribed training course. The reasons for this academic requirement are two. First, membership in a local Committee of Correspondence would not be only a civic honor. It would also be a job entailing several serious responsibilities: members would be required to attend regular meetings; to keep informed, especially on those developments that might lead to war; and to speak to local groups seeking information and guidance on any declarations of war that Congress might debate. Second, the drafting and evaluation of fully reasoned declarations of war requires training. It is an art that must be learned, not an inborn instinct acquired without effort. I emphasize this point even more strongly in the following section when I discuss Congress, but clearly not everyone possesses the judgment, the experience, and the knowledge to make the moral and grand strategic decisions that a fully reasoned declaration of war demands. Hence, some minimal training is necessary. Just as no one would suggest sending raw recruits into combat without some minimal basic training, so both those who draft fully reasoned declarations of war in Congress and those who sit in ultimate judgment in the general public also require some minimal basic training.

The content of the training course would be the responsibility of the training or educational section of the national committee, which would develop the necessary classroom materials and essay tests for certification based upon the results obtained by the research section. For example, one of the first questions that the research section would want to investigate is whether a fully reasoned declaration of war must always take the form of a petition, as the Declaration of Independence did, or can it instead begin with demands.

Based upon the results of research such as this, the training section would shape various curricula for the members of Congress, the applicants for the local Committees of Correspondence, and other groups of interested students. In general, the pattern for these courses of study would be as follows. After providing some theoretical grounding in the difference between war and combat, the just-war criteria, and the form and function of fully reasoned declarations of war, the syllabus would shift to case studies, various ancient and modern wars being studied with an eye to their grand strategic factors. The lens through which each war would be studied would be the formal or informal declarations of war by which the leadership attempted to articulate its grand strategy. The appropriate declaration would be identified (which is not always an easy task) and evaluated to see whether it accurately or inaccurately analyzed the grand strategic situation. Those that accurately analyzed the grand strategic situation, such as Woodrow Wilson's 1914 informal declaration against Mexico, would be held up as models to be emulated. Those that did not, such as all the congressional declarations of war, would be critiqued and the drafting of a more adequate declaration set as a class exercise. At the end of the course, a case would be set as an examination and the students evaluated on the quality of their grand strategic analysis, including, perhaps, their proposed draft for a fully reasoned declaration of war.

After having passed this course of study and their forty-fifth birthdays, individuals would be eligible for membership in one of the local Committees of Correspondence, the current members voting on their permanent membership after a period of probation. As the organization's membership grew, one could imagine the Committees of Correspondence developing along the following lines. After several years of private initiative, a sufficient number of local chapters would have been developed so that they could successfully pressure Congress to adopt new rules and procedures to allow it to debate and vote fully reasoned declarations of war. With these new rules in place, the stage would be set for confrontation with the commander-in-chief, who, it must be assumed, would be most reluctant to surrender the royal prerogative without a fight. Inasmuch as commanders-in-chief have won every battle on this issue for the last two hundred years, one must assume that they would initially prevail in these first skirmishes. Still, if the Committees of Correspondence could hold their ground, they should eventually be able to swing public opinion around and force the commanders-in-chief to give up the royal prerogative and accept the need for the people's representatives to articulate the nation's grand strategy by means of a fully reasoned declaration of war.

Once the proper subordinate relationship had been established between the people's representatives and the commander-in-chief, the Committees of Correspondence could then concentrate upon their primary task of informing and shaping public opinion in specific situations. The principal means for doing this would be talks with local groups, appearances in the local broadcast media, and articles in the local newspapers. For example, as a situation deteriorated in some part of the world, members in each local committee would debate the issues among themselves. The natural result of these debates would be division among the members: some would conclude that one course of action was required; some, that another course was required; and others would advocate inaction. "Leave well enough alone," the last group would insist. Thus prepared to present the full range of alternatives, the members would wait until the situation became a matter of more general concern, at which time they would accept invitations to speak before various groups and through the broadcast media, in addition to preparing articles, pro and con, for the local newspapers.

Should the situation deteriorate still further, to the point that Congress began debating a declaration of war, the local committees would intensify their activities. As soon as the draft declaration became available, the members would analyze it and publicize their critiques. Again, one would expect sharp differences in opinion: some members would endorse the draft declaration, and others would reject it. To influence the members of Congress more directly, though, each local committee would organize a number of meetings in collaboration with other groups. At these meetings the draft declaration would be debated, opposing members of the local committee leading the discussion. At the conclusion of each meeting, a vote would be taken and the results forwarded to the group's representatives in Congress:

> Fifty-two members of the First Baptist Church (or the Downtown Lions Club) having met and discussed the pending draft declaration of war against Fiji on the evening of 2 February, a secret ballot taken at the end of the discussion showed that, excluding the two members of the Committee of Correspondence present, thirty-three of the participants opposed the draft declaration, fourteen supported it, and five abstained.
>
> The principal arguments of those opposing the draft declaration were. . . .
> The principal arguments of those supporting the draft declaration were. . . .

As these reports—supplemented by the reports of votes taken within each Committee of Correspondence—flowed into Congress, not only would the members learn how many of their constituents supported the proposed draft declaration of war and how many opposed it, but more important, they would learn the reasons that motivated their constituents to take one position or another. The difference between these informed reports of actual votes and commercial opinion polls is obvious. One must assume that these reports, and not the commercial opinion polls, would have a preponderant, if not decisive, influence upon the members who received them as they formulated their own responses to the draft declaration.

In conclusion, then, the Committees of Correspondence would work to create an informed public opinion. A trained cadre would move the process beyond commercial opinion polls and generate informed opinions sufficiently powerful both to force commanders-in-chief to subordinate themselves to the people's representatives and to influence the members of Congress as they prepared to vote on draft declarations of war. In the end, it is to be hoped, the members of the Committees of Correspondence would develop an ethos similar to that of the early Roman *collegium fetialis*. Trained in the *jus fetiale,* the members of this sacred college saw it as their responsibility to act as the conscience of the Roman Senate and people, ensuring that Rome did not venture into impious wars to begin with or violate the laws of war thereafter. For example, in 300 B.C. Quintus Ambustus of the Fabii clan attacked a Gaul during a truce. This clear violation of the laws of war, of a solemn oath given before the gods, provoked the following reaction:

> When the senate convened in Rome, many denounced the Fabii, and especially the priests called *fetiales* were insistent in calling upon the senate in the name of all the gods to turn the curse of what had been done upon the one guilty man, and so to make expiation for the rest. . . .
>
> The senate referred the matter to the people, and although the [fetial] priests with one accord denounced Fabius, the multitude so scorned and mocked at religion as to appoint him military tribune, along with his brothers. (Plutarch, *Camillus,* 18.1–2; cited in Watson 1993, 40)

The fetials were not always successful, as the example illustrates. Yet theirs is the ethos that ideally would develop: a body of citizens not directly responsible for the question of war or peace but sufficiently knowledgeable, eminent, and respected to act as the nation's conscience, to guide and advise their fellow citizens as they direct their representatives on how to decide the question of war and peace.

Congress: Creating a Council of War

Speculating on how Congress might organize itself so as to fulfill its constitutional duties under article 1, section 8, is an exercise in imagining the unimagined. There is no obvious starting point, no precedent, no example, no model or illustration. Absolutely none. One cannot begin with the congressional practices of the last two hundred years, since these procedures, such as they are, constitute a recipe for allowing the commander-in-chief to do the work of Congress. Nor can one begin with the two councils of Gilgamesh, the debates in the Athenian Ecclesia, or the procedures of the *jus fetiale*. In these and every other case, either the precedent is irrelevant to the problems of an indirect democracy or the existing sources lack the required detail.

Still, although precedent may fail, a touchstone nevertheless does exist. War is not peace, which is only to say that the social, legal, and political conditions created by enmity are different from the social, legal, and political conditions created by amity. Different conditions naturally require different responses. They require social, legal, and political actors to organize and conduct themselves differently in war than in peace.

The principle is obvious, yet Congress alone among the three branches of government has ignored it. With respect to the judicial power, the Constitution recognizes the difference between war and peace by establishing two different types of courts, courts civil and martial, the latter operating whenever conditions do not permit the former to function. With respect to the executive power, although it vests power in the same person in both war and peace, the Constitution clearly recognizes the difference between the two. Whenever a state of amity exists, a civil president discharges those functions necessitated by peace. Whenever a state of enmity exists, a commander-in-chief discharges those functions necessitated by war or its preparation. Only Congress ignores the difference between enmity and amity in its organization and functioning. The same rules, the same organization, and the same committees govern its conduct in peace as in war. But war is not peace. It follows therefore that, should Congress ever be moved to discharge its constitutionally mandated war powers, it must organize itself in an entirely different manner, creating a parallel structure that is suited to the declaring of war but unsuited to the passing of ordinary appropriations and legislation.

The first step in imagining this parallel structure is to provide it with a name. Inasmuch as the *jus fetiale* has dominated all discussions on the declaring of war for over three millennia, the most obvious name is "Collegium Fetialis." Moreover, the House chamber is already decorated to accommodate a sitting of the fetiales, with its large gold fasces adorning the wall behind the Speaker's chair. Still, "Collegium Fetialis" is not an appropriate name. The fetiales did not decide the question of war or peace. The Roman Senate did. The function of the fetiales was to ensure the piety and justice of declarations after the Senate had decided on war. Had the Constitution given the commander-in-chief the power to declare war and then, as a check on this power, required that Congress sit in judgment on the piety and justice of the commander-in-chief's declaration, then "Collegium Fetialis" would be an appropriate name. But the Constitution does not do this. Instead, it gives the power to declare war uniquely to Congress. This being the case, the simplest name would appear to be the "Council of War on . . . ," the suspension points indicating the name of the country against which the declaration is being directed. For example, during World War II, Congress would have sat concurrently as six or seven different councils of war: the Council of War on Bulgaria, the Council of War on Hungary, the Council of War on Italy, the Council of War on Imperial Japan, the Council of War on Nazi Germany, the Council of War on Rumania, and possibly the Council of War on Finland. Since the role and circumstances of each country were different, the grand strategic analysis of each and the U.S. war aims for each should have been different, which is only another way of saying that the U.S. declaration of war against each should have been different from the others. To keep all of these differences clearly in mind, a separate council of war for each country should have sat until that country came to terms. Thus, during the course of World War II, the Council of War on Italy would have been the first to adjourn sine die and the Council of War on Imperial Japan would have been the last. This new name would, of course, also require a change in the enactment clause of the declaration, changing it from *Be it enacted by the Senate and House of Representatives of the United States of America in Congress assembled* to *Be it enacted by the Senate and House of Representatives of the United States of America in Council of War on . . . assembled.* In fine, then, whenever appropriations and normal legislation were considered, Congress would sit as "Congress," following its current rules and procedures. Whenever a declaration of war was under consideration, it would sit as "The Council of War on . . . ," following as yet undefined rules and procedures.

The name having been settled, the next consideration is dress. The declaring of war, in all cultures, for all times, has been regarded as a solemn and sacred proceeding. The solemnity of any performative is increased by the enacting of appropriate ritual, including the wearing of special dress. The suits and ties and the casual comings and goings that characterize the peacetime procedures of Congress are clearly inappropriate for the declaring of war. Consequently, when sitting as a council of war on some nation, the members would wear judicial or academic robes, entering and leaving the chamber in solemn procession led by a color guard. Each session would begin with the color guard standing at ease on the floor of the chamber, the members in black robes arrayed before their seats, and the chaplain intoning a prayer. A formal processional and recessional means that attendance would be mandatory. Members could not come and go as they please. The purpose of mandatory attendance is not primarily to increase the solemnity of the performance. Rather, it is to underline the extraordinarily serious nature of the decision under discussion. The absence of a member from a council of war should therefore be noted at the time; if it cannot be explained by illness or other exceptional circumstances, it should become a campaign issue in the next election: "Senator Smith cares so little for the lives of those he sends into combat that he could not even be bothered to attend the Council of War on. . . . How can you possibly reelect such a man?"

The increased formality of the proceedings highlights another hurdle that needs to be overcome: a lack of training. The members of Congress come to Washington for the most part well trained in the ways and means of passing peacetime legislation, having learned these skills in local and state legislatures. State and local legislatures do not declare war, however. Hence, with respect to this unique responsibility, the members arrive, as it were, as "raw recruits." But just as no one would dream of sending raw recruits to battle without adequate training, so the members of Congress should not be allowed to declare war without at least minimum training. To met this need, the first week of every session would include an extended debate on a mock declaration of war. Responsibility for organizing and conducting the mock debate would fall on the shoulders of the newly arrived first-term members of Congress, since they would be the primary targets of this training. During this training session, they would begin their study of the type of grand strategic analysis that is needed to compose a fully reasoned declaration of war. Indeed, the materials prepared by the training or educational section of the Committee of Correspondence for the mock declaration of war would have been selected so as to instruct all members of Congress on some difficult facet of grand strategic analysis. In addition, during this mock debate the new members would also learn the rules and procedures used in a council of war.

Just what these rules and practices might be is extremely difficulty to imagine, as I have already noted. The only certainty is that the councils of war could not be organized as Congress is presently organized. First and foremost, the present organization of Congress is inappropriate because war is not peace. Precisely because its current organization works so well during peacetime, it is ill suited for wartime. Moreover, to overcome any possible doubt about just how unsuited its current organization is for the declaring of war, one need only recall the fact that Congress has made but five unreasoned declarations in over two hundred years, which demonstrates beyond a shadow of a doubt that its present organization simply does not work. Given this single certainty, the first organizational change would be for both the Senate and the House to sit together whenever a council of war was called into session. The second change would be for the members to sit as state delegations and for the delegations to be seated alphabetically from Alabama on the right to Wyoming on the left of the chamber. In effect, the council of war would sit as a unicameral legislature. The primary reason for this is that Congress is not currently organized in this way, but the Second Continental Congress was. A secondary reason is to facilitate debate and voting, which should be by state delegation, as I will explain shortly.

Having brought the Senate and the House together in a single chamber, the council of war would be presided over by a moderator elected at the beginning of each Congress by a two-thirds vote of the state delegations. As the title indicates, this office would be largely ceremonial. The moderators would occupy the place of honor in the processional and recessional that respectively begins and ends each sitting of a council of war. They would recognize speakers during the debate and announce the results of any vote, listing the states that voted aye and those that voted nay. The moderator would also be the only permanent officer of the council of war. All other positions and committees would be ad hoc, appointed by the council to satisfy the contingencies of each case.

More specifically, the impetus for calling a council of war into session would originate with the individual members. Whenever a member felt that a situation in some part of the world called for a declaration of war, that individual would sound out his colleagues. As soon as 10 percent of the membership of one of the chambers concurred, this group would draft a petition to that effect praying the moderator to call to order a session of the council of war on the relevant nation. In addition to containing a brief justification, the petition would identify the ad hoc committees that would be appropriate for debating the case at hand and suggest the names of members willing to serve. At a minimum, the petition would establish two committees—a committee of five to draft the declaration and a committee, also of five, to act as the devil's advocate. The drafting committee would be composed of two members from the Senate and two from the House, one from each party, and the principal drafter. To distinguish themselves from the other members of that council of war, the drafting committee might wear blue or green robes. This committee would model itself on the Committee of Five established by the Second Continental Congress on 11 June 1776. The principal drafter would, like Jefferson, be responsible for producing the text of the declaration, whereas the other four members would provide a maximum amount of support and a minimum amount of criticism. The committee acting as the devil's advocate would also be composed of two members from the Senate and two from the House, one from each party, and the principal advocate. To distinguish themselves from the other members of that council of war, the devil's advocates might wear scarlet robes. The function of this committee would be to argue the case against the war, especially from the viewpoint of the prospective enemy. Other members would naturally raise arguments against the war during the course of the debate on the draft declaration, but this committee would be given a special responsibility to bring all these arguments together and present them as forcefully as possible.

Again, these two committees would be mandatory, but the promoters of the petition might want to suggest other committees to the council of war. For example, if economic sanctions are contemplated as the principal means of conducting the war, the promoters might want to establish a committee to investigate the economic impact upon both the United States and the target country. The results of such an analysis would be of considerable importance to the debate.

Once the promoters of the petition had determined how the council of war should be organized, identified the people to serve on the committees, and obtained the signatures of 10 percent of the members of their chamber, they would present the petition to the moderator. Several days later the moderator would call to order the initial session of that particular council of war, the business of which would be to consider the petition for adoption. During this initial session, the petition and its suggested committee structure would be presented, debated, modified if necessary, and voted upon by state delegation. Should the vote go against the petition, that would be the end of the matter. Should the vote be favorable, then the council of war would adjourn and the committees just established would commence their work. A minimum of three weeks later, the moderator would reconvene the war council. The reports of the various committees would be presented, including the draft declaration of war. The three-week minimum reflects the time Jefferson and the Committee of Five were allotted by the Second Continental Congress to draft the Declaration of Independence. Should the principal drafter or one of the other committees require more time, the moderator could delay the convening of the second session. When all was ready and after a full debate, the amended draft declaration of war would be put to a vote by state delegation. Should the vote go against the draft, that would be the end of the matter and the council of war would adjourn sine die. Should the vote be favorable, the declaration would be sent to the commander-in-chief for approval. Should the commander-in chief disapprove, that would be the end of the matter and the council would adjourn sine die. The reason for not attempting to override a veto is that no one should begin a war that the commander-in-chief opposes. It is a recipe for disaster, as the Sicilian expedition demonstrates. Should the commander-in-chief approve, however, war would be declared against the country in question and the council of war would adjourn until such time as developments might occur that would cause it to reconsider its decision—for example, the entrance of new belligerents into the war, such as the entry of the Chinese into the Korean War; the suffering of a crippling defeat, such as the sack of Washington during the War of 1812; the reaching of a stalemate, such as in Vietnam; or anything else that might cause the council of war to modify its grand strategic analysis and hence change its war aims.

This quick synopsis of the workings of a council of war leaves numerous loose ends unexplained. The first of these loose ends is the manner in which the debates would be conducted. During a debate, current congressional practice calls for members to be recognized by the Speaker of the House or president of the Senate as individuals and then to speak their minds. It must be noted that this was also the practice during the Second Continental Congress. Members were recognized as individuals and spoke their minds themselves. Only when it came time for a vote did the members of the same delegation bend their heads together to decide which way the delegation would vote, the head of the delegation then answering yea or nay when the clerk called the roll of states.

Notwithstanding these precedents, it would be more appropriate for a council of war to adopt a different procedure. Specifically, after the chaplain has finished the invocation, the moderator would recognize not individuals but the senior member of each delegation. Any member who wanted to add something to the debate would prepare a statement and hand it to the head of his delegation, who would request that it be entered into the record along with all the other statements of the other members of the delegation. The only statements that would actually be read by the heads of delegations on the council floor would be collective statements of the entire delegation—that is, statements that had been drafted and debated within the delegation as expressing the sentiments of the entire delegation, not the sentiments of any one individual. Needless to say, this is an extremely cumbersome and tedious way to hold a debate. All spontaneity is lost; all rhetorical skill and flourish is lost; and the spoken word is clothed with a certain air of insincerity, because the speaker most probably does not believe that which he is reading, it being the compromised thoughts of the group. Moreover, the debate would soon lose much of its logic and continuity since not all the prepared statements would speak to the issues of the moment, often referring to issues already discussed or yet to be broached.

But this formality is just the point. By depending upon prepared statements, the council would replace the spoken with the written, which in turn would reduce the role of emotion to a minimum. Indeed, so tedious is this method that one imagines that sessions of the council of war would consist of a solemn processional, a thoughtful invocation, a slow polling of the state delegations during which each head would announce how many prepared statements he wanted read into the record, a final meditative prayer, and a dignified recessional. More important than its reducing the role of emotion— a factor that too easily distorts deliberations over a declaration of war—this cumbersome method would have the effect of shifting the site of the debate from the floor of the chamber to the caucuses of the state delegations and, not incidentally, the general public.

To understand the full impact of this shift, one must also consider the impact of voting by delegation, not by individual. Current congressional practice is for each member to vote as an individual. The principal advantage of this is to maximize individual accountability. Constituents know where their representatives stand on various issues by looking at how they voted on those issues. However, war is not peace. Although it is perfectly acceptable to hold legislators to account for individual votes during peacetime, the same cannot be said for war. The problem is emotion. Both war and the rumors of war stir strong and often unhealthy public sentiments. Depending upon circumstances, these public sentiments may encourage politicians to vote for declarations of war that are unwise and unnecessary or discourage them from voting against declarations that are wise and necessary. As an example of the former, on 7 August 1964, the Gulf of Tonkin Resolution passed in the House unanimously and in the Senate eighty-eight to two; only Senators Wayne Morse, Democrat from Oregon, and Ernest Gruening, Democrat from Alaska, possessed the courage of their convictions and voted against the resolution. Needless to say, both paid the penalty for their unpopular votes. Both were defeated when they next came up for reelection in 1968 and never again held elective office.

As an example of the latter, after Hitler's invasion of Poland in September 1939, there could be little doubt that the United States would soon be drawn into war. President Roosevelt had indeed been attempting to prepare the country for this inevitability since at least October 1937. Yet isolationist sentiment was so strong that no politician dared to advocate openly a willingness to go to war. The best that the bravest among them would advocate publicly was an increase in defense preparedness, an increase in the monies appropriated to the army and the navy, and a modest peacetime conscription law. Isolationist sentiment notwithstanding, one cannot help but feel that stronger action might have been possible if only the members of Congress had been protected from the fate that befell Senators Morse and Gruening and allowed to vote their consciences. As it was, the U.S. declaration of war was delayed until public sentiment changed. On Sunday, 7 December 1941, the Japanese attacked Pearl Harbor. In an instant the previous implacable isolationist sentiment was transformed into an equally implacable internationalist sentiment, which allowed the members of Congress to do the right thing at last.

This stunning lack of political courage in the face of such an obvious danger was so disillusioning that Clinton Rossiter (1948) wrote a strange book after World War II entitled *Constitutional Dictatorship: Crisis Government in the Modern Democracies.* In this book Rossiter calls for a revival of the ancient Roman practice of electing a dictator to serve for a specified period of time during national crises, because, he argues, no "democracy at peace will prepare for war" (50). The value of this ancient practice, Rossiter suggests, is great and should not be gainsaid just because it was misused by Sulla or Caesar during the later republic or because President Paul von Hindenburg invoked article 48 of the Weimar Constitution, allowing him to rule by decree as a dictator, as part of the series of events that eventually brought Hitler to power. Instead of focusing on those negative examples, one should consider the positive examples of the dictatorships of T. Larcius Flaccus or Cincinnatus during the early republic or the positive effects that a Roosevelt dictatorship would have had upon the course of World War II.

Whatever the positive effects of a Roosevelt dictatorship might have been, a simpler, more democratic way to have achieved the same positive response to Nazi aggression would have been to protect the members of Congress from the fury of public sentiment through a secret vote. Voting by delegation with a secret ballot within each caucus seems to be the best way to do this. Moreover, that is the way the Second Continental Congress voted, and the practice is still found in article 2, section 1, and in the Twelfth Amendment to decide the winner of a presidential election whenever a tie in the electoral college throws the election into the House of Representatives. The only problem with this method is that the smaller congressional delegations, such as the delegation from Montana, are too small to provide the necessary protection. This could be remedied by having the smaller delegations caucus together in combinations large enough to protect the anonymity of the individual members, each state delegation to the combined caucus agreeing to abide by the vote of the combination.

As a result of voting by state delegation, the rhythm of sessions would be one of formal sittings alternating with informal caucuses, where the real debates and votes would take place. Thus, both houses of Congress would sit as a council of war whenever new reports, statements, or amendments were presented by committees or the heads of the state delegations, after which members would meet in informal caucuses at which the material just received would be debated and, when necessary, put to a secret ballot, the results of which would then be reported by the head of each state delegation at the next formal sitting of the council. After five or six cycles of these formal and informal gatherings, the climax would be reached when the state delegations proceeded into the chamber, the clerk called the roll, and the heads of delegations voted yea or nay on the draft declaration of war.

In harmony with this rhythm, a parallel process of debate and reaction would be taking place in the country at large, animated and structured by the members of the local Committees of Correspondence. As new materials became available in Washington, the members of the local committees would lead discussions among various groups, as described in the previous section. At the conclusion of these discussions, the local committees would ensure that the groups' representatives in Congress were informed of the results. Nourished by informed opinion for their districts and protected from uninformed public sentiments by a secret ballot in their respective caucuses, the members of the council of war should be in a position to make the best possible decision, or at least the best decision that sound procedure could procure.

Turning from process to substance, it should be clear that the preceding process would make it difficult to amend the draft declaration of war after it was presented to the council of war by the principal drafter. To further increase the difficulty of amending the draft declaration, the principal drafter would be given the privilege of withdrawing the draft from consideration if he felt that certain amendments had gone too far. With this withdrawal, the entire process would collapse, and the moderator would adjourn the council of war sine die. The promoters of the council of war would then have to begin all over again if they felt strongly that the circumstances necessitated a declaration of war. The reasons for this privilege are three: First, the object is to make it as difficult as possible to declare war. Second, amendments seldom strengthen a declaration of war, although the evidence for this is skimpy and contradictory. In the case of the Declaration of Independence, the amendments made by the Second Continental Congress greatly strengthened Jefferson's draft, his great angst over the deletions made notwithstanding. Yet both times that the U.S. Senate has amended a declaration of war—in 1898 and 1914—the amendments significantly weakened the House draft. Until such time as one could be confident that the members of Congress possessed the wisdom and skill of the Second Continental Congress, the safer course is to restrict the ability of members to amend the draft declaration.

Third, there is a substantive reason for limiting amendments. The role of the council of war is not to conduct the war. That is the function of the commander-in-chief. The role of the council of war is to compose a good declaration of war. This involves making a good grand strategic analysis and framing appropriate war aims in a fully reasoned formal declaration. One of the consequences of a good grand strategic analysis and appropriate war aims is to justify the war morally. A paradox now arises. On the one hand, war *is* justified whenever it is an appropriate response to some situation. On the other hand, the draft declaration will frequently not capture this fact. Either the grand strategic analysis will be faulty, or the war aims will be inappropriate. For example, the congressional declaration of war against Japan on 8 December 1941 was fully justified by the situation, the attack on Pearl Harbor. Nonetheless, the unreasoned declaration voted by the Seventy-seventh Congress should have been defeated because it contained neither a grand strategic analysis nor any war aims. The war was justified; the declaration of war was not. In fine, the duty of the council of war is not so much to determine whether war is called for in any particular case; rather, its primary duty is to determine whether the draft declaration before it actually justifies a resort to the *ultima ratio regum*. By restricting the ability of the members to amend the draft declaration, their ability to turn a sow's ear into a silk purse is also restricted. In the name of expediency, members would not be able to take a draft declaration that fails to justify a justified war and attempt to turn it into one that does. Texts tortured in this way seldom work.

More specifically, the primary duty of the council of war is to determine whether the draft declaration successfully addresses the *jus ad bellum* criteria as discussed in chapter 2. Whenever the *ad bellum* criteria are honestly addressed, the likelihood is that both the situation and the draft will justify a resort to war. The model for doing this is, of course, the Declaration of Independence, as was also discussed in chapter 2. An important point not discussed there, however, is the fact that Jefferson's draft was so successful in large part because it was so unoriginal. Had Jefferson's composition been original, it probably would not have been so successful. Jefferson was fully aware of his lack of originality, and he took considerable pride in the fact, as he wrote to Madison on 30 August 1823: "I did not consider it as any part of my charge to invent new ideas altogether, and to offer no sentiment which had not been expressed before" (in Ford 1905, 12:307–8). This lack of originality is crucial because it touches not only on the role and method of the principal drafter of the declaration but also on the frequency with which a council of war should be called into session.

With respect to the principal drafter's method, the ideal is expressed in the following excerpt from a letter Jefferson wrote to Henry Lee on 8 May 1825:

> This was the object of the Declaration of Independence. Not to find out new principles, or new arguments, never before thought of, not merely to say things which had never been said before; but to place before mankind the common sense of the subject, in terms so plain and firm as to command their assent, and to justify ourselves in the independent stand we are compelled to take. Neither aiming at originality of principle or sentiment, nor yet copied from any particular and previous writing, it was intended to be an expression of the American mind, and to give to that expression the proper tone and spirit called for by the occasion. All its authority rests then on the harmonizing sentiments of the day, whether expressed in conversation, in letters, printed essays, or the elementary books of public rights, as Aristotle, Cicero, Locke, Sidney, &c. (in Ford 1905, 12:409)

But before the "harmonizing sentiments of the day" can be placed before humankind, they must be identified and articulated and, through a process of frequent repetition, constant argumentation, and growing refinement, become "the common sense of the subject." For Jefferson, identifying these harmonizing sentiments was not a problem. Since at least the Stamp Act Congress of October 1765, the colonists had been arguing about and refining their grievances against the Crown. The First Continental Congress had drafted six different documents to this purpose in 1774, including the Bill of Rights [and] a List of Grievances and their Petition to the King. The Second Continental Congress was even more active. During 1775 it drafted eight documents, including A Declaration [of] . . . Causes and Necessity . . . , written by Jefferson himself, and the Olive Branch Petition, addressed to the king. In addition to these documents from the Continental Congresses, there were numerous documents drafted by the individual state legislatures, and Thomas Paine had published his *Common Sense* on 1 January 1776. Thus, by the time Jefferson sat down to draft the Declaration of Independence, his job was more one of summarizing and collating than of original composition. Indeed, except for its inclusion of the most recent events of the war, the Declaration of Independence's list of grievances is not original; it echoes those already found one or more of the 1774 Bill of Rights [and] A List of Grievances, the 1774 Petition to the King, his own 1774 Summary View of the Rights of British Americans, or his 1775 Declaration [of] . . . Causes and Necessity, among other documents (see Wills 1978, 68–72).

The difficulties that occur when one attempts "to invent new ideas altogether and to offer sentiments which had not been expressed before" in a declaration of war are perhaps best illustrated in Commander-in-Chief Wilson's 1917 declaration against Imperial Germany. Wilson's first innovation was to turn Jefferson on his head. Instead of beginning with a statement of purpose and following this with a list of grievances and war aims, as Jefferson did, Wilson began with a list of grievances and war aims and then concluded with a statement of principles, Wilsonian idealism in this case. This format worked quite well in 1914 when Wilson used it to declare war on Mexico. In 1917 he was not so lucky. One of the reasons for this failure was Wilson's second innovation: being unsure how he should frame the issues, he tried several different methods in the same declaration. The reason for this experimentation was that Wilson had just finished a campaign in which he had all but promised to keep the United States out of the war. Now, however, he had changed his mind, seizing upon the renewal of unrestricted submarine warfare by the Germans as the casus belli. Feeling no doubt that this simple and straightforward casus belli was inadequate either to explain his change in policy or to drum up enthusiasm for the war, Wilson did not stop there. He continued and introduced a number of idealistic reasons for warring against Imperial Germany, the most famous of which was his call to make the world safe for democracy. Unfortunately, though, the simple and idealistic justifications soon became entangled one within another such that no one was quite sure why Wilson had entered the war, a fact that became clear at the Versailles Peace Conference and its aftermath.

As can be seen, Wilson's problem was one of finding "the common sense of the subject." Precisely because there had been so very little public debate, and no official debate, over the casus belli that would trigger a U.S. entry into World War I, there were no "harmonizing sentiments of the day." Wilson, unlike Jefferson, was forced to be original and innovative in the substance of his declaration, with predictably unsatisfactory results.

The key to finding the common sense of the subject, then, is to have the issues involved debated frequently over a long stretch of time, refining the arguments and building the harmonizing sentiments within the general public, before the principal drafter sits down to write a declaration of war. The colonists did this officially through their numerous petitions to the king and unofficially through their vigorous pamphleteering, of which *Common Sense* is but the most enduring example. Pamphleteering is still possible for the unofficial side of the equation. But what about the official side? If it is no longer possible to petition the king, then how is Congress to debate and formulate the list of grievances and war aims such that the principal drafter can

avoid originality, as Jefferson did? The answer is found by returning to a previously asked question: how frequently should a given council of war be called
into session on any given situation?

Two cases arise, the normal and the abnormal. War has a long gestation
period. Incidents, tensions, and disagreements grow and develop over a number of years or decades. Normally these developments are noted, and it comes
as no surprise to anyone when amity changes to enmity and war or even combat begins. The Revolutionary War, both World Wars, and most other wars
followed this normal pattern. Infrequently, though, the developments that
lead to enmity go unnoticed, and everyone is surprised when war or combat
breaks out. The Korean War and the American invasion of Grenada are examples of this relatively abnormal situation. The abnormal cases are intractable.
Having already lost the chance for the debate to mature, the best that the
council of war can do is to make a formal absolute unreasoned declaration as
soon as possible so as to recognize the current state of enmity and to provide
a legal sanction for whatever the commander-in-chief is doing to meet the
emergency. Then, having taken care of the immediate situation, it should
organize itself and spend the next two or three months debating a fully reasoned declaration of war. Since this fully reasoned declaration will unavoid-
ably contain much that is original, it must be regarded with great suspicion.
The council of war should therefore hold itself unusually vigilant, tracking the
diplomatic and military situations closely and calling itself back into session
whenever new war aims or a new strategic analysis appears to be appropriate.

The normal cases are much more tractable. Inasmuch as the council of war
can no longer petition the British Crown, one alternative would be to substitute the United Nations Security Council. Instead of declaring war, the council of war could draft a petition identifying some serious breech of the peace
in a country and pray the Security Council to redress the situation just as the
First Continental Congress did with its 1774 Petition to the King. In this way
the harmonizing sentiments of the day could be developed and refined without the need to threaten war.

Alternatively, the council of war could threaten war. It could call itself into
session frequently for the purpose of debating and refining its list of grievances
and aims. That is, a council of war could be called into session for any troubling situation, it being understood by all that the purpose of such a session
would not be to declare war against a given country but rather to review the
situation and develop the grand strategic analysis and war aims that might
constitute a harmonizing sentiment at some later date, if things take a turn
for the worse. For example, instead of dealing with China's most-favored-
nation status through Congress's annual brouhaha on the issue, a better way

to handle these trade and human rights tensions would be for a Council of War on the Peoples Republic of China to sit annually to debate U.S. grievances and aims with respect to China. The conclusion of such a debate would be that, although the tensions were serious, insufficient enmity existed to justify a resort to war at the present time. To take a slightly different case, a case in which war in the form of economic sanctions had already been declared from at least June 1948, when the Berlin Airlift began, until November 1989 when the Berlin Wall came down, a Council of War on the Soviet Union should have sat annually to debate U.S. grievances and aims with respect to the Soviet Union. The conclusion of this debate would have been that, although the enmity between the two countries was deep and serious, the war should not go beyond the imposition of economic sanctions.

The principal danger in this second procedure is that the members of the council of war might lose control of the voting and accidentally vote a declaration of war against China or against the Soviet Union. As a check on this sort of accident, the commander-in-chief would have to exercise the veto, or should that individual lack the political courage to do so, the Joint Chiefs of Staff would have to resign, pointing out why war was inappropriate in the given case. Whatever the dangers might be, the need for frequent debate on issues of war and peace is even greater; otherwise, it is impossible to develop the common sense of the subject. Given this necessity, during the two-year life of any given Congress, one would anticipate that declarations of war against six or seven different countries would be debated by the same number of councils of war. Most of these declarations would be defeated, but perhaps one declaration would pass every five or six years. Of those declarations that passed, perhaps every second or third would eventuate in combat, judging by the frequency of wars over the last two hundred years.

With this I conclude my speculation on how Congress might possibly reorganize itself to fulfill its constitutional responsibilities under article 1, section 8. One can, of course, imagine other ways to accomplish the same objective, but the touchstone of any such restructuring must be the recognition that the current congressional rules and practices are totally inappropriate to the serious business of denouncing war because war is not peace.

Appendix:

U.S. Declarations of War

In two hundred years the commander-in-chief has requested a total of twelve declarations of war from Congress that led to combat on five different occasions—in 1812 for the War of 1812, in 1846 for the Mexican-American War, in 1898 for the Spanish-American War, in 1917 for World War I against Imperial Germany and the Imperial and Royal Austro-Hungarian Government, and in 1941 for World War II against Japan, Nazi Germany, Italy, Bulgaria, Hungary, and Rumania.

For the sake of simplicity, however, in the text I spoke of the five occasions and not the twelve declarations. The reason for this is that the declaration against Austro-Hungary in 1917 is a carbon copy of the declaration against Imperial Germany, and all six World War II declarations follow the pattern set by the first, the declaration against the Empire of Japan. The two declarations against Spain in 1898 are significantly different—the Joint Resolution of 20 April being conditional and reasoned, whereas the declaration of 25 April is both absolute and unreasoned—but this does not in any way affect my argument. The declaration of 25 April is curious primarily for the fact that it post-dated the start of the war to 21 April, which is rather unusual. The Joint Resolution of 20 April 1898, which McKinley used as an ultimatum, is of interest because it appears to be reasoned, yet the excessive vagueness of the arguments used in the amended Senate version that finally passed render it inadequate. All the other eleven declarations are both unreasoned and absolute in character.

For the War for Independence

In CONGRESS, July 4, 1776.
A DECLARATION
By the REPRESENTATIVES of the
UNITED STATES OF AMERICA,
In GENERAL CONGRESS assembled.

WHEN in the Course of human Events, it becomes necessary for one People to dissolve the Political Bands which have connected them with another, and to assume among the Powers of the Earth, the separate and equal Station to which the Laws of Nature and of Nature's God entitle them, a decent Respect to the Opinions of Mankind requires that they should declare the causes which impel them to the Separation.

We hold these Truths to be self-evident, that all Men are created equal, that they are endowed by their Creator with certain unalienable Rights, that among these are Life, Liberty, and the Pursuit of Happiness—That to secure these Rights, Governments are instituted among Men, deriving their just Powers from the Consent of the Governed, that whenever any Form of Government becomes destructive of these Ends, it is the Right of the People to alter or to abolish it, and to institute new Government, laying its Foundation on such Principles, and organizing its Powers in such Form, as to them shall seem most likely to effect their Safety and Happiness. Prudence, indeed, will dictate that Governments long established should not be changed for light and transient Causes; and accordingly all Experience hath shewn, that Mankind are more disposed to suffer, while Evils are sufferable, than to right themselves by abolishing the Forms to which they are accustomed. But when a long Train of Abuses and Usurpations, pursuing invariably the same Object, evinces a Design to reduce them under absolute Despotism, it is their Right, it is their Duty, to throw off such Government, and to provide new Guards for their future Security. Such has been the patient Sufferance of these Colonies; and such is now the Necessity which constrains them to alter their former Systems of Government. The History of the present King of Great Britain is a History of repeated injuries and Usurpations, all having in direct Object the Establishment of an absolute Tyranny over these States. To prove this, let Facts be submitted to a candid World.

He has refused his Assent to Laws, the most wholesome and necessary for the public Good.

He has forbidden his Governors to pass Laws of immediate and pressing Importance, unless suspended in their Operation till his Assent should be obtained; and when so suspended, he has utterly neglected to attend to them.

He has refused to pass other Laws for the Accommodation of large Districts of People, unless those People would relinquish the Right of Representation in the Legislature, a Right inestimable to them, and formidable to Tyrants only.

He has called together Legislative Bodies at Places unusual, uncomfortable, and distant from the Depository of their public Records, for the sole Purpose of fatiguing them into Compliance with his Measures.

He has dissolved Representative Houses repeatedly, for opposing with manly Firmness his Invasions on the Rights of the People.

He has refused for a long Time, after such Dissolutions, to cause others to be elected; whereby the Legislative Powers, incapable of Annihilation, have returned to the People at large for their exercise; the State remaining in the mean time exposed to all the Dangers of Invasion from without, and Convulsions within.

He has endeavoured to prevent the Population of these States; for that Purpose obstructing the Laws for Naturalization of Foreigners; refusing to pass others to encourage their Migrations hither, and raising the Conditions of new Appropriations of Lands.

He has obstructed the Administration of Justice, by refusing his Assent to Laws for establishing Judiciary Powers.

He has made Judges dependent on his Will alone, for the Tenure of their Offices, and the Amount and Payment of their Salaries.

He has erected a Multitude of new Offices, and sent hither Swarms of Officers to harrass our People, and eat out their Substance.

He has kept among us, in Times of Peace, Standing Armies, without the consent of our Legislatures.

He has affected to render the Military independent of and superior to the Civil Power.

He has combined with others to subject us to a Jurisdiction foreign to our Constitution, and unacknowledged by our Laws; giving his Assent to their Acts of pretended Legislation:

For quartering large Bodies of Armed Troops among us:

For protecting them, by a mock Trial, from Punishment for any Murders which they should commit on the Inhabitants of these States:

For cutting off our Trade with all Parts of the World:

For imposing Taxes on us without our Consent:

For depriving us, in many Cases, of the Benefits of Trial by Jury:

For transporting us beyond Seas to be tried for pretended Offences:

For abolishing the free System of English Laws in a neighbouring Province, establishing therein an arbitrary Government, and enlarging its Boundaries, so as to render it at once an Example and fit Instrument for introducing the same absolute Rule into these Colonies:

For taking away our Charters, abolishing our most valuable Laws, and altering fundamentally the Forms of our Governments:

For suspending our own Legislatures, and declaring themselves invested with Power to legislate for us in all Cases whatsoever.

He has abdicated Government here, by declaring us out of his Protection and waging War against us.

He has plundered our Seas, ravaged our Coasts, burnt our Towns, and destroyed the Lives of our People.

He is, at this Time, transporting large Armies of foreign Mercenaries to compleat the Works of Death, Desolation, and Tyranny, already begun with circumstances of Cruelty and Perfidy, scarcely paralleled in the most barbarous Ages, and totally unworthy the Head of a civilized Nation.

He has constrained our fellow Citizens taken Captive on the high Seas to bear Arms against their Country, to become the Executioners of their Friends and Brethren, or to fall themselves by their Hands.

He has excited domestic Insurrections amongst us, and has endeavoured to bring on the Inhabitants of our Frontiers, the merciless Indian Savages, whose known Rule of Warfare, is an undistinguished Destruction, of all Ages, Sexes and Conditions.

In every stage of these Oppressions we have Petitioned for Redress in the most humble Terms: Our repeated Petitions have been answered only by repeated Injury. A Prince, whose Character is thus marked by every act which may define a Tyrant, is unfit to be the Ruler of a free People.

Nor have we been wanting in Attentions to our British Brethren. We have warned them from Time to Time of Attempts by their Legislature to extend an unwarrantable Jurisdiction over us. We have reminded them of the Circumstances of our Emigration and Settlement here. We have appealed to their native Justice and Magnanimity, and we have conjured them by the Ties of our common Kindred to disavow these Usurpations, which, would inevitably interrupt our Connections and Correspondence. They too have been deaf to the Voice of Justice and of Consanguinity. We must, therefore, acquiesce in the Necessity, which denounces our Separation, and hold them, as we hold the rest of Mankind, Enemies in War, in Peace, Friends.

We, therefore, the Representatives of the UNITED STATES OF AMERICA, in General Congress, Assembled, appealing to the Supreme Judge of the World for the Rectitude of our Intentions, do, in the Name, and by Authority of the good People of these Colonies, solemnly Publish and Declare, That these United Colonies are, and of Right out [sic] to be, Free and Independent States; that they are absolved from all Allegiance to the British Crown, and that all political Connection between them and the State of Great-Britain, is and ought to be totally dissolved; and that as Free and Independent States, they have full Power to levy War, conclude Peace, contract Alliances, establish Commerce, and to do all other Acts and Things which Independent States may of right do. And for the support of this Declaration, with a firm Reliance on the Protection of divine Providence, we mutually pledge to each other our Lives, our Fortunes, and our sacred Honor.

For the War of 1812

The declaration of 1812 is reproduced in chapter 2, p. 40 (Pub. L. No. 12-102, 2 Stat. 755).

For the Mexican-American War

This most bizarre of all declarations of war requires a word of introduction. In 1812 the Twelfth Congress had declared war and then almost immediately adjourned without appropriating any money to fight the war. Needless to say, this had caused enormous difficulties. Thirty-four years later the Twenty-ninth Congress did not want to repeat the same embarrassing mistake, which explains all the money clauses. In addition, the Mexican-American War is arguably the most "political" war in American history; that is, it involved the petty politics of pork and personal advantage, as is reflected, for example, in section 6 of the act.

> An Act providing for the Prosecution of the existing War between the United States and the Republic of Mexico.
>
> Whereas, by the act of the Republic of Mexico, a state of war exists between that Government and the United States:
>
> *Be it enacted by the Senate and House of Representatives of the United States of America in Congress assembled,* That, for the purpose of enabling the Government of the United States to prosecute said war to a speedy and successful termination, the President be, and he is hereby, authorized to employ the militia, naval, and military forces of the United States, and to call for and accept the services of any number of volunteers, not exceeding fifty thousand, who may offer their services, either as cavalry, artillery, infantry, or riflemen, to serve twelve months after they shall have arrived at the place of rendezvous, or to the end of the war, unless sooner discharged, according to the time for which they shall have been mustered into service; and that the sum of ten million dollars, out of any moneys in the treasury, or to come into the Treasury, not otherwise appropriated, be, and the same is hereby, appropriated, for the purpose of carrying the provisions of this act into effect.
>
> Sec. 2. *And be it further enacted,* That the militia, when called into the service of the United States by virtue of this act, or any other act, may, if in the opinion of the President of the United States the public interest requires it, be com-

pelled to serve for a term not exceeding six months, after their arrival at the place of rendezvous, in any one year, unless sooner discharged.

Sec. 3. *And be it further enacted,* That the said volunteers shall furnish their own clothes, and, if cavalry, their own horses and horse equipments; and when mustered into service shall be armed at the expense of the United States.

Sec. 4. *And be it further enacted,* That said volunteers shall, when called into actual service, and while remaining therein, be subject to the rules and articles of war, and shall be in all respects, except as to clothing and pay, placed on the same footing with similar corps of the United States army; and in lieu of clothing, every non-commissioned officer and private in any company, who may thus offer himself shall be entitled, when called into actual service, to receive in money a sum equal to the cost of clothing of a non-commissioned officer or private (as the case may be) in the regular troops of the United States.

Sec. 5. *And be it further enacted,* That the said volunteers so offering their services shall be accepted by the President in companies, battalions, squadrons, and regiments, whose officers shall be appointed in the manner prescribed by law in the several States and Territories to which such companies, battalions, squadrons, and regiments shall respectively belong.

Sec. 6. *And be it further enacted,* That the President of the United States be, and he is hereby, authorized to organize companies so tendering their services into battalions or squadrons, battalions and squadrons into regiments, regiments into brigades, and brigades into divisions, as soon as the number of volunteers shall render such organization, in his judgment, expedient; and the President shall, if necessary, apportion the staff, field, and general officers among the respective States and Territories from which the volunteers shall tender their services, as he may deem proper.

Sec. 7. *And be it further enacted,* That the volunteers who may be received into the service of the United States by virtue of the provisions of this act, and who shall be wounded or otherwise disabled in the service, shall be entitled to all the benefits which may be conferred on persons wounded in the service of the United States.

Sec. 8. *And be it further enacted,* That the President of the United States be, and he is hereby, authorized forthwith to complete all public armed vessels now authorized by law, and to purchase or charter, arm, equip, and man, such merchant vessels and steamboats as, upon examination, may be found fit, or easily converted into armed vessels fit for the public service, and in such number as he may deem necessary for the protection of the seaboard, lake coast, and the general defense of the country.

Sec. 9. *And be it further enacted,* That whenever the militia or volunteers are called and received into the service of the United States, under the provisions of this act, they shall have the organization of the army of the United States, and shall have the same pay and allowances; and all mounted privates, non-commissioned officers, musicians and artificers, shall be allowed 40 cents per day for the use and risk of their horses, except of horses actually killed in action; and if any mounted volunteer, private, non-commissioned officer, musician, or artificer, shall not keep himself provided with a serviceable horse, said volunteer shall serve on foot.

Approved 13 May 1846. (Pub. L. No. 29-16, 9 Stat. 9)

For the Spanish-American War

House Resolution 233 was introduced in the House on 13 April 1898 but completely revised by the Senate. The original resolution read as follows:

Joint resolution (H. Res. 233) authorizing and directing the President of the United States to intervene to stop the war in Cuba, and for the purpose of establishing a stable and independent government of the people therein.

Whereas the Government of Spain for three years past has been waging war on the Island of Cuba against a revolution by the inhabitants thereof without making any substantial progress towards the suppression of said revolution, and has conducted the warfare in a manner contrary to the laws of nations by methods inhuman and uncivilized, causing the death by starvation of more than 200,000 innocent noncombatants, the victims being for the most part helpless women and children, inflicting intolerable injury to the commercial interests of the United States, involving the destruction of the lives and property of many of our citizens, entailing the expenditure of millions of money in patrolling our coasts and policing the high seas in order to maintain our neutrality; and

Whereas this long series of losses, injuries, and burdens for which Spain is responsible has culminated in the destruction of the United States battle ship Maine in the harbor of Havana and the death of 260 of our seamen;

Resolved by the Senate and the House of Representatives of the United States of America in Congress assembled, That the President is hereby authorized and directed to intervene at once to stop the war in Cuba to the end and with the purpose of securing permanent peace and order there and establishing by the free action of the people thereof a stable and independent government of their own in the Island of Cuba; and the President is hereby authorized and empowered to use the land and naval forces of the United States to execute the purpose of this resolution (*Cong. Rec.* [House] 18 April 1898, p. 4041, where the Senate amendments are also recorded.).

—

Joint Resolution For the independence of the people of Cuba, demanding that the Government of Spain relinquish its authority and government in the Island of Cuba, and withdraw its land and naval forces from Cuba and Cuban waters, and directing the President of the United States to use the land and naval forces of the United States to carry these resolutions into effect.

Whereas the abhorrent conditions which have existed for more than three years in the Island of Cuba, so near our own borders, have shocked the moral sense of the people of the United States, have been a disgrace to Christian civilization, culminating, as they have, in the destruction of a United States battleship, with two hundred and sixty of its officers and crew, while on a friendly visit in the Harbor of Havana, and cannot longer be endured, as has been set forth by the President of the United States in his message to Congress of April eleventh, eighteen hundred and ninety-eight, upon which the action of Congress was invited: Therefore,

Resolved by the Senate and the House of Representatives of the United States of America, in Congress assembled, First. That the people of the Island of Cuba are, and of right ought to be free and independent.

Second. That it is the duty of the United States to demand, and the Government of the United States does hereby demand, that the Government of Spain at once relinquish its authority and government in the Island of Cuba, and withdraw its land and naval forces from Cuba and Cuban waters.

Third. That the President of the United States be, and he hereby is, directed and empowered to use the entire land and naval forces of the United States, and to call into the actual service of the United States the militia of the several States to such extent as may be necessary to carry these resolutions into effect.

Fourth. That the United States hereby disclaims any disposition or intention to exercise sovereignty, jurisdiction, or control over said island except for the pacification thereof, and asserts its determination, when that is accomplished, to leave the government and control of the island to its people.

Approved, April 20, 1898. (The Joint Resolution was passed at 1:30 A.M. on 19 April 1989; Pub. Res. No. 55-24, 30 Stat. 738)

—

An Act Declaring that war exists between the United States of America and the Kingdom of Spain.

Be it enacted by the Senate and House of Representatives of the United States of America in Congress assembled, First. That war be, and the same is hereby, declared to exist, and that war has existed since the twenty-first day of April, anno Domini eighteen hundred and ninety-eight, including said day, between the United States of America and the Kingdom of Spain.

Second. That the President of the United States be, and he hereby is, directed and empowered to use the entire land and naval forces of the United States, and to call into the actual service of the United States the militia of the several States, to such extent as may be necessary to carry this Act into effect.

Approved, April 25, 1898. (Pub. L. No. 55-189, 30 Stat. 364)

For World War I

The State Department's draft as approved by Wilson and submitted to the House leadership on 2 April 1917:

JOINT RESOLUTION, Declaring that a State of War Exists Between the Imperial German Government and the Government and People of the United States and Making Provisions to Prosecute the Same.

Whereas. The recent acts of the Imperial German Government are acts of war against the Government and people of the United States:

Resolved. By the Senate and House of Representatives of the United States of America in Congress assembled, that the state of war between the United States and the Imperial German Government which has thus been thrust upon the United States is hereby formally declared; and

That the President be, and is hereby, authorized and directed to take immediate steps not only to put the country in a thorough state of defense but also to exert all of its power and employ all of its resources to carry on war against the Imperial German Government and bring the conflict to a successful termination. (*New York Times* 3 April 1917, p. 1)

After passing in the House, the State Department draft was amended in the Senate and then accepted by the House:

Joint Resolution Declaring that a state of war exists between the Imperial German Government and the Government and the People of the United States and making provision to prosecute the same.

Whereas the Imperial German Government has committed repeated acts of war against the Government and people of the United States of America: Therefore, be it

Resolved by the Senate and House of Representatives of the United States of America in Congress assembled, That the state of war between the United States and the Imperial German Government which has thus been thrust upon the United States is hereby formally declared; and that the President be, and he is hereby, authorized and directed to employ the entire naval and military forces of the United States and the resources of the Government to carry on war against the Imperial German Government; and to bring the conflict to a successful termination all the resources of the country are hereby pledged by the Congress of the United States. (Approved 6 April 1917; Pub. Res. No. 65-1, 40 Stat. 1)

The declaration of war against the Imperial and Royal Austro-Hungarian Government (approved 7 December 1917; Pub. L. No. 65-1, 40 Stat. 429) is identical to the declaration against the Imperial German government.

As a sign of the times, it is of interest to note that the declarations for World War I contain, for the first time, the novel idea that it is possible for the Imperial German government to make war on the *people* of the United States, whereas the United States makes war only on the Imperial German government, but not its *people.* This sentiment occupied a long and much acclaimed passage in Wilson's 2 April 1917 address to the Joint Session of the

Congress. All six of the World War II declarations also reproduce the same novel distinction.

For World War II

The declaration against the imperial government of Japan (approved 8 December 1941, 4:10 P.M., EST; Pub. L. No. 77-328, 55 Stat. 795) is reproduced in chapter 2. The other five declarations are identical except for two changes: the name of the country concerned changes, and the "Whereas" clause reads, "has committed unprovoked acts of war" in the declaration against Japan and "has formally declared war against" in the other five. The other five declarations are against the governments of Germany (approved 11 December 1941, 3:05 P.M., EST; Pub. L. No. 77-331, 55 Stat. 796), Italy (approved 11 December 1941 3:06 P.M., EST; Pub. L. No. 77-332, 55 Stat. 797), Bulgaria (approved 5 June 1942; Pub. L. No. 77-563, 56 Stat. 307), Hungary (approved 5 June 1942; Pub. L. No. 77-564, 56 Stat. 307), Rumania (approved 5 June 1942; Pub. L. No. 77-565, 56 Stat. 307).

References

Adams, Robert P. 1962. *The Better Part of Valor: More, Erasmus, Colet and Vives on Humanism, War and Peace, 1496–1535.* Seattle: University of Washington Press.

Arendt, Hannah. 1972. "On Violence." *Crises of the Republic.* New York: Harcourt Brace Jovanovich.

Arnold, Hugh M. 1975. "Official Justifications for America's Role in Indochina, 1949–67." *Asian Affairs* 3, no. 1 (Sept.-Oct.): 31–48.

Aron, Raymond. 1985. *Clausewitz, Philosopher of War.* Trans. Christine Booker and Norman Stone. Englewood Cliffs, N.J.: Prentice-Hall.

Asakawa, Kanichi. 1904. *The Russo-Japanese Conflict: Its Causes and Issues.* Boston: Houghton, Mifflin.

Blackstone, William. 1969 [1803]. *Blackstone's Commentaries. With notes of reference to the Constitution and Laws of the Federal Government of the United States, and of the Commonwealth of Virginia, by St. George Tucker.* 5 vols. South Hackensack, N.J.: Rothman Reprint.

Blechman, Barry M., Stephen S. Kaplan, et al. 1978. *Force without War: U.S. Armed Forces as a Political Instrument.* Washington, D.C.: The Brookings Institution.

Bodin, Jean. 1951. *Œuvres philosophiques de Jean Bodin.* Ed. Pierre Mesnard. Tome 5, numéro 3, *Corpus Général des Philosophes Français, Auteurs Modernes,* publié sous la direction de Raymond Bayer. Paris: Presses Universitaires de France.

———. 1962. *The Six Bookes of a Commonweale: A facsimile reprint of the English translation of 1606, corrected and supplemented in the light of a new comparison with the French and Latin texts.* Ed. and intro. Kenneth Douglas McRae. Cambridge, Mass.: Harvard University Press.

Bonet, Honoré. 1949. *The Tree of Battles.* Trans. G. W. Coopland. Liverpool: Liverpool University Press.

Brodie, Bernard. 1973. *War and Politics.* New York: Macmillian.

Brown, Philip Marshall. 1939. "Undeclared War." *The American Journal of International Law* 33, no. 3 (July): 538–41.

Burger, James A. 1978. "Review of *International Law—The Conduct of Armed Conflict and Air Operations,* Department of the Air Force Pamphlet 110-31. . . ." *Military Law Review* 80 (Spring): 259–65.

Bynkershoek, Cornelius van. 1930. *Quæstionum Juris Publici Liber Duo (1737).* Trans. Tenney Frank. The Classics of International Law No. 14 (2). Publications of the Carnegie Endowment for International Peace. Oxford: Clarendon. (The reformed Dutch spelling, under which Bynkershoek is often catalogued, is "Bijnkershoek, Cornelis van.")

Churchill, Winston. 1941. "Text of Prime Minister Churchill's Speech in Commons on Japan's Attack." *New York Times,* 9 December, 14.

Cicero. 1912. *Letters to Atticus.* Vol 2. Trans. E. O. Winstedt. Loeb Classical Library. London: Heinemann.

———. 1967. *On Moral Obligation: A New Translation of Cicero's "De Officiis."* Trans. John Higginbotham. Berkeley: University of California Press.

Clausewitz, Carl von. 1976. *On War.* Trans. and ed. Michael Howard and Peter Paret. Princeton, N.J.: Princeton University Press.

Committee on Foreign Affairs. 1970. *Background Information on the Use of United States Armed Forces in Foreign Countries.* Washington, D.C.: USGPO.

"Congress, the President, and the Power to Commit Forces to Combat." 1968. *Harvard Law Review* 81, no. 8 (June): 1771–1805.

Congressional Globe. 1833–73. Washington, D.C.

Congressional Record. 1873– . Washington, D.C.

De Louter, J. 1920. *Le Droit International Public Positif.* Dotation Carnegie pour la Paix internationale. Oxford: University of Oxford Press.

Department of the Air Force. 1984. *AFM 1-1, Basic Functions and Doctrine of the United States Air Force.* Washington, D.C.: USGPO.

Department of Defense. 1985. *U.S. Casualties in Southeast Asia: Statistics as of April 30, 1985.* Washington, D.C.: USGPO.

Department of State. *Foreign Relations of the United States 1861–.* Washington, D.C.: USGPO.

Department of State, Bureau of Public Affairs, Office of Media Services. 1971. *Current Foreign Policy: Congress, the President, and the War Powers: Statement by Secretary of State William P. Rogers before the Senate Committee on Foreign Relations, May 14, 1971.* General Foreign Policy Series, no. 235. Washington, D.C.: USGPO.

Department of State Bulletin. 1939–89. Washington, D.C.

Draper, Theodore. 1990. "The Constitution in Danger." *New York Review of Books,* 1 March, 41–47.

———. 1991. "Presidential Wars." *New York Review of Books,* 26 September, 64–74.

Eagleton, Clyde. 1933. "The Attempt to Define War." *International Conciliation* 291 (June): 237–87.

———. 1938. "The Form and Function of the Declaration of War." *The American Journal of International Law* 32, no. 1 (Jan.): 19–35.

Erasmus, Desiderius. 1957. *Ten Colloquies.* Trans. Craig R. Thompson. New York: Liberal Arts.

———. 1986. *Literary and Educational Writings 5, Panegyricus, Moria, Julius Exclusus, Instituto Principis Christiani, Querela Pacis.* Ed. A. H. T. Levi. Vol. 27 of *Collected Works of Erasmus.* Toronto: University of Toronto Press.

Farrand, Max, ed. 1911. *Records of the Federal Convention of 1787.* Vol. 2. New Haven, Conn.: Yale University Press.

Fisher, Louis. 1995. "The Korean War: On What Legal Basis Did Truman Act?" *American Journal of International Law* 89, no. 1 (Jan.): 21–39.

Fissel, Mark Charles. 1994. *The Bishops' Wars: Charles I's Campaigns against Scotland, 1638–1640.* Cambridge: Cambridge University Press.

Ford, Paul Leicester, ed. 1905. *The Works of Thomas Jefferson.* Vols. 1–12. New York: Putnam's.

Gentili, Alberico. 1933. *De Iure Belli Libri Tres.* 1612 ed., trans. John C. Rolfe. The Classics of International Law No. 16. Publications of the Carnegie Endowment for International Peace. Oxford: Clarendon.

George, Alexander L. 1991. *Forceful Persuasion: Coercive Diplomacy as an Alternative to War.* Washington, D.C.: United States Institute of Peace Press.

Glennon, Michael J. 1984. "The War Powers Resolution Ten Years Later: More Politics Than Law." *The American Journal of International Law* 78, no. 3 (July): 571–81.

Grotius, Hugo. 1925. *De Jure Belli ac Pacis Libri Tres.* Vol. 2. Trans. Francis W. Kelsey. The Classics of International Law No. 3. Publications of the Carnegie Endowment for International Peace. Oxford: Clarendon.

Gudridge, Patrick O. 1995. "Ely, Black, Grotius, and Vattel." *University of Miami Law Review* 50, no. 1 (Oct.): 81–106.

Hall, William Edward. 1924. *A Treatise on International Law.* 8th ed. Ed. A. Pearce Higgins. London: Humphrey Milford, for Oxford University Press.

Hamilton, Alexander. 1969. *The Papers of Alexander Hamilton: Volume XV: June 1793–January 1794.* Ed. Harold C. Syrett, Jacob E. Cooke, Jean G. Cooke, Cara-Louise Miller, Dorothy Twohig, and Patricia Syrett. New York: Columbia University Press.

Hart-Dyke, David. 1986. "HMS Coventry—The Day of Battle." *The Guardian Weekly,* 27 July, 17–18.

Herring, George C. 1994. *LBJ and Vietnam: A Different Kind of War.* Austin, Tex.: University of Texas Press.

Hobbes, Thomas. 1946. *Leviathan or the Matter, Forme, and Power of a Commonwealth Ecclesiasticall and Civil.* Reprint of 1651 ed. (London: Andrew Crooke). Ed. Michael Oakeshott. Oxford: Blackwell.

Johnson, James. 1981. *Just War Tradition and the Restraint of War: A Moral and Historical Inquiry.* Princeton, N.J.: Princeton University Press.

Johnson, Lyndon B. 1966. *Public Papers of the Presidents of the United States: Lyndon B. Johnson, 1965, Book 1.* Washington, D.C.: USGPO.

Keegan, John. 1976. *The Face of Battle*. Harmondsworth: Penguin.

Kennedy, John F. 1963. *Public Papers of the Presidents of the United States: John F. Kennedy, January 1 to December 31, 1962*. Washington, D.C.: USGPO.

Kimball, Jeffrey P., ed. 1990. *To Reason Why: The Debate about the Causes of U.S. Involvement in the Vietnam War*. Philadelphia, Pa.: Temple University Press.

Kinnard, Douglas. 1977. *The War Managers*. Hanover, N.H.: University Press of New England.

Kluckhohn, Frank L. 1941. "Unity in Congress." *New York Times,* 9 December, 1.

Kohn, Richard H., and Joseph P. Harahan, eds. 1988. "U.S. Strategic Air Power, 1948–1962: Excerpts from an Interview with Generals Curtis E. LeMay, Leon W. Johnson, David A. Burchinal, and Jack J. Catton." *International Security* 12, no. 4 (Spring): 78–95.

Lehman, John. 1976. *The Executive, Congress, and Foreign Policy: Studies of the Nixon Administration*. New York: Praeger.

Lenin, V. I. 1964. "The Collapse of the Second International." *Collected Works*. Vol. 21, *August 1914–December 15*. Ed. Julius Katzer. Moscow: Progress.

Lincoln, Abraham. 1907. *Abraham Lincoln: Complete Works*. 2 vols. Ed. John G. Nicolay and John Hay. New York: Century.

Livy. 1919. *Livy in Fourteen Volumes*. Trans. B. O. Foster. Loeb Classical Library. London: Heinemann.

Lobel, Jules. 1995. "'Little Wars' and the Constitution." *University of Miami Law Review* 50, no. 1 (Oct.): 61–79.

Locke, John. 1963. *The Works of John Locke: A New Edition, Corrected, in Ten Volumes*. Vol. 5. Aalen, Germany: Scientia.

Lofgren, Charles A. 1972. "War-Making under the Constitution: The Original Understanding." *The Yale Law Journal* 81, no. 4 (Mar.): 672–702.

Losman, Donald L. 1979. *International Economic Sanctions: The Cases of Cuba, Israel, and Rhodesia*. Albuquerque: University of New Mexico Press.

Madison, James. 1906. *The Writings of James Madison*. Vol. 6, *1790–1802*. Ed. Gaillard Hunt. New York: Putnam's.

Manicas, Peter T. 1989. *War and Democracy*. Oxford: Blackwell.

Martin, Lisa L. 1992. *Coercive Cooperation: Explaining Multilateral Economic Sanctions*. Princeton, N.J.: Princeton University Press.

Maurice, J.F., Brevet-Lt. Col. 1883. *Hostilities without Declaration of War: From 1700 to 1870*. London: H. M. Stationery Office.

Mearsheimer, John J. 1988. *Liddell Hart and the Weight of History*. Ithaca, N.Y.: Cornell University Press.

Miller, Richard I., ed. 1975. *The Law of War*. Lexington, Mass.: Lexington.

Molloy, Charles. 1672. *De Jure Maritimo or Treatise of Affairs Maritime and of Commerce*. 2 vols. London.

Moore, John N. 1969. "The National Executive and the Use of the Armed Forces Abroad." *Naval War College Review* 21, no. 5 (Jan.): 28–38.

More, Thomas. 1965. *Utopia*. Vol. 4 of *The Complete Works of St. Thomas More*. Ed. Edward Surtz, S. J., and J. H. Hexter. New Haven, Conn.: Yale University Press.

Naval War College. 1918. *International Law Documents: Neutrality, Breaking of Diplomatic Relations, War, with Notes, 1917.* Washington, D.C.: USGPO.

O'Brien, Tim. 1978. *Going after Cacciato.* New York: Delacorte.

Paine, Thomas. 1989. *Political Writings.* Ed. Bruce Kuklick. New York: Cambridge University Press.

Pisan, Christine de. 1937. *The Book of Fayttes of Armes and of Chyualrye (Le Livre des Faits d'Armes et de Chevalerie).* Trans. William Caxton (1489). Ed. A. T. P. Byles. Published by the Early English Text Society. London: Humphrey Milford, for Oxford University Press.

Plutarch. 1948. *Plutarch's Lives.* 11 vols. Trans. Bernadotte Perrin. Loeb Classical Library. London: Heineman.

Powers, Thomas. 1984. "Nuclear Winter and Nuclear Strategy." *The Atlantic Monthly,* November, 53–64.

Pritchard, James B., ed. 1955. *Ancient Near Eastern Texts, Relating to the Old Testament.* 2d ed. Princeton, N.J.: Princeton University Press.

Reagan, Ronald. 1985. *Public Papers of the Presidents of the United States: Ronald Reagan, 1983, Book II, July 2 to December 31, 1983.* Washington, D.C.: USGPO.

Roosevelt, Franklin D. 1938–50. *The Public Papers and Addresses of Franklin D. Roosevelt.* 13 vols. Compiled by Samuel I. Rosenman. New York: Random House (vols. 1–5, 1938); Macmillan (vols. 6–9, 1941); Harper and Brothers (vols. 10–13, 1950).

Rossiter, Clinton L. 1948. *Constitutional Dictatorship: Crisis Government in the Modern Democracies.* Princeton, N.J.: Princeton University Press.

Rostow, Eugene V. 1972. "Great Cases Make Bad Law: The War Powers Act." *Texas Law Review* 50, no. 5 (May): 833–900.

Schlesinger, Arthur M. Jr. 1972. "Congress and the Making of American Foreign Policy." *Foreign Affairs* 51, no. 1:78–113.

————. 1973. *The Imperial Presidency.* Boston: Houghton Mifflin.

Seymour-Ure, Colin. 1984. "British 'War Cabinets' in Limited Wars: Korea, Suez and Falklands." *Public Administration* 62 (Summer): 181–200.

Sharpe, Kevin. 1992. *The Personal Rule of Charles I.* New Haven, Conn.: Yale University Press.

Sofaer, Abraham D. 1976. *War, Foreign Affairs and Constitutional Power: The Origins.* Cambridge, Mass.: Ballinger.

Stone, Oliver. 1986. *Platoon.* Film. Hemdale.

Summers, Harry G. Jr. 1982. *On Strategy: A Critical Analysis of the Vietnam War.* Navato, Calif.: Presidio.

Takahashi, Sakuyé. 1908. *International Law Applied to the Russo-Japanese War, with the Decisions of the Japanese Prize Courts.* U.S. ed. New York: Banks Law.

Thucydides. 1982. *The Peloponnesian War: The Crawley Translation.* Ed. T. E. Wick. New York: Modern Library.

Tolstoy, Leo. 1966. *War and Peace.* Trans. Louise and Aylmar Maude. Ed. George Gibian. New York: Norton.

Truman, Harry S. 1965a. *Public Papers of the Presidents of the United States, Harry S. Truman, January 1 to December 31, 1950.* Washington, D.C.: USGPO.

————. 1965b. *Public Papers of the Presidents of the United States, Harry S. Truman, January 1 to December 31, 1951.* Washington, D.C.: USGPO.

Vattel, Emerich de. 1916. *The Laws of Nations or the Principles of Natural Law Applied to the Conduct and to the Affairs of Nations and of Sovereigns.* 1758 ed., trans. Charles G. Fenwick. Washington, D.C.: Carnegie Institution.

Virgil. 1951. *The Aeneid of Virgil.* Trans. Rolfe Humphries. New York: Scribner's.

Walzer, Michael. 1977. *Just and Unjust Wars: A Moral Argument with Historical Illustrations.* New York: Basic.

Ward, Robert. 1805. *An Enquiry into the manner in which the different Wars of Europe have commenced during the last two centuries. . . .* London: J. Butterworth and J. Stockdale.

Watson, Alan. 1993. *International Law in Archaic Rome: War and Religion.* Baltimore, Md.: Johns Hopkins University Press.

Wheaton, Henry. 1936. *Elements of International Law: Edition of 1866 by Richard Henry Dana, Jr.* Ed. George Grafton Wilson. The Classics of International Law No. 19. Publications of the Carnegie Endowment for International Peace. Oxford: Clarendon.

Wiedemann, Thomas. 1986. "The *Fetiales:* A Reconsideration." *Classical Quarterly* 36, no. 2:478–90.

Wills, Garry. 1978. *Inventing America: Jefferson's Declaration of Independence.* New York: Vintage.

————. 1992. *Lincoln at Gettysburg: The Words That Remade America.* New York: Simon and Schuster.

Wormuth, Francis D., and Edwin B. Firmage. 1989. *To Chain the Dog of War: The War Power of Congress in History and Law.* Urbana: University of Illinois Press.

Wright, Quincy. 1932. "When Does War Exist?" *American Journal of International Law* 26, no. 2 (Apr.): 362–68.

————. 1965. *A Study of War.* 2d ed. Chicago: University of Chicago Press.

Index

BRIEN HALLETT teaches at the Matsunaga Institute for Peace at the University of Hawai'i–Manoa. He is currently working on a second book that seeks to identify the procedural stumbling blocks that prevent Congress from exercising its war powers by examining selected nineteenth- and twentieth-century American wars.